AF598574

A Mysterious Guest for Dinner

EXPLORING TALMUDIC NARRATIVES

Moshe Sokol

A Mysterious Guest for Dinner

EXPLORING
TALMUDIC
NARRATIVES

Touro University
Maggid Books

A Mysterious Guest for Dinner
Exploring Talmudic Narratives

First Edition, 2024

Maggid Books
An imprint of Koren Publishers Jerusalem Ltd.

POB 8531, New Milford, CT 06776-8531, USA
& POB 4044, Jerusalem 9104001, Israel

www.korenpub.com

The publication of this book was made possible
through the generous support of *The Jewish Book Trust*.

ISBN 978-1-59264-674-6, *hardcover*

A CIP catalogue record for this title is
available from the British Library

Printed and bound in the United States

בס"ד

Touro College and University System
pays tribute to

RABBI DR. MOSHE SOKOL

DEAN, LANDER COLLEGE FOR MEN

Dean Sokol is an outstanding Rav, scholar and academician who is respected by his peers and beloved by his students.

This volume is yet another of his contributions to the corpus of Rabbinic scholarship. His insights will undoubtedly enhance understanding of the Talmud and advance Torah knowledge.

In memory of my beloved parents

Albert and Shirley Sokol

Contents

Acknowledgments

This volume, like the first volume I published on aggadic narratives, originated in a series of lectures delivered over a number of years to students at the Lander College for Men, and in some cases also to members of the Yavneh Minyan of Flatbush. I remain grateful to them not only for their enthusiastic interest, but for their insightful contributions to unraveling the oftentimes puzzling texts we studied together.

I am likewise grateful to the leadership of Touro University, which became my academic home shortly after I received my doctorate many years ago, and remains so until today. I have had the good fortune to teach its undergraduate and graduate students for many decades, and serve in various administrative capacities as well, including that of Dean of Lander College for Men for over two decades, in which position I continue to serve. I owe a special debt of gratitude to Dr. Alan Kadish, president and CEO of Touro University, and to Rabbi Moshe Krupka, executive vice president, not only for their extraordinary leadership of the university, but for their role in making possible the publication of this volume on aggadic narratives, as well as the previous volume.

I am also grateful to the Yavneh Minyan of Flatbush, where I have served as rabbi for over thirty years, and to its president Gordon Krauss-Friedberg and members of the board, not only for their leadership of such a special shul, but also for their role helping make the publication of this volume, and the first, possible.

Members of the Lander College for Men staff have likewise been most helpful, and I wish to thank Mr. Yeshaya Metal, the college librarian, for assisting me in tracking down many sources, and to Mrs. Elana Raskas Deutsch, Mrs. Samantha Friedman, and Mrs. Rachel Horowitz, for extensive assistance with the text.

Maggid Books did a wonderful job in publishing my first volume on aggadic narratives, and I am delighted to be publishing this second volume with them. Rabbi Reuven Ziegler, Editorial Director, Rabbi David Silverstein, Dr. Yoel Finkelman, Nechama Unterman, Tomi Mager, and Dvora Rhein all have been invaluable in bringing this volume to fruition.

Members of my family have read drafts of these chapters, and commented on them fruitfully, including my wonderful wife Chaya Sarah Sokol, and our children Rabbi Dov Zvi and Dr. Dina Sokol; Estee Schwab and her husband Rabbi Daniel Schwab; Dr. Aliza Rosenwasser and her husband Rabbi Uri Rosenwasser; Yonah Sokol and his wife Dr. Zehava Sokol; and Dr. Yosef Sokol and his wife Devorah Sokol. I have also benefited from the comments and suggestions of several of their older children, a supreme blessing in itself. Together with my dear brother Steven Sokol and sister Raisy Barnett and her husband David, they have nurtured me with their love and encouragement as I labored to bring these studies to light.

This volume is dedicated to the memory of my parents Albert and Shirley Sokol, both of whom passed away during this year, four months apart. They were deeply bonded in life and retrieved that bond in death. My mother, who loved, nurtured, and supported all her children, was also a gifted, magical teacher, who transformed the lives of countless students over the many decades she taught, redeeming many from the pits of failure. The remarkably moving testimonials we heard from so many of her students, and the magazine articles published about her before and after her death, bore the most eloquent testimony to the impact she had. Numerous students came to pay a *shiva* call, some more than fifty years after she had taught them as very young children in elementary school. Her impact on them, and on her own family, was indelible.

My father was a person of exceptional spirituality. He modeled the prayerful life, and movingly sang music he composed himself, or music composed by others, which all listeners could hear reverberated from the very depths of his soul. A gifted artist by profession, he was at the same time a remarkably diligent student of Torah. He overflowed with generosity of spirit, would invariably pull his car over at bus stops to offer rides to those waiting, and among many other acts of kindness put tefillin on a severely impaired person every week for over twenty-five years, often taking public transportation to do so. He was a man of good humor, joy, and equanimity, and despite the severity of his physical condition during the last years of his life, he never complained. Even at the very end of his life, when he couldn't move a finger due to severe Parkinson's disease, when we asked him how he was feeling his answer, invariably, was "Thank God, okay." He loved his family deeply, and was an inspiration to all with whom he came into contact.

May their memories be a blessing to their family, whom they loved so deeply and who amply returned their love, and to all whose lives they touched.

Finally, I wish to thank God for the many gifts He has bestowed upon me and my family. Each of us in our own distinctive ways endeavors to make the world a better place, and my prayer is that God continue to help us do so, with success, in good health, and in good cheer.

Introduction

This volume is my second one analyzing talmudic narratives, following upon *The Snake at the Mouth of the Cave: Exploring Talmudic Narratives.* The publication of that volume was widely reviewed and it generated many responses, thereby demonstrating to me that there exists a heretofore relatively untapped interest on the part of the English-reading public in the dramatic and profound narratives which abound in the Talmud.

Those unschooled in talmudic literature had rarely if ever encountered most of the narratives analyzed in that book, and those schooled in talmudic literature may have encountered them, but had rarely subjected them to rigorous analysis. Such is the way with most traditional students of the Talmud. They encounter an aggadic text during the course of their studies, may remark upon its mystery, and then quickly move on with their studies. Until I began to study aggada with great care, I confess that I personally was more or less amongst them. Yet I, and probably many others, felt a nagging sense that we were thereby missing something important, that the Talmud had something to teach us, but that our primary focus needed to be placed elsewhere, or that we lacked the tools to decipher these often mysterious texts.

No doubt some traditional students of the Talmud, upon encountering these texts and others like them, chose to consult one or more of the classical commentaries on the aggada, if they were especially interested, or if they possessed the time to do so. Yet as impressive as these commentaries might have been, at least this reader, and perhaps others as well, may still have experienced a lingering feeling that there was more to the aggada than met the eyes of even the greatest of its classic interpreters. First of all, these classical commentaries often disagreed amongst themselves. Second, many of the standard commentaries specializing in aggada were written hundreds of years ago, and as deeply informed and insightful as they may have been, they did not always speak to me as a student of the Talmud in the twentieth and twenty-first centuries. To take an example from the contemporary yeshiva world, those trained in the methods of what is called the "Brisker" approach to the analysis of rabbinic texts might not find the pilpulistic interpretations offered by many great sixteenth-century Polish Torah scholars very helpful to them. So too, contemporary students of talmudic narratives, with their own training and methods of analysis, might not find every classical interpretation to be as helpful to them as they would like. Of course, all such classical interpretations should be consulted and respected for the insight and knowledge they demonstrate, but each generation finds its own path into the intricacies and depths of the Talmud.

This seems especially true for talmudic narratives, for their subjects are human beings, not abstract principles of Jewish law. All human beings, as distinguished as they might be, possess a unique personal history, live in a particular period, in a particular geographic location, within a particular culture, and with the inner life that all human beings possess. Examining the context within which these figures lived provides extra insight into the narratives, and not every classical source made the fullest use of these contexts in interpreting the texts. Moreover, contemporary academic scholarship in the field of Talmud, as well as highly developed techniques of literary, psychological, and philosophical analysis available in modern scholarship, help provide fresh new perspectives as well, which have immeasurably enriched my own understanding of these narratives.

That said, I now wish to stress once again a point I made frequently in *The Snake at the Mouth of the Cave.* It is presumptuous for someone living in twenty-first-century New York to make any claims about some of the greatest religious figures in Jewish history. Who can even begin to penetrate the minds and spirits of such ancient rabbis as R. Yehuda HaNasi or Hillel, who lived in such different times and places, and whose lives as recounted in rabbinic sources epitomized extraordinary spiritual achievement and Torah knowledge? I wish to make this very clear: I make no assertions whatsoever about any of the talmudic figures featured in this volume, or its predecessor. Rather, my sole goal is to interpret the talmudic *text* which relates the narrative. The author or editor of the text possessed a message that he wished to convey, like the author or editor of any passage in the Talmud. Every rabbinic text calls for its interpretation, whether that text is halakhic or aggadic. What I seek to do in these volumes is to interpret these aggadic texts, to do my best to get at the messages they might convey. If the subject of the narrative is a talmudic great, then I seek to explore what that particular text might teach us about that individual, but that is altogether different from exploring what the talmudic Sage was truly like. The authors and editors of the Talmud often lived centuries after the protagonists of the narratives, and may have had their own personal point of view, or even axe to grind, about the issues at hand. We cannot know. All we can do is read the text as carefully and honestly as we can, and rigorously confront the many questions to which these narratives give rise, then struggle to the very best of our abilities to answer them. That is what I seek to do in this volume, no more, but no less.

Several reviewers of *The Snake at the Mouth of the Cave* noted that I frequently provide generous interpretations of the motives or behavior of the rabbinic protagonists in the narratives I analyze. Now I certainly do not seek to whitewash the sometimes-negative portrayals of rabbinic greats as they appear in the narratives, for to do so would be intellectually dishonest. However, these reviewers are correct in that where possible I often do provide generous readings. The stature of such figures as R. Akiva or R. Yoḥanan is amply attested to in their voluminous, inspirational teachings recorded in the Talmud, their vast knowledge of Torah, and in the many stories about them which appear in both Talmuds.

It was Maimonides who wrote in his *Commentary to the Mishna,*[1] on R. Yehoshua ben Peraḥya's teaching, that one should judge all people with the scale weighted in his favor. "If the person is known to be famously righteous and of good deeds, and an action of his is seen that all of its aspects indicate that it is a bad deed and a person can only determine it to be good with great stretching and distant possibility, it is fit that you take it that it is good, since there is some aspect of a possibility that it is good." This is quite a strong reading of the mishna, and I for one do not mean to maintain that all talmudic greats are perfect or never err, for that is true of no human being. However, I do maintain that generous readings of the narratives are indeed appropriate, but of course only where the context warrants this. The readers of that volume and this one will judge whether the readings I offer are indeed warranted.

Likewise, several reviewers noted that I analyze the texts as they appear in the classical edition of the Talmud, without examining their origins in time and space and how they took the form they did. This is correct; I noted this explicitly in the introduction to that volume, and I repeat it here. While such an endeavor can be very fruitful indeed, I leave it to those scholars who specialize in this undertaking, and like other scholars, I take the narratives as literary units in their own right, edited and placed as they were in the editions of the Talmud most widely read, referring occasionally to variant readings only where it seems especially warranted.

The Snake at the Mouth of the Cave was in many ways primarily biographical, in that over three chapters each, it traced the evolving lives of two leading figures from the rabbinic period, R. Eliezer and R. Yoḥanan. The remaining two chapters were biographical as well, focusing on narratives about two other Sages, Akavya ben Mahalalel and Ḥoni. This volume is more thematically than biographically focused, although since the narratives are about rabbinic Sages, they necessarily involve biographical elements as well.

The first theme of the book is entitled "Confronting the Other." In the first chapter, Rav Sheshet, who is blind, meets up with a heretic who sharply criticizes Rav Sheshet's behavior. The heretic, probably one

1. *Pirkei Avot* 1:5.

who denied the authority of the Oral Law, is surely outside the rabbinic mainstream, and is therefore an "other" to the Rabbis of the Talmud. Interestingly, Rav Sheshet's own blindness renders him, in his own way, outside the mainstream as well, and so each mirrors his interlocuter's otherness. The narrative suggests that their puzzling encounter reveals much about the true nature of sight and blindness, as it reveals much about the deeper significance of the Oral Law in Judaism.

In the second chapter, the great Sage Hillel confronts a man who does his very best to harass, annoy, and anger him. Hillel demonstrates his own remarkable approach to confronting those who seek to make our lives miserable, while at the same time revealing the limits of that approach as well.

In the third chapter, Rav Yannai meets up with a distinguished-looking man on the road and invites him to dinner. Rav Yannai then becomes so distraught at the man's apparent abject ignorance that he actually calls him a dog, only to regret doing so after he learns more about his guest, whose true identity nevertheless remains shrouded in enigma through the very end of the tale. This aggada teaches the reader much about the eternal mysteries of the human condition, as well as the moral implications of those mysteries.

The second section of the book is entitled "Piety, Poverty, and Wealth." The first chapter in this section presents the question of who deserves charity during a famine. The great R. Yehuda HaNasi, a wealthy man, opened his storehouses of food to the poor, but initially excluded those who were Jewishly ignorant from receiving his largesse. R. Yehuda HaNasi then struggled with that choice after a poor man, who was an apparent ignoramus, pushed his way into the storehouse, begging for food. "Feed me like a dog or a raven," he begged. After changing his mind multiple times, R. Yehuda HaNasi eventually opened his storehouses to all. Why did R. Yehuda HaNasi repeatedly change his mind? What motivated his decisions? Can we trace the sinuous passage of his thinking and feelings about this critical issue? And what does R. Yehuda HaNasi's journey teach the reader about the very nature of morality?

The next two chapters in this section focus on the experiences of the wives of two holy men who choose a life of divine service over a life of material well-being. What were their feelings about their husband's choices? What roles did they play in making crucial decisions for the household? Should one make extreme sacrifices for the sake of a life of extreme holiness? Miraculous events occur in each narrative, which serve to illuminate the dilemmas, the choices made, and the very different roles each wife played in the pious aspirations of their husbands, and in their own pious aspirations as well. These two narratives are uncommon in talmudic literature, in that they focus on the personal experiences of women rather than men, and therefore take on extra significance for students of talmudic literature.

The third and final section of the book is titled "Confronting the Past and Future." The first chapter in this section tells of a deathbed encounter between the great R. Yoḥanan ben Zakkai, the man most responsible for the survival of Judaism after the destruction of the Second Temple, and his students. He cries upon seeing them, expresses fears that he will not merit the World to Come, offers them altogether enigmatic advice before his death, and dies after uttering several very puzzling words. Why did a man who accomplished so much cry and fear for his own future in the afterlife, and what is the meaning of his enigmatic deathbed advice and mysterious final words? I shall argue that this dramatic scene makes most sense as a confrontation with a deeply troubling scene from R. Yoḥanan's past.

The second chapter in this section examines the breakdown of a marriage, the great R. Meir's role in that failure, and his attempt to repair the marriage through personal atonement. Here too, R. Meir must confront his own past in order to make healing possible in the future.

The third chapter in this section likewise involves confronting the past, in this case that of King David. King David goes on a hunt, encounters a giant who wishes to kill him, and is miraculously saved by his nephew and colleague, Avishai. The story abounds in fantastical events. One element of this chapter is methodological: How should the reader interpret talmudic narratives that at first glance seem to be fantastical? I examine various approaches taken by Jewish scholars throughout the ages, consider briefly their strengths and weaknesses, then propose an alternative method, according to which the narratives should be seen as dreams, or as dream-like sequences. This approach, likewise based upon classical, but far less well-known, sources, provides an exceptionally rich and revealing framework for analyzing these narratives, and I use that method to interpret the strange tale told in this aggada. This is a method I also employed in *The Snake at the Mouth of the Cave,* but here I give it more systematic treatment and a fuller methodological context.

The final chapter in this section, and the last one in the book, appropriately looks forward to the future rather than backward to the past, the future here being the Messianic Era. In this deeply puzzling narrative, R. Yehoshua ben Levi meets up with Elijah and asks him, *inter alia,* where he can find the Messiah and how he will identify him. Told that the Messiah awaits at the gates of Rome, R. Yehoshua finds him and asks him when he will come to redeem the Jews, but is deeply chagrined and puzzled by the answer he receives. When after all will the Messiah come? The narrative both answers and fails to answer that very crucial question.

The title of this volume is drawn from the aggada about Rav Yannai and his mysterious guest. This particular aggada is a resonant metaphor for the role of aggadic narratives in the lives of those who study them. Many of these narratives, upon both superficial and then careful reading, seem enigmatic, intricate, and difficult to penetrate. They are mysterious guests at the dinner table of all students of the Talmud, as they should be mysterious guests at the dinner tables of all human beings who wish to penetrate the hidden recesses of the life, times, moral and religious dilemmas, and teachings of some of the greatest Rabbis of the talmudic era. The mysterious guest at Rav Yannai's table taught him a set of complex moral and religious lessons about the human condition and about Judaism. It is my hope that this volume too will offer its readers insight into the complex moral and religious dimensions of the human condition, and of Judaism, that are encoded in these riveting texts.

Confronting the Other

Chapter 1

Who Is the Blind Man?

Berakhot 58a

INTRODUCTION

The capacity to see is usually considered to be a great gift, and indeed early in the daily liturgy the reader blesses God as the King of the Universe who gives sight to the blind. While sight is truly a blessing, and those who are blind must meet great challenges, it is nevertheless worth pondering whether sight is indeed an unqualified blessing. Might the blind person "see" what the sighted person cannot?

The story told in this aggada focuses on Rav Sheshet, a leading scholar from Babylonia in the late third–early fourth century, who at some point in his life became blind. He was an unparalleled master of the halakhic teachings of his predecessors, committed to memory as a result of unstinting effort, and a man of great piety and the firmest convictions, which he did not hesitate to share with even the senior political leadership of the community.[1] Rav Sheshet meets up with a

1. For an extensive biographical discussion with many primary and secondary sources cited, see Binyamin Lau, *The Sages, Volume V: The Yeshivot of Babylonia and Israel* (Jerusalem, 2022), 173–205.

heretic, who attacks him with the nastiest of language. This encounter as it unfolds poses important questions not only about the meaning of sight, but at a deeper level, about how best to approach the Divine in a world so far removed from Him.

רַב שֵׁשֶׁת סַגִּי נְהוֹר הֲוָה. הֲווֹ קָאָזְלִי כּוּלֵּי עָלְמָא לְקַבּוֹלֵי אַפֵּי מַלְכָּא, וְקָם אֲזַל בַּהֲדַיְיהוּ רַב שֵׁשֶׁת. אַשְׁכְּחֵיהּ הָהוּא צָדוֹקִי[2] אֲמַר לֵיהּ: חַצְבֵי לְנַהֲרָא, כַּגְנֵי לְיָיא? אֲמַר לֵיהּ: תָּא חֲזִי דְּיָדַעְנָא טְפֵי מִינָּךְ. חֲלַף גּוּנְדָּא קַמַּיְיתָא. כִּי קָא אָוְשָׁא, אֲמַר לֵיהּ הָהוּא צָדוֹקִי: אֲתָא מַלְכָּא. אֲמַר לֵיהּ רַב שֵׁשֶׁת: לָא קָאָתֵי. חֲלַף גּוּנְדָּא תִּנְיָינָא. כִּי קָא אָוְשָׁא, אֲמַר לֵיהּ הָהוּא צָדוֹקִי: הַשְׁתָּא קָא אָתֵי מַלְכָּא. אֲמַר לֵיהּ רַב שֵׁשֶׁת: לָא קָא אָתֵי מַלְכָּא.

The Gemara relates: **Rav Sheshet was blind. Everyone was going to greet the king and Rav Sheshet stood up and went along with them. This Sadducee found him** there and **said to him:** The intact **jugs** go **to the river, where do the broken** jugs **go?** Why is a blind person going to see the king? Rav Sheshet **said to him: Come see that I know more than you** do. **The first troop passed,** and **when the noise grew louder, this Sadducee said to him: The king is coming. Rav Sheshet said to him:** The king **is not coming. The second troop passed,** and **when the noise grew louder, this Sadducee said to him: Now the king is coming. Rav Sheshet said to him: The king is not coming.**

חֲלֵיף תְּלִיתַאי. כִּי קָא שָׁתְקָא, אֲמַר לֵיהּ רַב שֵׁשֶׁת: וַדַּאי הַשְׁתָּא אָתֵי מַלְכָּא. אֲמַר לֵיהּ הָהוּא צָדוֹקִי: מְנָא לָךְ הָא? אֲמַר לֵיהּ: דְּמַלְכוּתָא דְאַרְעָא כְּעֵין מַלְכוּתָא דִרְקִיעָא, דִּכְתִיב (מְלָכִים א יט, יא–יג): "צֵא וְעָמַדְתָּ בָהָר לִפְנֵי ה׳ וְהִנֵּה ה׳ עֹבֵר וְרוּחַ גְּדוֹלָה וְחָזָק מְפָרֵק הָרִים וּמְשַׁבֵּר סְלָעִים לִפְנֵי ה׳ לֹא בָרוּחַ ה׳ וְאַחַר הָרוּחַ רַעַשׁ לֹא בָרַעַשׁ ה׳. וְאַחַר הָרַעַשׁ אֵשׁ לֹא בָאֵשׁ ה׳ וְאַחַר הָאֵשׁ קוֹל דְּמָמָה דַקָּה".

2. Note that I have changed the text and translation for this word that is used in the *Sefaria* edition of the Talmud and translation, in use throughout this book, from "*min,*" which is translated as "heretic," to "*Tzadduki,*" translated as "Sadducee." This is to conform to the text in the classic edition of the Talmud. See note 4 below for discussion.

The third troop **passed,** and **when there was silence, Rav Sheshet said to him: Certainly now the king is coming. This Sadducee said to him: How do you know this?** Rav Sheshet **said to him: Royalty on earth is like royalty in the heavens, as it is written** with regard to God's revelation to Elijah the Prophet on Mount Horeb:

"And He said: Go forth,
and stand upon the mount before the Lord.
And, behold, the Lord passed by,
and a great and strong wind rent the mountains,
and broke in pieces the rocks before the Lord;
but the Lord was not in the wind;
and after the wind an earthquake;
but the Lord was not in the earthquake;
and after the earthquake a fire;
but the Lord was not in the fire;
and after the fire a still small voice.

And so it was, when Elijah heard it, that he wrapped his face in his mantle and went out, and stood in the entrance of the cave" (I Kings 19:11–13). God's revelation was specifically at the moment of silence.

כִּי אֲתָא מַלְכָּא, פְּתַח רַב שֵׁשֶׁת וְקָא מְבָרֵךְ לֵיהּ. אֲמַר לֵיהּ הָהוּא צְדוֹקִי: לְמַאן דְּלָא חָזֵית לֵיהּ קָא מְבָרְכַתְּ? וּמַאי הֲוֵי עֲלֵיהּ דְּהָהוּא צְדוֹקִי? אִיכָּא דְּאָמְרִי: חַבְרוֹהִי כַּחְלִינְהוּ לְעֵינֵיהּ, וְאִיכָּא דְּאָמְרִי: רַב שֵׁשֶׁת נָתַן עֵינָיו בּוֹ, וְנַעֲשָׂה גַּל שֶׁל עֲצָמוֹת.

When the king came, Rav Sheshet began to bless him. The Sadducee mockingly **said to him: Do you bless someone you do not see?** The Gemara asks: **And what ultimately happened to this Sadducee? Some say** that **his friends gouged out his eyes, and some say** that **Rav Sheshet fixed his gaze upon him, and** the Sadducee **became a pile of bones.**

RAV SHESHET MEETS A HERETIC

The aggada begins by providing crucial biographical background to the story, particularly mentioning Rav Sheshet's blindness. While the translation of the text uses the word "blind" to describe Rav Sheshet's condition, the original Aramaic text means literally "clear of vision," a widely used talmudic euphemism, or metaphor, for blindness. Thus, the original text asserts literally that Rav Sheshet possessed clear vision, although the connotation of the phrase in context is that he was blind. However, as we shall eventually see, the thesis of the aggada is precisely to subvert the euphemistic connotation of the phrase, and to assert that the literal, as well as the connotative metaphoric meaning, are both literally true. That is, while Rav Sheshet was indeed literally blind – the connotative meaning of the phrase – he also possessed, in his own way, literal clarity of vision – the literal meaning of the phrase. Thus, the very first words of the aggada subtly telegraph its ultimate message.

The aggada proceeds to relate that the king was approaching, the populace went out to greet him, and Rav Sheshet arose to join them. This was a conscious decision on the part of Rav Sheshet: The text asserts not only that he joined them, but that he *arose* to join them, no doubt from sitting in the study hall, engaged in Torah. Why did Rav Sheshet choose to leave the study hall merely to greet the king? Was he just following the crowd? This is hardly likely, given what we know about his intense and unflagging commitment to Torah study.

While the aggada itself does not directly answer this question, the context of the aggada certainly provides an important clue. In the passage just prior to the narrative, R. Yoḥanan is quoted as teaching: "One should always strive to run toward the kings of Israel [to greet them]. And not only toward the kings of Israel, but also toward the kings of the nations of the world, so that if he will be privileged he will distinguish between the kings of Israel and the kings of the nations of the world." While the exact meaning of the reason R. Yoḥanan gives for his teaching is somewhat obscure,[3] its import is not. The Talmud records our aggada immediately following the teaching of R. Yoḥanan, to exemplify it in Rav Sheshet's practice. Thus, it seems more than likely that Rav Sheshet indeed chose to greet the king because he was following the teaching of

3. See Rashi, ad loc., that the Jewish king here is a reference to the Messiah. I shall return to this point later in the chapter.

his great predecessor R. Yoḥanan. All this begs the question, of course, as to the meaning of R. Yoḥanan's teaching, a point we shall return to later.

Now a heretic, a Sadducee in the text of the classic edition of the Talmud,[4] meets up with Rav Sheshet on his way, and makes a startling and altogether nasty comment: "Intact jugs go to the river, where do broken jugs go?" He meant to say that by virtue of his blindness, Rav Sheshet is like a broken jug. While it does make sense to take a whole jug to the river to fill it with water, what sense does it make to take a broken jug to the river, if it cannot be filled with water? By analogy, the Sadducee meant to say, what sense does it make for Rav Sheshet to greet the king if he cannot even see him?

Of course, this is a very hurtful statement to make to a blind person, and one wonders what might have precipitated it. Is it attributable to no more than the clash of beliefs between them? Certainly, people with divergent religious beliefs can be rather nasty to one another. According to some textual variants, the Sadducee in question was raised as a

4. Most manuscripts do not read "Sadducee," but rather either "heretic" [*min*] or "heretic the son of a master's house" [*mina bar bei rav*]. See *Dikdukei Soferim* and other sources cited in R. Kalmin, *Jewish Babylonia: Between Persia and Roman Palestine* (Oxford, 2006), 222, n. 50. However, we must ask on what account the person in the aggada here is a heretic. While the term "*min*" in the Talmud is frequently a reference to Christians, Barak Cohen has argued that Christianity had not yet spread to the relevant parts of Babylonia during this period. (See his "'In Nehardea There Are No Heretics': The Purported Jewish Response to Christianity in Nehardea," in Dan Jaffe, ed., *Studies in Rabbinic Judaism and Early Christianity* [Leiden, 2010], 29–44.) Of course, another candidate for *min* would be a Sadducee, and several scholars have argued that proto-Karaites, often called Sadducees because both denied the legitimacy of the Oral Law, did exist at that time and place. (See the sources cited in Kalmin, p. 245, n. 37, although Kalmin himself is unsure of this.) Thus, it is altogether likely that the editor of the classic edition of this text either had a variant manuscript which read "Sadducee," or that he inserted "Sadducee" in lieu of the original text which read "*min,*" in order to more precisely identify the heresy of which the person was guilty, an identification which has considerable historical plausibility. Our analysis will seek to unpack the broader significance of this particular form of heresy to the overarching themes of the aggada. I might add that even if the reference here is to a Gnostic or Manichean heresy, the framework of the analysis offered below obtains, as we shall see. In any case, I conform to the text as it appears in the classic Vilna edition of the Talmud.

rabbinic Jew, then abandoned the faith of his fathers.[5] If so, as a renegade he may have felt anger toward those who represent the faith he had rejected. This too is hardly unknown in history. Indeed, some of the most vicious inquisitors during the Spanish Inquisition were Jews who had converted to Christianity. It is also possible that there was some previous, if unreported, history of cantankerous dialogue between them. We cannot say for sure.

Whatever the reason for the Sadducee's cutting comment, Rav Sheshet responds with a challenge: "Come see that I know more than you do." Note that Rav Sheshet introduces his challenge with the phrase "Come see," surely ironic in context. The Sadducee had attacked Rav Sheshet on account of his inability to see, and Rav Sheshet challenges him to see, as if to say, "You maintain that I cannot see. However, come see that I can indeed see, and that you are the one who cannot see." Of course, after saying "Come see," Rav Sheshet goes on to assert that he "knows more" than the heretic, not that he can see better than he can. However, as I shall argue, what this really means is that for Rav Sheshet, seeing without knowing has no value, and knowing even without visually seeing is what matters. Put differently, knowing is a kind of seeing, and the only kind of seeing of ultimate worth.

We would do well to recall here that in common parlance we frequently use the term "seeing" to mean "knowing" or "understanding." For example, after a teacher explains a difficult concept to a student, he or she might ask "Do you see that?" to mean "Do you understand or grasp that point?" "Seeing" is a metaphor here for "understanding" or "knowing."[6] When Rav Sheshet said "Come see that I know more than you do," he was probably intentionally playing on this metaphoric use of the term for sight, saying that while I cannot see, I challenge you to come see that I possess knowledge, which is a kind of sight.

Twice a troop of soldiers passes by, making all the noise that troops of soldiers can make; twice the Sadducee asserts to Rav Sheshet that the king is coming; twice Rav Sheshet informs him that he is wrong;

5. See note 4, above.
6. This is a theme in Maimonides' *Guide for the Perplexed* I:4 (Chicago, 1963), trans. S. Pines, 27–28, for numerous examples of this in Scripture.

and twice Rav Sheshet is vindicated: The king does not come. When the third troop passes, this time in silence, Rav Sheshet informs the Sadducee that the king will now come, and indeed he does. The Sadducee, no doubt astounded by the blind Rav Sheshet's perspicacity, asks Rav Sheshet how he knew this, and Rav Sheshet responds by quoting a verse from I Kings 19. God revealed Himself to Elijah the prophet in a "still, small voice," a symbol for silence, not tumult. Rav Sheshet maintains that there is an analogy between royalty in the heavens and royalty on earth. Therefore, if royalty in heaven – divine royalty – appears in silence, so too would human royalty. The king passes by, and Rav Sheshet then recites the blessing on a king, described in the talmudic passage just preceding the teaching of R. Yoḥanan.

At first blush, the use of this analogy by Rav Sheshet appears problematic. While there may be certain similarities between divine and human kings, surely there are many dissimilarities as well, a point Rav Sheshet would no doubt vigorously affirm. How then can Rav Sheshet predict with any certainty that the analogy holds for silence, but not for so many other qualities, such as incorporeality , omniscience, omnipotence, and so on? In fact, one might argue that the manifold differences between God and human kings are so overwhelming in scope that analogies between them would be difficult to draw. How then could Rav Sheshet so confidently predict when the human king would or would not arrive?

A possible answer to this question emerges from the broader context of the aggada, which is embedded in a halakhic discussion about obligatory blessings (the very name of the tractate in which it appears). The Talmud lists a variety of blessings in this discussion, including blessings on wise Jews and wise gentiles, and, of particular relevance to the aggada, blessings on Jewish and gentile kings. The blessings for kings of Israel, which Rav Sheshet recited, reads as follows:

> "Blessed... who has shared of His glory with those who revere Him." One who sees kings of the nations of the world recites "Blessed... who has given of His glory to flesh and blood."

A key word in these blessings is "glory" or "honor," "*kavod*" in Hebrew. These blessings assert that the glory possessed by a king, Jewish or gentile, derives from God Himself, who shares or grants His own glory to human kings. These blessings thus maintain that no glory or honor would accrue to a mortal king but for the fact that God provides it from His very own glory. With respect to glory, then, the blessings overtly affirm not only a similarity between the glory of the divine and human kings, but a unity between them, for God takes of His own glory to provide it to them. Their glory is really His. The language of the blessings thus provides the logic behind Rav Sheshet's analogy.

I shall have more to say about these blessings and their underlying meaning shortly, but this analysis for now provides a perfect segue into the next episode related in the aggada. The Sadducee, it turns out, was not defanged by Rav Sheshet's superior knowledge, and he levels yet another attack on Rav Sheshet and his blindness. "Do you bless someone you cannot see?" he mockingly asks. Interestingly, Rav Sheshet provides no verbal retort to this challenge. The next we hear, in a passage to be analyzed toward the end of this chapter, is that the Sadducee is physically attacked, either by his friends, or by Rav Sheshet himself.

But why did Rav Sheshet not respond verbally to the Sadducee's verbal attack on him, exactly as he did the first time? We cannot say for sure, but it is possible that by now he had discovered the limits of dialogue. If Rav Sheshet's demonstrably superior knowledge did not daunt the Sadducee, what then could? Many of us tend to think that enduring conversation with opponents is a good thing. Just keep on talking, so the theory goes, and eventually rapprochement may emerge. That may indeed be true sometimes, but it is hardly true always. There are some opponents who are so closed-minded, so obtuse to reason and evidence, so vehemently entrenched in their opinions, that dialogue is futile. If the Sadducee mocked Rav Sheshet even after his wisdom had been so brilliantly demonstrated, then Rav Sheshet may well have seen no gain to further conversation. No matter what he might have said, the mocking Sadducee would remain the mocking Sadducee.

Let us now consider more carefully the Sadducee's argument. Whether or not the Sadducee was knowledgeable in rabbinic law,[7] the

7. He might well have been knowledgeable in halakha, if he had been a heretic who started out as a rabbinic Jew. See n. 3, above.

author of the aggada no doubt was, and, as cited above, the law that kings must be blessed reads that "one who *sees* kings" must recite the relevant blessing.[8] This is a teaching that the author of the aggada, and possibly the Sadducee himself, would likely have known. But if seeing the king is what occasions the blessing, and Rav Sheshet, being blind, did not see the king, then Rav Sheshet should not have made the blessing, and *prima facie* the Sadducee was correct! Is the reason Rav Sheshet did not respond because in point of fact he had no response?

This is highly unlikely. Rav Sheshet was a master of halakha, and everything we know about him suggests that here, as elsewhere, he knew exactly what he was doing. The answer to this question almost certainly hinges upon the multiple meanings of the word "see." I argued above that "see" possesses both a literal and a metaphoric meaning. While Rav Sheshet was literally blind, metaphorically he was sighted, because he possessed knowledge; he knew when the king was present even if he could not literally see him. Rav Sheshet thus "saw" (metaphorically) the king through his knowledge, and could indeed make the blessing.[9] Let us remember that while the blessing is occasioned by seeing the king, the blessing is made not to the king, but to God, the King of Kings. God cannot be seen literally, but he can be "seen" metaphorically. That is, God can be known – if only in the profoundly limited way that any human being can really know Him. There is then a strict analogy between a blessing *for* a king, and all blessings, which are *to* the King of all Kings. Blessings can be uttered based upon (limited) knowledge, even without either the king, or the King of all Kings, being literally seen.

8. These blessings are classified in halakhic literature as "*birkhot hare'iya,*" blessings occasioned by seeing.
9. The *Pri Megadim, Eshel Avraham* (224:6) maintains that even if a blind person may generally not make *birkhot hare'iya,* blessings occasioned by seeing (of which there are many), he or she may still make the blessing on the king. This is because the blind person can sense the king's presence by the reaction of those who can see him, the awe and silence he provokes in others. Similarly, Ben Yehoyada, in his commentary to our passage in the Talmud, distinguishes between visual and cognitive sight. It should be noted that there is an extensive halakhic discussion of the status of a blind person with regard to such blessings, in the commentaries to *Shuḥan Arukh, Orḥ Ḥayim* 224.

As we shall see, this is a crucial point with respect to the overall theme of the aggada, but for now let us examine some of its implications by returning to R. Yoḥanan's teaching, which gave rise to Rav Sheshet's decision to greet the king. It will be recalled that R. Yoḥanan taught that one should strive to greet kings of Israel as well as kings of the nations of the world, so that if one merits, one will discern the difference between the two. What is the meaning of R. Yoḥanan's reasoning? Rashi suggests that the reference here is to the Messianic Era. If someone merits experiencing the Messiah, having already seen a gentile king, he or she will discern just how much more glory accrues to those who fulfill God's commands than accrues to the nations of the world in the pre-Messianic Era. Rashi in his interpretation thus shifts the focus from the difference in honor accruing to two kings to the difference in honor accruing to those who obey God's commands, and those, not Jewish, who do not. This seems a bit distant from a simple reading of the text itself, as does the insertion of the Messiah into R. Yoḥanan's teaching.[10]

However we are to understand Rashi, another reading does suggest itself, which takes us back to the original teaching about the blessings, the very teaching which had occasioned the Talmud's citation of R. Yoḥanan's teaching. What are the key linguistic differences between the blessing on a king of Israel and the blessing on a king of the nations of the world? The former asserts that God *shared* of His glory with *those who revere Him*, while the latter asserts that God *has given* of His glory to *flesh and blood*. Kings of Israel are called "those who revere God," while kings of the nations of the world are called "flesh and blood." God "shares" His glory with kings of Israel, but He "has given it" to kings of nations of the world. What do these differences amount to?

First, the status of the two kinds of kings is radically different. Israelite kings are assumed to revere God,[11] a status which places them in a living relationship with Him. Kings of nations of the world are no

10. R. Kalmin, p. 100, suggests that the king in the aggada about Rav Sheshet stands for the Messiah, whose eventual arrival will be heralded in silence.

11. Of course, the prophetic literature makes amply clear that many Israelite kings did not exactly fit this idealized description, unless one hypothesizes that at some murky level, no matter how corrupt they were, all Israelite kings did in fact revere God. Such a reading, though, would be far from straightforward.

more than flesh and blood, and in this respect no different from all living creatures, animals included. Second, and probably a consequence of the first, the means whereby God graces the two kinds of kings with His glory is different. If I share something with you, then you and I are both using what I still own. We are bound together by shared usage of the very same object. Thus, if I share my book with you, then I still retain its ownership, even as you use the very book that I own and may still use too. However, if I give you my book, then the book is no longer mine. There is no shared usage of the same object, and therefore donor and recipient are no longer bound together. Once the gift is given, it is given.

What this implies, then, is that if Israelite kings share in God's glory, then the very same glory that is God's is in some sense that of the Israelite king too, like two people who share the very same book. This is because Israelite kings revere God. The very glory that God the King possesses is manifest in the lives of those kings who revere Him too. A person who meets up with such a king will sense in his reverent, awe-filled presence the glory of the God this king reveres, in the same way that someone who has the good fortune to meet a saintly individual will feel God's presence in his or her life. A king who stands in awe of the King of Kings would naturally evoke awe in the religiously sensitive person who observes him. However, none of this is true for the kings of the nations of the world. Since they do not revere God, the glory they possess is not shared with Him. Their glory is temporal but not religious, unlike the glory of the king of Israel, whose temporal and religious glory merge.[12]

We are now positioned to understand why R. Yoḥanan taught that one should run to witness a king, so that if privileged he will distinguish between the two kinds of kings. The privilege here is the capacity to discern that the glory of the Israelite king is not only temporal but a glory shared with God Himself. The religiously sensitive person who observes a reverent Israelite king will experience God's own glory in the

12. While this formulation is mine, many classic rabbinic commentaries articulate similar ideas. See the commentaries of the *Beit Yosef* and *Baḥ* to *Arba Turim, Oraḥ Ḥayim* 224 on the passage dealing with blessings for wise men of Israel and gentile wise men. See too the commentaries of the *Taz* and *Magen Avraham* to *Shulḥan Arukh* 224:6. While these sources focus on blessings for wise men, their logic would apply to blessings for kings, and the *Baḥ* makes this connection explicit.

king's temporal glory, for the Israelite king's glory is not only temporal, but a manifestation of the glory of God whom the king reveres. In order to experience this difference, one must run to experience the glory of both kings, so that they may be contrasted.[13] Only the privileged person will succeed in penetrating to the true difference between them, and will succeed in experiencing God's glory in the glory of the Jewish king.

That said, the glory of the gentile king is also derived from God. Indeed, it was God's glory until He gifted it to the gentile king. What this likely means is that God's glory possesses a temporal element too. Whatever other qualities God has, He also possesses sheer might, power, and honor, which can be transferred over to a gentile king. In so doing, they lose some of their original meaning in God, for whom these qualities are inextricably linked with who He truly is. Nevertheless, enough of their significance can be retained to survive their transfer to a flesh and blood person. For this reason, Rav Sheshet could argue that kingly glory, divine or human, is kingly glory, and if God's glory is manifest in silence, so too would the glory of a flesh and blood king.

What then enabled Rav Sheshet to make all these inferences and distinctions? His understanding of God, the only real "sight" that possesses value. The Sadducee could never see beyond sight. That is, he was imprisoned by the limitations of physical sight. He could not comprehend why Rav Sheshet would bother to greet the king if Rav Sheshet could not visually see the king, nor could he understand how a blessing could be made on the king if the king could not be seen. For the Sadducee, visual sight exhausted the possibilities of seeing. But of course, for Rav Sheshet, that was entirely wrong. The only sight that matters is understanding. This understanding makes for him greeting the king valuable, and makes his blessing on greeting the king possible.

13. According to this analysis, one might ask why R. Yoḥanan did not also teach that people should run to experience wise men of Israel and gentile wise men too. The answer may well be that the wisdom which accrues to a Jewish wise man is the wisdom of Torah (as the commentators cited above note), and that kind of wisdom is so manifestly different from the wisdom of gentiles that no comparison is necessary.

THE MANY MEANINGS OF AN ENCOUNTER

Let us now examine the aggada in its broadest contours. Three inversions shape the development of the story. First, and the one on which we have focused so far, is the inversion of sight and blindness. Rav Sheshet is blind but "sees" the king, while the Sadducee is sighted but fails to know when the king arrives. Phrased differently, Rav Sheshet lacks sight but possesses insight, while the Sadducee possesses sight but lacks insight.[14] In the aggada, sight and insight stand in an inverse relationship. Sight blinds the Sadducee from insight, while the blindness of sight liberates insight. The Sadducee was imprisoned by sight, by what his eyes revealed to him, and therefore did not have the insight to know that kings are accompanied by silence. Nor did the Sadducee have enough insight to know that blessings may be made even on, and to, what cannot be seen. Put more broadly, the author of the aggada might mean to suggest that all human beings are sometimes misled by sight. The best evidence for the truth of a proposition for many people is that it can be empirically verified through observation. Conversely, the truth value of that which cannot be empirically verified through observation is suspect. At one level, this perspective seems like common sense. What cannot be seen may be a figment of the imagination.

However, consider the limitations of this perspective too. Much of modern science and scientific theory operate not on the basis of what can be empirically observed, but rather on what can be inferred from observation. No one can see electrons, nor can anyone see kinetic or atomic energy, yet these phenomena, amongst many others like them, shape our understanding and use of the world around us. To base one's picture of the world only upon what can be empirically observed would make contemporary science, so dependent upon abstract mathematical modeling, impossible. Indeed, one way to think about the history of science is as a story of the slow liberation of human

14. This theme emerges in classical literature as well. For example, in *Oedipus the King,* Tiresias the blind prophet knows Oedipus' origins and the cause of the plague in Thebes, while the sighted Oedipus does not. When Oedipus discovers the truth, he blinds himself. Sight and insight are inversely related.

beings from the prison of sight. Ironically, people who are blind will find it easier than people with sight to achieve that liberation. For a blind person to function in the world, he or she must be preternaturally attuned to sound, to reflecting or intuiting what occurs around them, to knowing without seeing.

If this is true of science, it is true for other dimensions of life as well. Thus, we see that Rav Sheshet understood what kings are like because he could not see them, and therefore was constrained to reflect about them, to understand what they are like at a deeper than sensory level of perception. To achieve this understanding Rav Sheshet would naturally look to the Torah for guidance in a sightless world. And that is exactly where he found it, in the verses from Kings. In short, while sight is a gift from God, upon which a daily blessing from the liturgy is made, it is nevertheless at the same time a prison. Sight inhibits insight, and Rav Sheshet's blindness therefore helped liberate him from the prison of sight.

This then is the first inversion, and it harkens back to the euphemism with which the aggada began, for let us recall that Rav Sheshet was called a person who is "clear of vision," a euphemism for blindness. This first inversion, and the overall theme of the aggada, is that behind the euphemism, behind the metaphor, lies a literal truth. Rav Sheshet really does possess clarity of vision, of insight, if not sight. This is a central teaching of the aggada which is adumbrated from its very beginning, and is the deeper truth that lies behind the euphemism.

The second inversion involves not sight but sound. The Sadducee – and probably many others like him as well – expected that the king would arrive amidst the sounds of trumpets blaring, the tumult of crowds, and the troops marching noisily. Yet this expectation was false. Silence accompanies the king, not sound. Rav Sheshet draws the explicit analogy between God and human royalty. Power, honor, and glory do not require physical manifestation. The greatest power is masked by silence, because it does not require noise to prove its power. The less power or talent a person has, the more he or she must make an effort to trumpet the power or gifts that the person possesses. This is one way (among others) to interpret Queen Esther's choice to abstain from excessive use of makeup and other ointment in preparation for her meeting with the king.[15] Secure people do not need to brag; it is only the insecure who must. It was Alfred Adler who said that "if we inquire into a superiority complex ... we can always find a more or less hidden inferiority complex."[16] A mark of a truly powerful king (or any person), divine or human, is that he does not need to proclaim that he is powerful.

In this sense, then, the second theme echoes the first. Both blindness and silence push down deeper to what lies behind mere sense perception. Both themes teach that reality is masked by those sense perceptions, by sight or by sound. Those who can penetrate beyond that mask achieve a Rav Sheshet wisdom. They know that silence, not sound, marks true power, and that sight blocks rather than reveals the deepest truths. Where there is silence, there is nothing to be heard, and where there is blindness there is nothing that can be seen. Yet it is precisely where sense perception is absent, where there is silence or blindness, that wisdom and insight emerge, as they did for Rav Sheshet but not for the Sadducee.

It is worth observing here that not only can sight block insight, but sound can block true listening as well. For just as there is a distinction between sight and insight, there is a parallel distinction between what we might call hearing and listening. Someone can hear what you say, but not really listen to you, not pay close attention, or not attend to what you are trying to communicate. Unfortunately, that is hardly a rare occurrence. Conversely, someone can listen to what you are really trying to communicate even if they cannot hear the words you are saying. They get it, by paying careful attention to your intonations or your facial expression and other non-verbal cues. People often say one thing but mean to communicate something else entirely, for which reason what is heard, the words that are actually articulated, can be misleading. For example, someone might stress again and again that she is perfectly happy living alone. However, as Shakespeare said, "The lady doth protest too much, methinks."[17] What this person really may mean to com-

---

15. Esther 2:15.
16. H. and R. Ansbacher, ed., *The Individual Psychology of Alfred Adler: A Systematic Presentation in Selections from His Writings* (NY, 1956), 259.
17. William Shakespeare, *Hamlet,* Act III, Scene II.

municate, despite her many words to the contrary, is that she is lonely. The person who listens rather than merely hears will not be misled by words. Thus, the two inversions, of sight and sound, echo one another and communicate the same theme.

There is yet a third inversion, but to see what that is we must examine the dramatic conclusion of the aggada. It will be recalled that after the Sadducee mockingly challenged Rav Sheshet on blessing someone he cannot see, the Talmud asks, "And what ultimately happened to this Sadducee?" The Talmud records two traditions.[18] The first is that the Sadducee's friends gouged out his eyes, and the second, that Rav Sheshet fixed his gaze upon the Sadducee, whereupon the Sadducee became a pile of bones. Let us examine each tradition more carefully.

At one level, of course, the Sadducee's blindness is a fitting *quid pro quo*. He mocked a blind man, and a perfectly fitting punishment would be for him to go blind himself. However, there is more to it than that, because in point of fact, the language in the original text does not literally mean that the Sadducee's friends gouged his eyes out. That is a euphemistic rendering of the original, which means literally that they applied makeup to his eyes. It is Rashi in his commentary who interprets this to mean that they gouged out his eyes.

Why does the author of the aggada choose a euphemism for blindness? Probably because it echoes the euphemism for blindness with which the aggada began. Rav Sheshet's blindness was ultimately clarity of vision, true insight. The Sadducee's sight was good, but his insight was poor. He could achieve insight only if he lost sight, so his eyes were gouged out, and this is literally denoted as beautifying his eyes. By losing his sight his eyes were beautified, because he gained the most important sight of all, insight. Now, like Rav Sheshet, the Sadducee too could learn to truly "see." In this respect, then, the first inversion discussed above, of blindness and sight, is true not only for Rav Sheshet, but is thematically recapitulated in his nemesis, the Sadducee. Rav Sheshet in his person

18. Y. Frankel, in "Bible Verses Quoted in Tales of the Sages," *Scripta Hierosolmitana*, Vol. XXII (Jerusalem, 1971), 98, n. 73, notes yet a third tradition recorded in many manuscripts, according to which sparks of fire came forth and singed the heretic's eyes.

demonstrates that lack of sight makes true "sight" possible, while the Sadducee, in his person, demonstrates that he must lose sight in order to gain sight, to achieve a beautification of his eyes.

But if this analysis is correct, why then does the Talmud not use the same euphemism for blindness as it used for Rav Sheshet? Why not say that his friends provided him with clarity of vision, the standard euphemism for blindness in the Talmud? This suggests that the Sadducee may not really have achieved true clarity of vision, and is therefore not the perfect parallel to Rav Sheshet. Moreover, why do his friends blind him? Of course, this may have been what actually happened. Yet the great care manifest in the writing of this aggada, and the symbolism which recurs, suggests there may be more to it than that. After all, the author could have written merely that his eyes were gouged out. Why was it important to note that the culprits were his friends?

To answer these questions, let us first reflect upon the difference between the two euphemisms: clarity of vision and beautification of eyes. The former is substantive, the latter superficial. If the primary function of eyes is to see, then eyes that possess clarity of vision function well. That is not true for beautified eyes. While they will appear to an outsider as attractive, they will function for sight no better than non-beautified eyes. Upon careful analysis, then, it turns out that the Sadducee never really achieved what Rav Sheshet had, for Rav Sheshet possessed clarity of vision, but the Sadducee possessed no more than beautified eyes. Put differently, the blinding of the Sadducee's eyes never achieved for him true reform, never enabled him to gain the insight of Rav Sheshet. His eyes were indeed improved by their blinding – they were "beautified" – but never to the extent of Rav Sheshet's eyes.

Let us now turn to the question regarding friends. Why were his friends the vehicles for his partial reform? At one level, their role serves to exclude Rav Sheshet as the person responsible for gouging out the Sadducee's eyes, in contrast to the second tradition recorded in the Talmud, according to which Rav Sheshet himself is responsible for the Sadducee's punishment. But to make that point, the author of the aggada could simply have written that others gouged out his eyes. Why insert "friends" specifically?

While we cannot say for sure, since there is no evidence from the text itself, it is possible that the Talmud wishes to convey that the Sadducee had broken the norms of discourse even within his own Sadducean society. The Sadducees were opponents of Rav Sheshet and his rabbinic brethren. Yet does religious disagreement warrant nasty behavior toward a blind man? On this reading the Talmud wishes to communicate that there are limits to theological debate. No matter how vigorously the Sadducees disagreed with the rabbis, certain language and speech should never be acceptable. A blind person may never be mocked, even if you sincerely believe that the blind person is a heretic who is leading others down the path of heresy. The Sadducee's friends understood the limits of religious debate, were shocked by the outrageous behavior of their friend and colleague which shattered the norms of civilized discourse, and they blinded his eyes in revulsion. Through the vehicle of the Sadducee's friends, the Talmud vigorously condemns his morally outrageous behavior.

According to the second tradition recorded in the Talmud, Rav Sheshet himself punishes the Sadducee. He gazes at him, and the Sadducee becomes a pile of bones. Herein then is the third great inversion of the aggada. At the outset, the Sadducee was the victimizer, mocking Rav Sheshet twice, and Rav Sheshet was the victim. By the end of the aggada, Rav Sheshet aggressively avenges his mistreatment by the heretic, and the Sadducee is no longer the victimizer but the victim, hoisted by the petard of his own moral and religious failures. The Sadducee's bones fall lifeless to the ground, but Rav Sheshet remains alive and erect, as vital as the Oral Law he embodies.

Note the irony in the use of the verb "gaze." Rav Sheshet, who cannot see, looks at the Sadducee, and with this look, kills him. This is yet another inversion of sight in the aggada. Rav Sheshet possesses no sight, yet his gaze can be deadly, for visual sight is not what true seeing is. Even if one possesses no visual sight, one's gaze can still be potent, for seeing is not all there is to gazing. Rav Sheshet possessed no sight, but did possess insight; he could penetrate to the deepest meaning of a person's life and thereby, where warranted, transform that life to death. Put differently, Rav Sheshet's insight, his "gaze," revealed the deep spiritual void within the Sadducee, the absence of moral and religious vitality, and thereby transformed his outer life to correspond precisely to his inner life. The Sadducee turned into an empty, desiccated pile of bones, the physical embodiment of his true inner spiritual and moral state, which only Rav Sheshet could apprehend.

This in turn leads us to reflect more carefully on the image of a pile of bones. That image is a vivid and powerful one, not uncommon in the Talmud,[19] and it would be valuable to consider it specifically in light of the Sadducee's beliefs. For is it not likely that Rav Sheshet's encounter with a Sadducee described here would be part and parcel of a rabbinic polemic against Sadducism, and that Rav Sheshet's two victories would be understood as two victories against this heresy? If we understand the aggada in this way, then we must ask ourselves what the image of a pile of bones might mean in that polemical context.

Recall now the core belief of the Sadducees: They denied the existence of the Oral Law, and lived only according to their literal and strict reading of the Written Law as recorded in the Torah. The Rabbis might ask us to imagine what Jewish life would be like if the Sadducees had emerged dominant over the Rabbis. They would argue that those who observe halakha can find their lives saturated with God, for every movement, every choice, every behavior is governed by halakha as developed and recorded by the Rabbis. The scope of rabbinic law is so sweeping that it touches almost every moment of the day. This makes for what can be a remarkably vital and rich religious life.

Sadducean Judaism, by contrast, is bereft of the richness of rabbinic law, and therefore would leave large stretches of the day devoid of that encounter with God. The rabbinic Jew, of course the author of the aggada included, would argue that Sadducean religious life is relatively empty of God and therefore spiritually desiccated. Exactly like a dry heap of bones, a brilliantly apt metaphor for Sadducean Judaism in the eyes of the Talmud. Rav Sheshet, a leader of the rabbinic Judaism of his day, saw exactly that. His gaze transformed the Sadducee into what he truly was: a pile of religiously empty bones. This reading thus suggests a powerful if subtle polemic against Sadducean Judaism.

---

19. E.g., Sanhedrin 100a, Shabbat 33b.

From this paerspective, the image of dry bones takes on yet another layer of meaning. For what is the relationship between the Oral and Written Law? One apt metaphor for this relationship is the relationship between the flesh of a human being and the skeletal structure on which the flesh rests. Bones are the scaffolding which holds up and gives shape to the flesh, muscles, tendons, and ligaments of the body. The Written Law, similarly, is the divinely revealed structure, the scaffolding, which holds up the infinite riches of the Oral Law. Yet it is the Oral Law which gives practical meaning, guidance, fullness, and spiritual beauty to Jewish practice and life. For rabbinic Jews, unlike for Sadducees, one without the other is unimaginable. From the perspective of the Talmud, then, Rav Sheshet's gaze illuminates the true essence of all Sadducees: They are no more than a heap of bones.

We can now deepen this point even further. When the Sadducee reads the Torah, he sees no more than what inheres in the simple reading of the text. For him, Judaism is what appears in the text. However, when the rabbinic Jew reads the Torah, he sees within its contours, its subtle and sometimes elusive language, its apparent contradictions and repetitions, the explication and development of Torah at the hands of rabbinic scholars throughout the ages. Rashi's classic commentary to the Torah is a brilliant example of the rabbinic organicity of the Written and Oral Law.

The difference between the Sadducean and rabbinic modes of reading the Torah exactly recapitulates the difference between sight and insight, which is one of the great themes of this aggada. The Sadducee possessed only sight but no insight. This is of a single theological and psychological piece with his Sadducism. To possess sight but no insight is to be imprisoned by appearances, by what the eyes visually see. The Sadducee, who possessed sight, could read, and he was trapped by the words of the text. For him, there could be no truth but what his eyes saw, and what they saw was only the Written Law. The very same narrowness of vision which prevented him from knowing when the king came, and from acknowledging that a blind person can make a blessing on a king that he does not see, also prevented him from seeing the possibility of an Oral Law within the Written Law. Not only is visual sight not a criterion for truth, it can even block its very apprehension.

This leads us back to the blessing on kings. As I noted above, the blessing is *for* a king, but it is made *to* the King of Kings, and for Rav Sheshet there is a strict analogy between them. God cannot be seen, and the king need not be seen, because the presence of both is apprehended, is known by faculties other than the visual. If the Jew can make a blessing to God, even if he cannot see Him, that is because the Jew affirms that there are modes of knowledge that do not require empirical evidence. And if there are modes of knowledge that do not require empirical evidence, such as "seeing" without visual sight, then why not make a blessing for a king who is not seen by visual sight, but is "seen" by apprehension?

It might be argued that this analogy cuts to the very heart of the enduring theological debate between the Sadducees and the Rabbis. The difference between the Sadducee and Rav Sheshet over the blessing may be much more than a technical legal dispute. Rather, one might argue that it rests on two fundamentally different conceptions of the role of sense perception in life and in religion, and indeed very different conceptions of the meaning of reality. The Sadducee's vision was this-worldly and proto-scientific, empirically grounded in what can be seen. God's word is what appears in the Written Torah, and no more. Life is restricted to a world we can see, and does not admit to an ethereal life after death which cannot be seen. The Rabbis, of course, affirmed belief in the World to Come, a tenet which the Mishna canonized as central to rabbinic Judaism.[20] While God Himself cannot be seen, He is the exception that proves the rule, which is that all else other than Him is centered around what can be perceived by the senses. Therefore, while a blessing may be made to an invisible God, it cannot be made occasioned by an invisible king.

However, the Rabbis re-centered that conception of life and religion, around what cannot be seen by sight, but what can be apprehended by insight. For the Rabbis, the deepest truths rest not in the wind, the earthquake, or the fire, but in the "still, small voice," the far more magnificent reality which lurks behind what can be perceived by the senses. Jewish life is guided by the Oral Law, hidden within the crevices of the

20. Sanhedrin 11:1.

Written Law, not by the Written Law alone; it is guided by what cannot be seen but can only be apprehended. The Rabbis looked beyond sense perception to an alternate reality, which shaped their experience of the sensual reality in which they lived. For the Rabbis, God was not the exception that proved the rule, but the very highest expression of a rule that governed all.

For this reason, the analogy following from the text of the blessing between the King of Kings and the human king is strict. If a blessing can be made *to* an invisible King of Kings, it can be occasioned *by* an invisible king as well. This may be the deepest meaning of Rav Sheshet's teaching, that "royalty on earth is like royalty in the heavens." Judaism looks to an existence beyond what can be perceived by the senses as the most apt model for understanding what can be perceived by the senses, for apprehending reality, and for living a Jewish life.[21] It turns out, then, that the reading offered here, while not directly entailed by the text, reveals an underlying theological unity to the entire story, and richly unpacks its symbolism.

Our aggada ends with the resounding victory of this rabbinic conception of the world over its nemesis, the Sadducean conception of the world. Yet the defeat of this Sadducee does not entail the defeat

---

21. As noted earlier, this entire analysis follows the text of the classic Vilna edition which reads "Sadducee" rather than "heretic." I believe it is likely that either the editor of this edition followed a manuscript to that effect, or that he inserted "Sadducee" in place of "heretic" to offer an interpretation of just what the heresy was, and a historically very plausible one at that. I would argue that the analysis offered in this chapter demonstrates the very rich interpretive meanings made possible by the Vilna version of the text. Nevertheless, it is at least possible that the heretic referred to in many other editions of the text is not a Sadducee but a Gnostic or Manichean, both dualistic worldviews. While the full analysis offered here would not apply, suffice to say that elements of it would, for within the classic Gnostic and Manichean worldviews, God as the force for good is hidden or not present in a world subject to other forces. This worldview strips the universe in which we live of its divine goodness. Sight yields only forces for evil, although insight – Rav Sheshet's vision – yields an apprehension of goodness that ultimately controls the world. The same insight/sight dichotomy thus plays out. Moreover, the motif of the pile of bones would also make sense, as a dualistic world leaves its inhabitants bereft of divine goodness, like desiccated bones. More could be said about this, but my focus in this chapter has been on the Sadducee reading, to which I adhere.

of his worldview. Karaism would emerge to revive similar beliefs and practices starting in the eighth century, and the tension between a this-worldly, quasi-"scientific" worldview and a pronounced otherworldly one continues to live on in Judaism to this very day. The pile of bones manages to endure.

Chapter 2

Hillel and the Harasser

Shabbat 30b–31a

INTRODUCTION

How should an educator respond to a harassing student? How should anyone respond to a person who actively seeks to annoy him or her? This question has bedeviled teachers and all human beings over the ages, and it is one that Hillel confronted just over two millennia ago. Hillel was one of the outstanding Torah scholars and leaders of all time whose teachings shaped and continue to shape rabbinic Judaism to this very day. Aside from Hillel's immense learning and devotion to spreading Torah to all interested Jews, he was also famous for his modest, tolerant, and welcoming character, in sharp contrast to his great halakhic antagonist Shammai, noted for his impatience. The aggada which is the focus of this chapter begins with the following teaching: "A person should always be patient like Hillel and not impatient like Shammai."

While this is a lovely thought, it nevertheless raises a variety of questions. Are there any limits to patience? Should there be? What is the value of patience? What practical steps might one undertake to preserve patience in the face of verbal assault? What are the responsibilities of a teacher to a disrespectful student? What strategies might the teacher employ to teach the student, and to influence him or her to improve? What is the cognitive basis that supports patience, and can it be learned?

Unfortunately, we cannot ask Hillel directly how he would answer these questions. Nevertheless, the Talmud relates a fascinating story about Hillel to exemplify the teaching cited above. As we shall see, its careful study may help illuminate just how Hillel himself might have responded to these questions, if we could have asked him.

תָּנוּ רַבָּנַן: לְעוֹלָם יְהֵא אָדָם עַנְוְותָן כְּהִלֵּל וְאַל יְהֵא קַפְּדָן כְּשַׁמַּאי. מַעֲשֶׂה בִּשְׁנֵי בְּנֵי אָדָם

Since the Gemara discusses the forbearance of Sages, who remain silent in the face of nonsensical comments, it cites additional relevant examples. **The Sages taught** in a *baraita*: **A person should always be patient like Hillel and not impatient like Shammai.** The Gemara relates: There was **an incident** involving **two people**

שֶׁהִמְרוּ זֶה אֶת זֶה, אָמְרוּ: כָּל מִי שֶׁיֵּלֵךְ וְיַקְנִיט אֶת הִלֵּל יִטּוֹל אַרְבַּע מֵאוֹת זוּז. אָמַר אֶחָד מֵהֶם: אֲנִי אַקְנִיטֶנּוּ. אוֹתוֹ הַיּוֹם עֶרֶב שַׁבָּת הָיָה, וְהִלֵּל חָפַף אֶת רֹאשׁוֹ. הָלַךְ וְעָבַר עַל פֶּתַח בֵּיתוֹ, אָמַר: מִי כָּאן הִלֵּל, מִי כָּאן הִלֵּל? נִתְעַטֵּף וְיָצָא לִקְרָאתוֹ. אָמַר לוֹ: בְּנִי, מָה אַתָּה מְבַקֵּשׁ? אָמַר לוֹ: שְׁאֵלָה יֵשׁ לִי לִשְׁאוֹל. אָמַר לוֹ: שְׁאַל בְּנִי. שָׁאַל: מִפְּנֵי מָה רָאשֵׁיהֶן שֶׁל בַּבְלִיִּים סְגַלְגַּלּוֹת? אָמַר לוֹ: בְּנִי, שְׁאֵלָה גְּדוֹלָה שָׁאַלְתָּ. מִפְּנֵי שֶׁאֵין לָהֶם חַיּוֹת פִּקְחוֹת.

who wagered with each other and **said: Anyone who will go and aggravate Hillel** to the point that he reprimands him **will take four hundred** ***zuz*. One of them said: I will aggravate him. That day** that he chose to bother Hillel **was Shabbat eve, and Hillel was washing** the hair on **his head. He went and passed the entrance to** Hillel's **house** and in a demeaning manner **said: Who here is Hillel, who here is Hillel?** Hillel **wrapped himself** in a dignified garment **and went out to greet him. He said to him: My son, what do you seek? He said to him: I have a question to ask.** Hillel **said to him: Ask, my son, ask.** The man asked him: **Why are the heads of Babylonians oval?** He was alluding to and attempting to insult Hillel, who was Babylonian. **He said**

to him: My son, you have asked a significant question. The reason is **because they do not have clever midwives.** They do not know how to shape the child's head at birth.

הָלַךְ וְהִמְתִּין שָׁעָה אַחַת, חָזַר וְאָמַר: מִי כָּאן הִלֵּל, מִי כָּאן הִלֵּל? נִתְעַטֵּף וְיָצָא לִקְרָאתוֹ. אָמַר לוֹ: בְּנִי, מָה אַתָּה מְבַקֵּשׁ? אָמַר לוֹ: שְׁאֵלָה יֵשׁ לִי לִשְׁאוֹל. אָמַר לוֹ: שְׁאַל בְּנִי. שְׁאַל: מִפְּנֵי מָה עֵינֵיהֶן שֶׁל תַּרְמוֹדִיִּין תְּרוּטוֹת? אָמַר לוֹ: בְּנִי, שְׁאֵלָה גְּדוֹלָה שָׁאַלְתָּ. מִפְּנֵי שֶׁדָּרִין בֵּין הַחוֹלוֹת.

That man **went and waited one hour,** a short while, **returned** to look for Hillel, **and said: Who here is Hillel, who here is Hillel?** Again, Hillel **wrapped himself and went out to greet him.** Hillel **said to him: My son, what do you seek?** The man **said to him: I have a question to ask. He said to him: Ask, my son, ask.** The man asked: **Why are the eyes of the residents of Tadmor bleary** [*terutot*]? Hillel **said to him: My son, you have asked a significant question.** The reason is **because they live among the sands** and the sand gets into their eyes.

הָלַךְ וְהִמְתִּין שָׁעָה אַחַת, חָזַר וְאָמַר: מִי כָּאן הִלֵּל, מִי כָּאן הִלֵּל? נִתְעַטֵּף וְיָצָא לִקְרָאתוֹ, אָמַר לוֹ: בְּנִי, מָה אַתָּה מְבַקֵּשׁ? אָמַר לוֹ: שְׁאֵלָה יֵשׁ לִי לִשְׁאוֹל. אָמַר לוֹ: שְׁאַל בְּנִי. שְׁאַל: מִפְּנֵי מָה רַגְלֵיהֶם שֶׁל אַפְרִקִיִּים רְחָבוֹת? אָמַר לוֹ: בְּנִי שְׁאֵלָה גְּדוֹלָה שָׁאַלְתָּ - מִפְּנֵי שֶׁדָּרִין בֵּין בִּצְעֵי הַמַּיִם.

Once again the man **went, waited one hour, returned, and said: Who here is Hillel, who here is Hillel?** Again, **he,** Hillel, **wrapped himself and went out to greet him. He said to him: My son, what do you seek? He said to him: I have a question to ask. He said to him: Ask, my son, ask.** The man asked: **Why do Africans have wide feet?** Hillel **said to him: You have asked a significant question.** The reason is **because they live in marshlands** and their feet widened to enable them to walk through those swampy areas.

אָמַר לוֹ: שְׁאֵלוֹת הַרְבֵּה יֵשׁ לִי לִשְׁאוֹל, וּמִתְיָרֵא אֲנִי שֶׁמָּא תִּכְעוֹס. נִתְעַטֵּף וְיָשַׁב לְפָנָיו. אָמַר לוֹ: כָּל שְׁאֵלוֹת שֶׁיֵּשׁ לָךְ לִשְׁאוֹל שְׁאַל. אָמַר לוֹ אַתָּה הוּא

הִלֵּל שֶׁקּוֹרִין אוֹתְךָ "נְשִׂיא יִשְׂרָאֵל"? אָמַר לוֹ: הֵן. אָמַר לוֹ: אִם אַתָּה הוּא, לֹא יִרְבּוּ כְּמוֹתְךָ בְּיִשְׂרָאֵל. אָמַר לוֹ: בְּנִי, מִפְּנֵי מָה? אָמַר לוֹ מִפְּנֵי שֶׁאִבַּדְתִּי עַל יָדְךָ אַרְבַּע מֵאוֹת זוּז. אָמַר לוֹ: הֱוֵי זָהִיר בְּרוּחֲךָ כְּדֵי הוּא הִלֵּל שֶׁתְּאַבֵּד עַל יָדוֹ אַרְבַּע מֵאוֹת זוּז וְאַרְבַּע מֵאוֹת זוּז, וְהִלֵּל לֹא יַקְפִּיד.

That man **said to him: I have many** more **questions to ask, but I am afraid lest you get angry.** Hillel **wrapped himself and sat before him,** and **he said to him: All of** the **questions that you have to ask, ask** them. The man got angry and **said to him: Are you Hillel whom they call** the *Nasi* **of Israel? He said to him: Yes. He said to him: If** it **is you,** then **may there not be many like you in Israel.** Hillel **said to him: My son, for what** reason do you say this? The man **said to him: Because I lost four hundred** *zuz* **because of you.** Hillel **said to him: Be vigilant of your spirit** and avoid situations of this sort. **Hillel is worthy of having you lose four hundred** *zuz* **and** another **four hundred** *zuz* **on his account, and Hillel will not get upset.**

A MAN COMES TO HILLEL'S DOOR

The troubling encounter described here took place after Hillel had already been appointed *Nasi*, leader of the Jewish community, and he would have been a famous, even revered figure.[1] Despite his high office, however, Hillel was a man of great modesty, patience, and tolerance, and his reputation for these qualities was so established and widespread that two troublemakers could offer the sum of four hundred *zuz* to anyone who would successfully aggravate him.

One man, whom we'll call the harasser, takes up the challenge, and approaches Hillel on Friday, as he was shampooing his hair in preparation for Shabbat. The timing here is crucial. Friday is typically known to be a very busy day, people rush to finish what they must before Shabbat begins, and tempers can sometimes fray. On top of that, the harasser chooses a most inopportune time to come to the door, as Hillel is washing his hair, and is no doubt full of soap and water. This is hardly a conducive time to be questioned, and would surely add to

1. See Rashi s.v. *Mikan.*

Hillel's annoyance. Who today would want to be bothered with someone banging on the door while he is showering? The reader might wonder whether the harasser knew that Hillel was shampooing his hair at that moment. While we cannot say for certain, it is surely possible that he chose a time when many people would be doing exactly that.

The harasser approaches the door to Hillel's home and shouts, probably at the top of his lungs, "Who here is Hillel, who here is Hillel?" This is demeaning to Hillel in several ways. First, he does not knock on the door respectfully, but rather stands outside the door and shouts. Second, he doesn't ask, even in a loud voice, whether he might pose some questions to Hillel. Rather he yells, demanding to know if anyone present is Hillel, as if to imply that Hillel is no more than an unknown servant around the house rather than the *Nasi*. Moreover, he repeats the phrase twice, adding insult to injury. Given Hillel's stature, this behavior is extremely disrespectful and entirely inappropriate.

Hillel's response is both revealing and fascinating. The first point to make is that Hillel actually does respond. Many of us in similar circumstances would be so repelled by the man's obnoxious behavior that we wouldn't even bother to meet with him, but that was not Hillel's way. He does respond, and the first action he takes is to wrap himself in a garment, probably a *tallit* or another dignified article of clothing, reflecting his elevated position in the community. This act is repeated no less than four times in the story. Why did he do so, and why is it so important as to warrant such repetition?[2]

First, wrapping oneself in a garment disposes the wearer to self-restraint and discipline. A person dressed casually is likely to be less on guard in his speech and behavior than someone dressed formally, especially someone wrapped in, and covered by, a large garment.

This would be especially true if what Hillel wore was the equivalent of professional attire. The Talmud teaches that in a Jewish court of law, a trial begins formally only when the judges wrap themselves in their cloaks. Rashi explains that judges wear their *tallitot* as an expression of

---

2. For an excellent discussion of the significance of wrapping oneself in a garment, and for this whole aggada, see R. Vaknin, "*What Your Heart Wants*" (Jerusalem, 2013), ch. 26 (Heb.).

their fear of God, and to help them focus their attention only on the litigants, with a settled mind.[3] Such attire conduces to this sensibility. Indeed, there is an ancient tradition in many countries continuing into the present that judges wear robes in court, probably for much the same reason. Other professionals too, such as physicians, wear their own characteristic attire. Hillel probably feared that the person yelling for him at the door might trigger an angry response on his part, and he dressed to help protect himself from impulsivity. He would be as measured in his words as he was in his dress.

Yet another element of this attire is that it expresses respect for oneself, and for the questioner too. If I dress with dignity, I carry myself with dignity. If I dress with dignity to greet someone, then I am also showing my respect for the person I am greeting. Hillel wanted to demonstrate via his dress that he took the questioner and his questions seriously. He was communicating, non-verbally, that the questioner deserved the same careful consideration as if he were a litigant before the court and Hillel were the honored judge. This humane attitude, represented initially by Hillel's dress, will become ever more apparent as the story unfolds. Indeed, it is one of the very themes of the aggada. How interesting, then, that such a deeply moral theme can be disclosed by a mere article of clothing.

Finally, by wrapping himself with such dignity, Hillel is signaling to the man at the door that he expects to be treated with the dignity his stature commands. Of course, this is not a matter of ego, for Hillel was a man of incomparable modesty, the very point of the aggada. Rather, it is a means for Hillel to help reshape a relationship that appears to have begun very poorly.

As an aside, it is worth pondering the implications of this teaching for contemporary educators. Ever since the 1960s, it has become commonplace for educators at all levels, from elementary school to university (and other professionals as well), to dress casually. This idea was born of the egalitarian impulse of the times. Are professors any better than the students they teach? If professors dress like their students, then an atmosphere of collegiality would ensue, in which everyone in

3. Shabbat 10a and Rashi s.v. *Dayanim*.

the classrooms are equal seekers after the truth. While this idea is surely noble, one wonders, after reflecting on Hillel's attire, if it has come at too great a cost. What inappropriate behavior or speech by professors might have been prevented had they dressed in more formal attire, keeping the boundaries between student and professor clearly delineated? Of course, this does not mean to suggest that there is a direct causal link between informal attire and inappropriate behavior, for that is far too simplistic. Rather, it is to note that formal attire may serve to remind instructors of the expectations attached to their role, and to encourage students to relate to them accordingly.

Hillel, now wrapped in his garment, emerges from the house to encounter the man who had yelled. He asks him, "My son, what do you seek?" Note that Hillel uses a term of endearment to address the harasser, calling him "my son." It is remarkable enough that Hillel goes out to greet him, given the disrespect he was shown, but he even calls him "my son"! Note also that he asks him what he seeks. A more natural question might have been "What would you like to ask me?" or "What do you want (in Hebrew, *rotzeh*)?" The word "seek," in Hebrew "*mevakesh,*" reaches broader and deeper. Hillel meant to ask him what he was really after. What was he seeking in treating Hillel with such disrespect, what lay behind his outrageous behavior? Was there something troubling deep within him which motivated his quest? And if there were, how could he, Hillel, help him?

Moreover, Hillel is treating the harasser with far more respect than the harasser has shown him. If the harasser is truly seeking something, then he must be serious. And if he is serious, then he should act that way too. By treating the harasser with respect, Hillel hopes to evoke respectful behavior in him. Students do sometimes rise to the higher bar that instructors set.

The harasser responds that he has a question to ask, and Hillel immediately says, "Ask, my son, ask." He calls the harasser "son" a second time, and utters the verb "ask" twice, both reflecting warmth and endearment. So far, Hillel reacts to the disrespectful harasser with words of love and respect, communication reinforced non-verbally by the garment in which he chose to wrap himself. We might read Hillel's message this way: "My son, I love and care about you as a fellow Jew and human being, despite your provocative behavior. I take you, your questions, and your life very seriously indeed. I want to understand you, understand what motivates you, what problems might be bothering you, and work with you to address them."

The harasser now poses his first question: "Why are the heads of Babylonians oval?" This is surely a surprising question to ask the greatest rabbinical leader of the generation! The shape of Babylonian heads is not a matter of Jewish law or lore, indeed has no obvious religious significance at all. Moreover, what is the urgency of the question? Must Hillel interrupt his preparations for Shabbat to answer what appears to be no more than an idle question? And does Hillel not have other things to do in the rush before Shabbat than answer a question like this? Moreover, Hillel himself was from Babylonia. Surely he might have taken umbrage at this less than subtle criticism of his origins.

Of course, this was exactly the harasser's intent: to harass Hillel. Yet Hillel does not respond as expected, and as most of us probably would have responded. He once again calls the questioner "my son," and even compliments him on asking something important, thus offering him positive reinforcement. Taking the question with utmost gravity, he proposes an answer, that Babylonian midwives are less than competent, and they mishandle babies' heads at birth. This satisfies the harasser, who then departs. He now waits an hour, Shabbat is even closer, and he returns once again to Hillel's home. The scene, with identical verbiage, repeats itself: He yells provocatively, "Who here is Hillel, who here is Hillel?" Hillel yet again emerges wrapped in a garment, and repeats the very same words, "My son, what do you seek?" The harasser again asserts that he has a question to ask, and again Hillel says, warmly, "Ask my son, ask." Why did the harasser leave, if only to return to ask yet another question? Probably because leaving, then returning, would be more annoying to Hillel than just posing another question right after the first one.

In any case, the harasser now poses another question: "Why are the eyes of the residents of Tadmor bleary?" Once again, the question appears idle and is about nothing obviously Jewish, yet once again Hillel addresses it with utmost gravity. He responds, again with warmth, that the question is significant, and offers an answer, that Tadmor is sandy, and the sand gets into the eyes of those who live there, leading to blurry vision. This too satisfies the harasser and he leaves, but only to return once again an hour later. The yelling at the door, the entire scene and language exactly recapitulate themselves. Hillel, showing the greatest imaginable patience, dresses again in his wrap, and responds exactly as he did before, despite the repeated provocations. This time the harasser asks another question, "Why do Africans have wide feet?" Hillel, ever respectful, takes the question seriously and answers that Africans walk in marshlands, for which wide feet are advantageous.

Finally, the harasser says that he has many more questions to ask, but fears that Hillel will get angry. Ironically, this statement in itself was probably designed to anger Hillel, for Hillel had just demonstrated how unfathomably patient he was, and now the harasser has the temerity to suspect him of veering into anger! Yet again, Hillel does not take the bait. He again wraps himself in his cloak, sits down – the first time in the aggada that he is described as sitting – and responds to the harasser: "All the questions you have to ask, ask them." The reader of our aggada will certainly be troubled by some things here: Why does Hillel sit? Why does he wrap himself yet again in his cloak, considering that he had just wrapped himself to answer the previous question, and no break occurs between the two questions? And why does Hillel not use the same warm words as before, "Ask my son, ask"?

Hillel may well have detected a subtle shift in the questioner's posture, and responded in kind. On the one hand, by sitting down, Hillel wishes to communicate to the harasser that he remains loyal to him and to what he "seeks," that he is ready to spend as much time with him as necessary to answer his endless idle questions, as if to say, "We have all the time in the world, so let's begin." He wants the harasser to know that he has Hillel's full attention and focus. On the other hand, this could take a great deal of time, and Shabbat was approaching quickly. By not using the same warm words that he had used during their previous three interactions, Hillel subtly conveys to the harasser that he has stepped just a mite too far. Not that Hillel would get angry at him, for Hillel would never lose his temper, but now he no longer wishes to show the harasser the same warmth. Moreover, Hillel knows that his tolerance would be more sorely tested than ever before, and so he rewrapped himself in his cloak to protect himself from anger. In the end,

Hillel still remains a rock of enduring patience in the face of pestering provocation, even if he subtly changes his language.

WHY IS HILLEL SO PATIENT?

Before examining the harasser's response to Hillel's offer, we must now ask ourselves just why Hillel behaved as he did. This is the crucial question in our aggada. No doubt Hillel was a man of expansive patience, and it was he who taught that "an impatient man cannot teach."[4] Nevertheless, it is difficult to understand what justified his extreme behavior. Even one patient encounter with the obnoxious harasser would have been beyond the call of duty. But three shouts at the door, three idle questions unrelated to Torah, all poorly timed and in immediate succession, finally capped by a fourth request for open-ended time, seems beyond the pale. The Talmud just prior to the outset of the story cites the teaching of Proverbs, "Answer not a fool according to his folly" (26:4). Surely this is an apposite critique of Hillel, as the Maharsha points out.[5] Moreover, why does Hillel exactly replicate his attire and language on the first three occasions? Even a patient person might alter his responses, to at least suggest subtly to the harasser that he had crossed the boundaries of civility. Why did Hillel wait until their fourth interaction to do so?

Rabbi Yaakov Reischer (late seventeenth- to early-eighteenth-century Prague) in his commentary to this passage in *Iyun Yaakov* (included in the standard editions of the *Ein Yaakov*) makes an interesting suggestion: If a student or parishioner approaches a rabbi with a foolish question, and the rabbi responds harshly, this person is unlikely to approach the rabbi for another question, one which might actually be of paramount importance. Every rabbi or teacher must offer positive reinforcement to one who asks even the silliest of questions, because

4. *Pirkei Avot* 2:6.
5. S.v. *Mipnei ma*. The Maharsha himself sees symbolic significance to the three questions. Misshapen heads symbolize arrogance, bleary eyes symbolize an evil eye, and wide feet symbolize greed. Hillel considered the harasser to be asking about these three character traits, which elevates the status of the questions, for which reason Hillel took them seriously. However, this interpretation seems at face value to be far removed from the simple reading of the aggada.

it is imperative that this questioner feel welcome to ask again. A rabbi's or teacher's door must always remain open. Perhaps not surprisingly, R. Reischer himself was a communal rabbi, occupying positions in Worms and Metz.[6] He may well have known from his own rabbinic experience just how important this approach can be.

While this may be part of the answer, it does not seem to go far enough, for why replicate the exact language and attire on each occasion? Why the love and terms of endearment? A respectful answer would keep the door open too.

Other factors may be at play here. Let us recall that the harasser is just that, a harasser. How then does a teacher cope with so provocative and obnoxious a student? One answer this aggada suggests is by offering him or her warmth and love. If a student is obnoxious it is likely that something is bothering him at home, with friends, or at school, so he vents in frustration and anger at the teacher. One way to help heal that anger is through love. If a teacher validates the student's questions, he is validating the student himself. Recall that Hillel asked what the harasser "seeks," what he is really after, what troubles him down deep. If a teacher communicates to the troubled student that he cares about and respects him or her, that he wants to work together with the student to address not only technical questions but what he or she really "seeks" deep down, then the teacher opens lines of communication that can begin a healing process. While there is much to be said in favor of this interpretation, one wonders if it adequately explains the aggada. What after all is the significance of these particular questions?

Another consideration is that if a teacher responds in anger to an obnoxious student, he or she has lost control of the teaching encounter. The obnoxious student emerges victorious, for he has triggered anger in the teacher, and anger can lead to impulsive comments or behavior on the part of the teacher, which may be regretted later. The class then belongs to the harassing student, not the teacher, and this reversal of roles can damage the teacher's effectiveness long into the future. Hillel remained in full control of their exchanges, because he retained his composure throughout.

---

6. *Encyclopedia of Great Men of Israel* (Tel Aviv, 1961), vol. 3, 883 (Heb.).

While there is important truth to this observation, it is also an insufficient explanation for Hillel's behavior, for it alone does not explain Hillel's extreme warmth, and his excessively positive response to the harasser's questions. Surely questions about wide feet and oval heads are not so "significant," in Hillel's language, and if Hillel had merely kept his composure he would have achieved his goal of maintaining control of the encounter without the excessive praise and warmth.

Once again, we are led back to the choice of these three questions and their "significance." Of course, they may really possess no significance at all; they may just happen to have been the questions that the harasser posed. Yet this aggada is crafted with such meticulous care, with language and behavior exactly repeating itself over and over again, that the reader must wonder if there is more to their choice than happenstance. After all, Hillel refers to them again and again as "significant." Might the author of the aggada not be signaling to the reader that he or she too must consider them significant, just as Hillel did? But then what is their hidden significance?[7]

The first point to make is that each of these questions is about a physical aberration of some sort. Misshapen heads, bleary eyes, and excessively wide feet are all examples, for someone living at that time and place, of the abnormal. Whatever the harasser's intent, Hillel answered each question with the utmost seriousness because he wanted to convey to the harasser a series of very important points: First, anything about the human condition is significant and worthy of attention, even deformities. After all, at that time and place people might think that there is no value to understanding the causes of misshapen heads, bleary eyes, and wide feet. While today attitudes are different, over two thousand years ago it is likely that most people would stop to notice the unusual

7. On this reading, the author of the aggada placed these questions in the mouth of the harasser for his own purposes, which I shall attempt to explicate below. Was there no tradition about what questions were actually asked by the harasser, so the author crafted his own questions? Were these the questions the harasser actually did ask, but he did not consciously understand their full import? We cannot say for sure. Note that the Maharsha, ad loc., likewise sees symbolic significance to the questions. I follow his overall approach, but read the symbolism differently.

and then move on, without stopping to reflect deeply about their causes, and seeking to provide a "scientific" explanation.

Hillel rejected this posture. While he may have harbored a proto-scientific sensibility, we have no evidence for that, and the more likely explanation is that he took every human being seriously, merely by virtue of their humanity, much as we saw in previous chapters about Rebbe and Rav Yannai. Hillel taught in *Pirkei Avot* (1:12): "Be among the disciples of Aaron, loving peace and pursuing peace, loving people (*briyot*) and drawing them close to the Torah." The term "people" here is a translation of the Hebrew word which literally means "creatures." Hillel does not distinguish between Jew and gentile here; all people must be loved. Hillel implemented this attitude in practice. Immediately following our aggada, the Talmud relates two encounters Hillel had with gentiles who wished to convert, one on condition that he accept only the Written Law, but not the Oral Law, and the second on condition that Hillel teach him the Torah while he, the prospective convert, stands on one foot. In both cases Hillel welcomed these gentiles with respect, despite their troubling, even disrespectful conditions that they proposed, and enabled them to convert, exactly exemplifying his teaching in *Pirkei Avot*. All human beings are creatures of God.

If all human beings are creatures of God, then each human being deserves love and respect for that status, and that includes the attempt by others to understand his or her condition, as aberrant as it might be. People with oval heads or bleary eyes are no less human for that condition, and they deserve our careful and respectful attention too. This then may be the first layer of meaning to the "significance" of the harasser's questions. They are significant because asking those questions demonstrates that every human being is worthy of respect and consideration. By explicitly affirming their significance, Hillel is challenging the harasser to see them as significant too. He subtly seeks to lead the harasser into reflecting about the very premise of his questions, that all human beings deserve respect, a core teaching of Hillel himself.

If the harasser does reflect on the significance of his questions, he may come to realize that he has violated their very premise. For how has the harasser treated Hillel? Hardly with the respect he deserves, not only as *Nasi* but as a human being, no different from those with oval heads or wide feet. To assert as Hillel does the significance of the questions is to point the harasser – and the reader – to the deep contradiction between the harasser's questions and his behavior. The questions he asks assume respect for all human beings, but his behavior demonstrates just the opposite. In this way, Hillel subtly rebukes the harasser, all the while welcoming him with warmth, love, and respect. For the only way to help the harasser to see the error of his ways is to welcome him exactly as Hillel did. To criticize the harasser directly would place him on the defensive, and if he is on the defensive he would never be open to self-reflection. To treat him with warmth and respect is to make him feel safe in the encounter with Hillel, and thereby give him emotional space to reflect on Hillel's words.

Is it likely that the harasser will see this deep contradiction on his own? Probably not, at least immediately. But Hillel, who taught the importance of loving all creatures, who was ever generous in his estimation of human worth, hoped that eventually, with time and space to reflect, he would. The reader can only admire Hillel for his teaching and his practice, and that is surely part of the message of the aggada.

Now consider the status of the harasser himself. From Hillel's perspective, his behavior is no less aberrant than the deformities of those about whom the harasser inquired. The harasser's deformity is moral, for he shows no respect for Hillel the *Nasi*. Their deformity, on the other hand, is physical. Yet each is aberrant and, we might ask, whose aberration is more serious? Surely that of the harasser, for he can control and correct his deformity, but those about whom he asked cannot. Yet Hillel treated the harasser with respect, tolerance, and support. Hillel's moral principles are consistent throughout.

The choice of these three questions illuminates the status of the harasser, for he, like they, suffers from a deformity. If the harasser raises questions about their deformity, then he should, to be consistent, reflect on his own deformity as well. That too is part of the "significance" of the questions. They are significant because they reflect back onto the questioner himself. When Hillel affirms their significance to the harasser, he is also subtly suggesting to him that he reflect on his own behavior in light of these "significant" questions. Whose eyes, whose vision, is blearier, the Tadmorians' or the harasser's himself, whose eyes are bleary to his own moral shortcomings? Whose head is more misshapen, the Babylonians' or the harasser's, whose head is misshapen with arrogance? Who has feet that are too wide, the Africans or the harasser himself, who steps upon those deserving of respect?

There is then another layer of meaning to the significance of the questions. They mirror back to the harasser his own moral deformities, and in so doing lead him to reflect, improve, and grow through his encounter with the great Hillel, who subtly and brilliantly provides both a context, as well as encouragement, for his reform.

DOES HILLEL SUCCEED, OR, WHO IS THE TRUE HILLEL?

It turns out that all of Hillel's efforts are for naught. The harasser responds to Hillel's offer to answer every question of his with apparent anger – exactly the emotion he is attempting to provoke in Hillel. Ironically, Hillel remains imperturbable, and the harasser's verbal bullets ricochet back upon himself. He blurts out, "Are you Hillel whom they call the *Nasi* of Israel?" Hillel responds in the affirmative, upon which the harasser exclaims, "If it is you, may there not be many like you in Israel!" Hillel asks him why, with the very same term of endearment he always uses – "my son." His love and warmth endure. The harasser answers that on account of Hillel's patience he lost the four hundred *zuz* he was to have earned in the wager.

Hillel's response to this explanation is shocking, for it represents a complete about-face. It is as if a new and unrecognizable Hillel emerges. He says, "Be vigilant of your spirit. Hillel is worthy of having you lose four hundred *zuz,* and another four hundred *zuz* on his account, and Hillel will not get upset."

Hillel, the Sage famous for his patience and modesty, vehemently asserts his self-worth in no uncertain terms. He refers to himself in the third rather than first person, a sign of self-respect, and the respect he now demands from the harasser. While Hillel may not be upset – and he concludes his comments by saying that he does not get upset – he expresses himself as if he were. Unlike the positive reinforcement and warmth of the past, which were accompanied by no more than subtle hints at reform, now he confronts the harasser forcefully, telling him to be vigilant about repeating such behavior in the future. His use of the term "spirit" is interesting and unexpected. Why not speak directly to his bad behavior itself, rather than to his spirit? Probably because Hillel understood that his bad behavior had its roots in a bad spirit, in arrogance, disrespect, and mockery. The cause, rather than the effect, must be addressed first.

Why then did Hillel change his approach to the harasser so dramatically? No doubt because he now understood the man's true motives, an insight which depends upon a distinction between obnoxiousness and mockery (or *letzanut* in Hebrew). When an obnoxious student approaches a teacher, the teacher must respond as Hillel did at first, to understand and respond to what the student was truly "seeking." But the harasser set out to mock Hillel. To wage a bet against Hillel's patience is to make a game out of his virtue, and to make a game out of Hillel's virtue is to mock it. For the harasser, virtue is not to be profoundly respected, but to be played with. Moreover, in playing with Hillel, the goal was to show that he would get angry, that he did not live up to his sterling reputation.

Why then is mockery so especially problematic? The first verse in Psalms praises the person who does not dwell amongst the mockers, but the talmudic rabbis judged mockers in very harsh terms indeed, asserting, *inter alia,* that they can never receive the Divine Presence,[8] that they bring annihilation to the world,[9] and that they fall directly into Gehenna.[10] But why did the rabbis react so negatively to mockery? At least part of the answer is that mockery blocks the ability to accept criticism, just like a shield smeared with oil deflects arrows, to use R. Moshe Hayim Luzzatto's metaphor.[11] If the harasser makes a game of Hillel, then how can Hillel ever succeed in reaching and helping him reform? When Hillel discovered that he was dealing with a mocker, he realized that his soft touch of warmth, respect, and love would never

8. Sota 42a.
9. Avoda Zara 18b.
10. Ibid.
11. *Mesilat Yesharim,* ch. 5.

succeed. The mocker will never take him, or anything else, seriously, and seriousness is the beginning of introspection and self-evaluation, which in turn are the beginning of reform. This is the deeper reason why the mocker falls directly into Gehenna.

It turns out, then, that a teacher who emulates Hillel must learn to balance patience with forcefulness, forgiveness with expectations of respect, love with rebuke. There are times when patience, forgiveness, and love are called for, and there are times when forcefulness, expectations of respect, and rebuke are called for. Hillel, with remarkable self-possession and self-control, modeled the capacity to marshal all these contradictory qualities and to deploy each as necessary. How did he achieve this?

Probably because these qualities emerged from choice. It was not as if Hillel's personality was fundamentally one or the other of these two poles, for people would have great difficulty altering their personality to suit the occasion. Rather, Hillel possessed mastery over his character. His behavior emerged from careful consideration of the circumstances, not from fixed personality traits. Of course, he could have possessed a natural inclination toward love and patience, but he controlled his love and patience; his love and patience did not control him.[12] Teachers who seek to emulate Hillel would seek to cultivate exactly this self-possession, together with the ability to understand the frequently masked motives of a difficult student. Remember that Hillel himself initially misread the harasser, and only discovered the truth much later. Reading a student can be far more difficult than reading a runic text.

That said, let us recall Hillel's final words in the aggada: "Hillel will not get upset." The Hillel of the second part of the aggada may be forceful, may insist on the respect due him as *Nasi*, and may issue a strong rebuke, but he never, ever gets upset. That too is self-mastery, perhaps the greatest self-mastery of all.

---

12. See *Guide for the Perplexed* I:54 (Chicago, 1963), trans. S. Pines, 123–128, for a Maimonidean perspective on this theme, and a discussion in Moshe Sokol, *Judaism Examined* (Boston, 2013), ch. 2.

Chapter 3

Rav Yannai and the Mysterious Guest

Leviticus Rabba 9:3

INTRODUCTION

Rav Yannai was an eminent Sage who lived during the third century CE and was for a time part of the circle surrounding the great Rebbe, R. Yehuda HaNasi, compiler of the Mishna.[1] In the aggada that is the subject of this chapter, R. Yannai meets up with a man on the street whose appearance is so extraordinary that Rav Yannai invites him for dinner. After examining the Torah knowledge of his guest, only to find him to be an apparent ignoramus, Rav Yannai actually calls him a dog! Questions abound: What was so extraordinary about the guest's appearance? Why exactly did he give off such airs if he was really an ignoramus? Why did Rav Yannai humiliate him? Surely on the face of it such behavior is troubling, and indeed Rav Yannai eventually regrets what he did. But

1. For a discussion of the relationship of Rav Yannai to Rebbe and to Rav Natan ben Amram, see Binyamin Lau, *The Sages, Volume IV: From the Mishna to the Talmud* (Jerusalem, 2015), 87–92. For more on this, see below.

how could a man as distinguished as Rav Yannai have engaged initially in such behavior? Why did the guest's actions appear to betray the claims he made about himself? The story unfolds in remarkable and surprising ways, and as we shall see, the questions about it continue to multiply. What lessons might the author of the midrash have sought to convey to the puzzled reader? Just who is the mysterious guest who forces Rav Yannai to change his ways?[2]

דָּבָר אַחֵר, וְשָׂם דֶּרֶךְ, אָמַר רַבִּי יַנַּאי וְשָׁם כְּתִיב דְּשָׁיֵם אָרְחֵיהּ, סַגֵּי שָׁוֵי, מַעֲשֶׂה בְּרַבִּי יַנַּאי שֶׁהָיָה מְהַלֵּךְ בַּדֶּרֶךְ וְרָאָה אָדָם אֶחָד שֶׁהָיָה מְשֻׁפָּע בְּיוֹתֵר, אֲמַר לֵיהּ מַשְׁגַּח רַבִּי מִתְקַבְּלָא גַּבָּן, אֲמַר לוֹ אִין, הִכְנִיסוֹ לְבֵיתוֹ הֶאֱכִילוֹ וְהִשְׁקָהוּ,

Another opinion regarding the verse (Psalms 50:23) "And to him who sets aright [*vesam*] the path, I will show him the salvation [of God]," Rav Yannai said: [The Hebrew word] *vesam* – "the one who sets aright" – can be read with a letter *shin* [and not the letter *sin*, meaning that] one who assesses his ways [*vesham*] will find the salvation [of God]. Rav Yannai was once walking along the road, and saw a man who was extremely well dressed. Rav Yannai said to him: Would my master look upon us favorably and agree to join us [for dinner]? The man replied: Yes. Rav Yannai brought him into his home, and gave him food and drink.

בְּדָקוֹ בְּמִקְרָא וְלֹא מְצָאוֹ, בְּמִשְׁנָה וְלֹא מְצָאוֹ, בְּאַגָּדָה וְלֹא מְצָאוֹ, בְּתַלְמוּד וְלֹא מְצָאוֹ, אֲמַר לֵיהּ סַב בְּרִיךְ, אֲמַר לֵיהּ יְבָרֵךְ יַנַּאי בְּבֵיתֵיהּ, אֲמַר לֵיהּ אִית בָּךְ אֲמַר מַה דַּאֲנָא אֲמַר לָךְ, אֲמַר לֵיהּ אִין, אֲמַר לֵיהּ אֱמֹר אָכוֹל כַּלְבָּא פִּיסְתָּיָא דְּיַנַּאי,

[As they were eating and drinking together,] Rav Yannai examined him in his knowledge of Bible, and found out that he had none; examined his knowledge of Mishna, and realized that he

2. A parallel to the story told in this midrash appears in Leviticus Rabba 16:2. There, Rav Yannai learns about the importance of refraining from evil talk about another from a visiting merchant. See Avigdor Shinaan, "Rabbi Yannai, the Merchant and the Man Who Was Extremely Well Dressed," in *Bikoret UMasoret*, 30, ed. Y. Elshtein (Ramat Gan, 1984), 15–23 (Heb.) for a comparison between these two aggadot.

had none; his knowledge of legends, and saw that he had none; his knowledge of Talmud and saw he had none. [Rav Yannai] then told him: Wash and recite grace. Said the guest: Let Yannai recite grace in his own home. [Seeing that he could not even recite a blessing,] Yannai asked him: Can you at least repeat what I say? Said he: Yes. Said [Rav Yannai]: Repeat [the following]: "A dog has eaten Yannai's bread."

קָם תַּפְסֵיהּ אֲמַר לֵיהּ יְרוּתָתִי גַּבָּךְ דְּאַתְּ מוֹנֵעַ לִי, אֲמַר לֵיהּ וּמַה יַרְתּוּתָךְ גַּבִּי, אֲמַר לֵיהּ חַד זְמַן הֲוֵינָא עָבַר קַמֵּי בֵּית סִפְרָא, וּשְׁמָעִית קָלְהוֹן דְּמֵנִיקַיָּא אָמְרִין (דברים לג, ד): תּוֹרָה צִוָּה לָנוּ מֹשֶׁה מוֹרָשָׁה קְהִלַּת יַעֲקֹב, מוֹרָשָׁה קְהִלַּת יַנַּאי אֵין כְּתִיב כָּאן אֶלָּא קְהִלַּת יַעֲקֹב. אֲמַר לֵיהּ לָמָּה זָכִיתָ לְמֵיכְלָא עַל פְּתוֹרִי, אֲמַר לוֹ מִיּוֹמַי לָא שְׁמָעִית מִילָּא בִּישָׁא וְחַזַרְתִּי לְמָרֵהּ, וְלָא חָמֵית תְּרֵין דְּמִתְכַּתְּשִׁין דֵּין עִם דֵּין וְלָא יְהַבִית שְׁלָמָא בֵּינֵיהוֹן.

[Offended,] the man stood up and grabbed Rav Yannai by the coat! He then said: My inheritance is with you, and you are withholding it from me! Said [Rav Yannai with puzzlement]: What legacy of yours is there with me? He replied: Once I passed by a school, and I heard the voices of the little children saying: "Moses gave us the Torah, the inheritance of the congregation of Jacob." They did not say "the inheritance of the congregation of Yannai," but the "congregation of Jacob." [Rav Yannai] asked: How then are you worthy to eat at my table? [The guest] replied: Never have I heard an evil word spoken and returned it. Never have I seen two people arguing without making peace between them.

אֲמַר לֵיהּ כָּל הָדָא דֶּרֶךְ אֶרֶץ גַּבָּךְ וְקָרִיתָךְ כַּלְבָּא, קָרָא עֲלֵיהּ שָׂם דֶּרֶךְ, דְּשָׂיֵם אָרְחֵיהּ סַגֵּי שָׁוֵי, דְּאָמַר רַבִּי יִשְׁמָעֵאל בַּר רַב נַחְמָן עֶשְׂרִים וְשִׁשָּׁה דוֹרוֹת קָדְמָה דֶּרֶךְ אֶרֶץ אֶת הַתּוֹרָה, הֲדָא הוּא דִכְתִיב (בראשית ג, כד): לִשְׁמֹר אֶת דֶּרֶךְ עֵץ הַחַיִּים, דֶּרֶךְ, זוֹ דֶּרֶךְ אֶרֶץ, וְאַחַר כַּךְ עֵץ הַחַיִּים, זוֹ תּוֹרָה.

[Rav Yannai] then said: You have so much *derekh eretz* and I called you a dog. On him [Rav Yannai] said the verse: "And there is a path," meaning that one who assesses his ways will find the salvation [of God], since R. Yishmael son of R. Naḥman said:

> *Derekh eretz* precedes Torah by twenty-six generations, since it is written: "And to guard the way to the Tree of Life" (Genesis 3). "Way" is *derekh eretz,* and only after that comes "Tree of Life," which is Torah.[3]

RAV YANNAI INVITES A GUEST TO DINNER, THEN CALLS HIM A DOG

The story the midrash tells is preceded by a verse in Psalms (50:23) which had been cited earlier in the chapter, and which reads: "And to him who sets aright [*ve'sam*] the path, I will show him the salvation of God." In the original Hebrew, the first part of the verse reads "*vesam derekh,*" with the letter *sin* in the word "*vesam.*" However, Rav Yannai, to make a point, reads the verse not with a *sin* but with the letter *shin,* the very slightest of orthographic changes, but a change with great significance nonetheless. Read in this way, the verse would be saying that the person who assesses his or her ways will find divine salvation, for such a person can adjust his behavior if found wanting. An example of this would be if someone determines that he or she had not behaved with *derekh eretz,* with civility and good manners toward others. Such a person, having assessed his ways and found them wanting, must improve. The story that unfolds in the midrash about Rav Yannai himself is such a case, and therefore exemplifies exactly this point.[4]

---

3. Like all texts in this volume the translation comes from Sefaria, but numerous changes have been made here by the author.
4. After Rav Yannai discovers that his guest is a master of *derekh eretz,* the text of the midrash reads that "on him Rav Yannai said the verse" about assessing one's ways. The phrase "on him" could refer either to the guest or to Rav Yannai himself, with Rav Yannai speaking about himself in the third person. Both are acceptable readings (see the commentary *Imrei Yosher,* ad loc.). I favor the second reading because we have no evidence that the guest assessed his ways, only that he behaved with *derekh eretz,* while Rav Yannai does assess his ways and regrets his behavior. I shall follow this reading throughout the chapter. Note, however, that even according to the first interpretation, Rav Yannai surely does regret his behavior and changes his view based upon his experience with the guest, and so the analysis presented in this chapter would apply equally to both interpretations.

Rav Yannai was walking along the road and passed a man whose appearance was so impressive that Rav Yannai invited him for dinner. What was so remarkable about his appearance? This is not altogether clear, as the midrash uses an obscure Hebrew phrase, "*meshupa beyoter.*" The classic commentaries to the midrash, printed in many standard editions, all struggle with its meaning.[5] Thus, the *Eitz Yosef* and *Matanot Kehuna* suggest that it means he dressed in the standard garb of a Torah scholar. However, this would not in itself explain why Rav Yannai was so struck by his appearance that he felt compelled to invite him for dinner. Surely others dressed that way too, unless this was one scholar in his community Rav Yannai had not met, whose acquaintance he therefore wanted to make. The *Imrei Yosher* proposes that it was his overall impressive appearance, not specifically his dress, which stood out, while the *Mesoret HaMidrash,* suggests that the man seemed exceptionally modest and refined.

Whichever way we are to understand the phrase itself, clearly Rav Yannai was impressed by something, for it was probably not all that common to invite someone to dinner merely upon passing him in the street, unless he looked especially needy, which here was not the case. The language Rav Yannai uses to extend the invitation is exceptionally ornate, something like "Would my master look upon us favorably and agree to join us?" Apparently, a simple invitation for a man who appeared so extraordinary would not be appropriate.

While the language Rav Yannai used for the invitation was ornate, the language the man used to accept the invitation could not have been any simpler. In fact, it was just one word, "Yes." Why the contrast? Is it because the man himself is simple, so his language is simple too? Or does the man subtly wish to make a point of his own, that Rav Yannai's baroque invitation may be off the mark? As we shall see, this guest may not be as simple as he appears.

Rav Yannai provides his guest with food and drink, then examines him on a range of Jewish sacred literature, from Tanakh to Mishna to aggada to Talmud, and in each domain he is found to be woefully

5. E.g., *Midrash Rabba,* vol. 4 (Jerusalem, 2001), 85.

ignorant.[6] Finally, Rav Yannai asks the guest to lead the *birkat hamazon,* the prayer said upon completing a meal, and he refuses even that, from which Rav Yannai infers that the guest does not know even so elementary a prayer.

Before considering Rav Yannai's reaction to his guest's ignorance, we might ask why he examined him in all these domains of Torah learning. Of course, it would not be out of the ordinary for Rav Yannai to engage the guest in conversation about Torah. Indeed, the Mishna compiled by Rav Yannai's teacher, Rebbe, teaches that every meal at which three people eat must be accompanied by words of Torah, for otherwise it is as if they had eaten the sacrifices of dead idols.[7] While at this dinner there is no evidence that more than two men were present, nevertheless, words of Torah are always in order. But that is not what Rav Yannai did. Rav Yannai actively examined him, probed his knowledge. Why?

We cannot know with certainty, for the text does not say, but it is likely that Rav Yannai was so struck by the man's appearance that he wanted to get to the bottom of just who this exceptional man was. Perhaps, too, he harbored a suspicion that the guest was not all he appeared to be. After all, sometimes people can look a bit ***too*** perfect. It is as if they are overcompensating, trying too hard, so as to mask a deficiency. For example, some people may be truly pious, but others may act with extreme piety in order to overcompensate for their religious deficiencies.

Rav Yannai's reaction when the guest refuses his invitation to lead the *birkat hamazon* is nothing short of astonishing. He asks him if he is capable of repeating the words that Rav Yannai is about to utter. This is a humiliating enough question. But the words Rav Yannai asks the guest to repeat are not only humiliating but even *prima facie* cruel: "A dog has eaten Yannai's bread." Rav Yannai was a man of exemplary learning and Torah scholarship, and he comes to regret those words later in the story, as we shall see. But what could have led him to say them now? Why would he treat his guest so harshly?

---

6. These different domains of Jewish learning appear elsewhere in the Talmud, e.g., Ḥagiga 14a. Note that the order in which Rav Yannai quizzed the guest seems odd. If he did not even know Bible, why would he know Talmud?

7. *Pirkei Avot* 3:4.

Part of the answer may have to do with the negative attitude that many Sages of the talmudic era held toward *amei ha'aretz,* ignoramuses, discussed more fully in the next chapter. Yet that probably does not tell the whole story. For why call the guest a dog? Why not just send him out, or express anger in some other way? Why specifically call him a dog? I think it is very likely that Rav Yannai felt such intense anger toward the guest because he believed he was *deceived* by him. The guest's mode of dress and his comportment suggested that he was a man of special stature, but in point of fact he was an utter ignoramus, an imposter posing as a superior person. Rav Yannai could not tolerate a poseur who wanted to scavenge a meal from passersby. Is this really any different than a dog? After all, dogs are scavengers, ferreting out scraps of food wherever they can find them. In this precise sense, then, Rav Yannai forced him to admit that he was no better than a craven dog. Let us recall that the Talmud calls dogs "brazen creatures."[8] Rav Yannai may have seen in the behavior of this scavenging imposter the brazenness of a dog. And what kind of dog? The Talmud distinguishes between two kinds of dogs, a regular dog and a bad one. Of the latter, the Talmud teaches that one may not raise such a dog in his home, because it can lead to harm.[9] Surely this ignoramus is no better than a bad dog, for he harms others by eating their food, and by engaging in brazen deception.

Consider now the fluidity of the guest's identity. He was an ignoramus posing as a superior man, but this posing in turn made him like a dog. Is he, then, a superior person, an ignoramus, or a dog? I shall argue that the question of murky identities is a crucial theme of the aggada as it develops.

Offended, the guest gets up and grabs Rav Yannai by the coat.[10] At first glance, this act of physical aggression is surprising, since the man's comportment and attire suggested exquisite refinement. While this behavior is surely understandable, it also seems to confirm Rav

---

8. Beitza 25b.
9. Ketubot 41b.
10. This is a play on words, for the Aramaic word for "grab" is "*tafsei*" and the Aramaic word for "bread" is "*pistiya.*" See Shmuel Faust, *Aggadeta* (Or Yehuda, 2011), 284–290.

Yannai's accusation – the very accusation the guest would no doubt wish to refute – that he is no better than a dog, no less capable than a dog of physical aggression. Even if the guest was angered, and well he might have been, would it not have been more prudent to avoid confirming Rav Yannai's accusation? His aggression thus undercuts the very identity he had so painstakingly sought to construct. What then does this behavior reveal about the man? Just who is he?

THE GUEST TEACHES RAV YANNAI *DEREKH ERETZ*

Before considering these questions further, we must examine the guest's response: He accuses Rav Yannai of withholding his inheritance from him. Not surprisingly, this accusation puzzles Rav Yannai, and the guest therefore explains that he had once passed a school and heard the voices of little children chanting the verse "Moses gave us the Torah, the inheritance of the congregation of Jacob" (Deuteronomy 33:4). The guest observes that the children did not say "the inheritance of the congregation of Yannai," but rather "the congregation of Jacob." This, of course, is a clever play on words, for the Hebrew for Jacob, Yaakov, sounds very much like Yannai.

What does the guest mean by this accusation? One possibility is that the guest meant to claim that God gave the Torah to all Jews, not only to the learned, and the Torah is the legacy of all Jews, even the ignorant. But if even the ignorant guest possesses the legacy of Torah, how could Rav Yannai denigrate him so harshly and call him a dog?[11] By calling him a dog, Rav Yannai was implying, counterfactually, that the guest possesses no Torah, and he was thereby withholding from him the rights to Torah that he truly possesses. While this is a very plausible reading, another possibility suggests itself as well, as we shall soon see.

Quite apart from the message the guest seeks to convey is the medium whereby he conveys it. Several observations are in order. First, for an ignoramus who cannot even recite *birkat hamazon,* this is quite an impressive performance. Not only did the guest need to recall what

---

11. See the commentaries of *Eitz Yosef* and *Matanot Kehuha* ad loc.

he happened to hear while passing a schoolhouse, a remarkable enough feat to begin with, he also needed to recognize that the sound of "Yaakov" is similar to the sound of "Yannai." Indeed, how likely is it that he would happen to have heard exactly the one verse he needed now to make his point? Moreover, he also needed to be capable of this kind of classic rabbinic reading of a verse, using a clever play on words to make a penetrating comment. How likely is it that an ignoramus would be capable of this kind of rabbinic reading, with a play on words, to sharply critique Rav Yannai, based upon a verse he once happened to overhear? To this reader, it seems unlikely indeed.

One begins to wonder now about the true identity of this mysterious guest, for on the evidence he might have been far more knowledgeable than he let on. Perhaps his appearance did not belie his true reality, but rather accurately conveyed it. While he may indeed have been an imposter, he was not the imposter we thought he was. On this reading, the mysterious guest would not have been an ignoramus posing as a learned man, but rather just the reverse, a learned man posing as an ignoramus. But why would he have posed as an ignoramus? Perhaps because he had an agenda, and that agenda may have been to teach Rav Yannai to assess his ways, and to teach him the value of *derekh eretz,* the central moral lesson of the midrash. The guest thus made certain that his appearance was so impressive that he could expect Rav Yannai to invite him for dinner, so that he could then have the opportunity to reprove Rav Yannai by posing as the ignoramus he was not.

On this reading, our midrash calls to mind another talmudic story, that of R. Shimon ben Elazar. R. Shimon ben Elazar happened upon an ugly man while riding along the riverbank, returning from an extended period of Torah study. R. Shimon ben Elazar makes this cutting comment to him: "How ugly that person is! Are the other inhabitants of your city as ugly as you are?"[12] The ugly man, not surprisingly, objects. R. Shimon ben Elazar realizes how wrong he had been, and the rest of the story describes his attempts to seek forgiveness from the man he offended.

---

12. Ta'anit 20a–b. Other texts read R. Shimon the son of R. Elazar. See *Mesoret HaShas* ad loc.

Now just who was this ugly man? No doubt he might have been just that, an ugly man whom R. Shimon ben Elazar coincidentally met. Yet the story seems almost too perfect for that reading, and both Rashi and *Tosafot* in their commentaries cite an alternative textual tradition, according to which the ugly man was none other than Elijah the Prophet, who made an appearance to provoke R. Shimon ben Elazar's moral improvement. While I do not mean to claim that the mysterious guest in our story was actually Elijah the Prophet, the phenomenon may be parallel. Sometimes outsiders may appear in disguise, to provoke the repentance of otherwise exemplary individuals, a theme which recapitulates in the next chapter about Rebbe, as we shall see.

But, we must now ask, has Rav Yannai really been changed by the guest's biting critique? Apparently, the answer is, not yet. For Rav Yannai responds by asking him how he, an ignoramus, merited eating at the table of a man as distinguished as himself. It is true that Rav Yannai's posture here has changed, for he is no longer biting in his comments, and he seems to ask this question in all earnestness. Nevertheless, at the same time, Rav Yannai retains a decidedly condescending and superior air, for he cannot imagine how an ignoramus could have found his way to dinner. The process of moral growth may have begun, but it has hardly reached its culmination, as the unfolding story makes amply clear.

The guest's answer is revealing, but in unexpected ways. He explains that he merited eating at the table of Rav Yannai for two reasons. First, he asserts that he never heard an evil word spoken without returning it to its source, and second, he never saw two people arguing without bringing peace between them. Each of these reasons deserves its own analysis.

The first claim is unclear in the original Hebrew, and two explanations which appear in the commentaries seem plausible.[13] One explanation is that the guest attests that after hearing person A speak ill – *lashon hara* – about person B, he never reported back to B what A had said about him. He kept the *lashon hara* to himself. To report back to B what A had said about him would be wrong – *rekhilut,* according

13. See *Eitz Yosef* and *Matanot Kehuna* ad loc.

to halakha[14] – and if the guest had committed *rekhilut,* he would have acted immorally and against halakha. So, by the guest's own testimony, the reader learns that the guest was not a sinner in that particular way. But this surely misses the mark, for such failure to sin is hardly worth bragging about! After all, the guest is attempting to justify access to Rav Yannai's table on grounds of his special virtues, and avoiding *rekhilut* by not reporting *lashon hara* back to its victim is hardly such a remarkable virtue. Moreover, one might ask why the guest was paying attention to that *lashon hara* in the first place, for according to many talmudic sources, and the halakha as it developed, listening to *lashon hara* is also forbidden.[15]

The second explanation offered by the classic commentaries is that the guest is asserting that if someone spoke ill or even cursed him directly, he never responded, but rather absorbed the verbal blow in humble and forgiving silence. This is surely a mark of great virtue, but the problem is that on the evidence we have, it is simply false. Consider the story at hand. Rav Yannai shames the guest and calls him a dog. Does the guest respond in forgiving and humble silence? Hardly! He responds with physical aggression, grabbing Rav Yannai by his coat. His behavior belies his claim.

Consider next the second claim the guest makes to justify his access to Rav Yannai's table: He never encountered people quarreling without bringing peace between them. This is indeed a remarkable claim which, if true, would surely bespeak extraordinary virtue on the part of the guest. The question begs itself, however, about the plausibility of the claim itself. If the guest had asserted merely that he had *endeavored* to bring peace to every quarrel, that would be virtue enough, and at least a plausible assertion. But here he makes the more striking claim, not only that he endeavored to bring peace, but that he actually succeeded in doing so. While this is not technically impossible, it is surely implausible. Anyone who has had the ill-fortune to witness a bitterly

14. For an extensive discussion of these laws see R. Yisrael Meir HaKohen, *Ḥafetz Ḥayim* (Jerusalem, 1982), 197–228 (Heb.).

15. See *Ḥafetz Ḥayim,* p. 121, and sources there in *Be'er Mayim Ḥayim,* n. 2. While it is possible that the guest never listened in ways strictly forbidden, nevertheless, the circumstances themselves may be less than morally pure.

divorcing couple, or two people engaged in an angry and enduring fight, would immediately wonder what magical potion the guest might have possessed if he could have brought peace even there. Just how credible, then, is the guest's claim?

In short, both justifications the guest offers for gaining access to Rav Yannai's table, according to all interpretations, seem at the very least questionable, if not downright problematic. Yet oddly enough, at least on the face of it, none of this seems to trouble Rav Yannai, who responds with both apparent remorse and alacrity, "You have so much *derekh eretz* and I called you a dog." He then cites the verse with which the midrash began, praising those who assess their ways. Rav Yannai has now assessed his ways, and found them wanting in his behavior toward the guest. The guest possesses great *derekh eretz,* Rav Yannai failed to recognize that, and he behaved toward his guest with a notable lack of that very virtue, *derekh eretz.* Rav Yannai has thus learned the value of *derekh eretz.* The midrash then cites a teaching of R. Yishmael the son of Rav Naḥman, that the imperative of *derekh eretz* preceded the revelation of the Torah by twenty-six generations.

The introduction of the moral category of *derekh eretz* here may shed light on the guest's somewhat puzzling critique earlier, that all Jews possess the inheritance of Torah, which Rav Yannai had unfairly withheld from him. Exactly what element of Torah is Rav Yannai withholding? Perhaps the answer is *derekh eretz* itself. In other words, one might argue that *derekh eretz* is not completely distinct from Torah, but rather sometimes overlaps with it. Consider the case at hand. Rav Yannai calls the guest a dog, clearly offending him. Is it permissible to verbally offend another person? That is a halakhic question, and the mishna teaches that it is wrong, based upon the verse in the Torah that forbids *ona'a,* which, because of an apparent duplication of verses, the talmudic rabbis maintained included not only economic overcharging but also verbal offense. The latter is called in the mishna "*ona'at devarim,*" and the mishna's own example of this is reminding a convert or penitent of his past.[16]

---

16. Mishna Bava Metzia 4:10.

If reminding a convert or penitent of his past is the kind of verbal offense which is not only contrary to the mandates of *derekh eretz*, but also contrary to halakha, then one might well argue that calling a person a dog in our text is likewise not only a violation of *derekh eretz*, but also a violation of halakha. If so, elements of *derekh eretz* overlap with biblically derived halakha, and would be part of the Torah itself.[17] The midrash claims that *derekh eretz* preceded the revelation of Torah at Sinai by twenty-six generations. However, it seems apparent that the Torah absorbed at least some elements of *derekh eretz* into its very corpus, at least as understood by the Rabbis, including, in all likelihood, Rav Yannai himself. The guest, even if ignorant of much of the Torah, still possesses his very own portion of it, *derekh eretz*, which Rav Yannai withholds from him. Rav Yannai maintains that the guest is ignorant of Torah, but in point of fact, the guest possesses more expertise in that domain of Torah than the great Rav Yannai himself.

While some elements of *derekh eretz* may not be halakhically mandated or forbidden, but are rather social conventions reflecting civility,[18] some elements of *derekh eretz* clearly do rise to that status. We might thus think of the relationship between the two bodies of norms like a Venn diagram, with some overlap between them. *Derekh eretz* and Torah are not entirely distinct, but overlap in important ways.

Returning to the text at hand, it seems fair to say that Rav Yannai's capacity to critique his own behavior with rigorous honesty and to change his ways is a morally impressive feat on Rav Yannai's part, and bespeaks his character. No doubt the author of the midrash intended to teach exactly this virtue to his readers. If even the eminent Rav Yannai

17. One might likewise argue that the evidence the guest cites for his own expertise in *derekh eretz*, which so impresses Rav Yannai, is itself embraced by Torah, but such a discussion would take us far afield.

18. See the minor tractates *Derekh Eretz* and *Derekh Eretz Zuta* for examples of such. See further Marcus van Loopik, *The Ways of the Sage and the Ways of the World: The Minor Tractates of the Talmud* (Tubingen: Mohr, 1991), 5–10, for a review of the meaning of the phrase "*derekh eretz*" in rabbinic literature, and the sources cited there. See too Aharon Lichtenstein, "Does Jewish Tradition Recognize an Ethic Independent of Halakha?" reprinted in *Contemporary Jewish Ethics*, ed. M. Kellner (NY, 1978), 103, and especially sources cited in n. 2.

could assess and improve his ways, then surely the readers of the midrash must do no less. All must assess their ways, follow the imperative of *derekh eretz,* and treat everyone with civility and respect, exactly as the great Rav Yannai had come to do himself. Let us recall that Rav Yannai believed that he had been deceived by the guest, had been duped into providing an unworthy man a meal, for which reason he called him a dog. Nevertheless, Rav Yannai came to see the shortcomings of his ways and regretted that behavior.

That said, we must consider this question: Suppose the guest had not demonstrated to Rav Yannai's satisfaction that he had deserved a seat at Rav Yannai's table. Suppose that he had not demonstrated that he was a master of *derekh eretz,* and that in point of fact he was a mere ignoramus. What would Rav Yannai's stance have been then? Would he have felt justified in calling him a dog? Put differently, if someone like the guest possesses no merits in particular, including *derekh eretz,* is it still consistent with the expectations of *derekh eretz* to call him names and to humiliate him? One reading of the midrash, and *prima facie* the simplest, would be to answer these questions in the affirmative. For Rav Yannai reassesses his behavior only *after* discovering that the guest is a master of *derekh eretz.* Indeed, he explicitly says, "You have so much *derekh eretz* and I called you a dog!" This phrase suggests a direct link between Rav Yannai's regret and his discovery that the guest is indeed a virtuous man. Without that discovery he would not have reassessed his behavior. While this reading may trouble some readers, perhaps the author of the midrash was not troubled by it himself. Indeed, this may be part of the lesson the midrash wishes to teach. Poseurs forfeit their right to civility and respect.

That said, and despite the plausibility of this reading, an alternative reading may be plausible as well. Let us recall that the points of defense the guest offered for access to Rav Yannai's table were themselves implausible. Could the guest have truly brought peace to every bitterly quarreling couple? Is it really such a remarkable feat not to report back *lashon hara* to its victim? Is he really the docile absorber of verbal abuse that he makes himself out to be? If we had doubts about the guest's claims, wouldn't Rav Yannai have had the same doubts as well, especially since he would instinctively have wished to defend his behavior anyway?

Perhaps the author of the midrash wishes subtly to suggest that Rav Yannai's reversal was much deeper than it first appears.

WHAT DID RAV YANNAI LEARN?

Let us return to the question of the elusive and murky identity of this mysterious guest. If the guest's points of defense, upon reflection, are problematic, so too is his identity. While he presented himself as an ignoramus, we questioned just how much of an ignoramus he could have been if he managed not only to recall a stray overheard verse but to interpret it as a caustic critique of Rav Yannai, with a clever rabbinic play on words. He presents himself as an ignoramus but acts otherwise, and presents himself as a master of *derekh eretz,* but in rather unconvincing ways. He even behaves in an unruly manner, which undercuts his very claim. The text ironically deconstructs its own simple reading, and leaves the reader more puzzled than ever. I wish to suggest now that the many ways in which this text deconstructs itself are central to its core message. These ironic subversions may be the author's subtle means of signaling that the reader must look ever deeper to ferret out the meanings of the text.

The first point to make is that if Rav Yannai clearly understood the weakness of the justifications the guest offered, and if he similarly understood the irony of the guest's claims, then he may have intended to respond with his own irony as well. Rav Yannai would have meant to say to the guest: "You claim, with some irony, that you are a master of *derekh eretz,* and I agree, with the very same irony you speak, that you are indeed, ironically, a master of *derekh eretz.* I will henceforth treat you with *derekh eretz.*[19]

19. For a discussion of the use of irony in aggada, see James Diamond, "King David and the Sages: Rabbinic Rehabilitation or Ironic Parody," *Prooftexts* 27 (2007): 373–426, especially pages 378–380, 398–399, and the relevant footnotes.

But the question now begs itself: Why then would Rav Yannai treat the guest with *derekh eretz* if he attributes *derekh* eretz to the guest only ironically? This leads us into what may be the moral heart of this complex midrash. Let us return to this question: If in fact the guest was a learned man, why then did he pose as an ignoramus? And why does he obfuscate and thereby undercut his very own claims that he is a master of *derekh eretz*? Let us recall that I suggested above that this mysterious guest might have had a mission, and that mission was to reprove Rav Yannai. His posing as a learned man to pique Rav Yannai's interest so as to gain an invitation for dinner, then his subterfuge of ignorance, were part of a plot. And that plot was to provoke Rav Yannai into calling him a name, which would in turn trigger a response on the part of the mysterious guest, a response which would contradict its very own overt message. All these contradictions may have been designed by the mysterious guest to convey to Rav Yannai a fundamental message: Just like I contradict myself, and I am masked, so too are all human beings.

The confusing masks the guest wears are indeed impenetrable, and neither Rav Yannai nor the reader can ever penetrate them. Indeed, precisely because the masks the mysterious guest wears are impenetrable, he must be treated with *derekh eretz*. Since neither Rav Yannai nor the reader can peel away the masks to get at the true identity of the guest, he must be treated with respect, because he just might be the kind of person who deserves respect. We can never know. The guest wears too many masks. While an omniscient God knows the guest's true identity, and what his true merits and demerits are, human beings like Rav Yannai and the reader do not possess God's omniscience, and in ignorance must treat all guests with respect.

It is not unlikely that the author of the midrash would want his readers to take a broader moral message from this story, to extrapolate beyond its narrow confines. For one could well argue that all human beings wear masks, not only the mysterious guest, indeed *all human beings are ultimately mysterious guests*. No one presents himself or herself as he or she truly is to everyone. At work, at play, with members of our families, while socializing, we all wear different masks, highlighting certain aspects of our personality and hiding others, or sometimes even artificially acting as if we were one kind of person, when we are not. But if all human beings wear masks, then how can we know what kind of treatment any person deserves?

The mysterious guest's message to Rav Yannai is that we cannot know. On this reading, *the very contradictions in the text are fundamental to the text's central message.* These contradictions bespeak the human condition, in all its complications, contradictions, and opacity. The masks the mysterious guest wore are brilliant manifestations of the midrashist's take on the human condition. Why treat the mysterious guest with civility and why not call him a dog? Because even this "ignorant" guest may possess *derekh eretz*, even *derekh eretz* of a compromised and equivocal nature, and he may even be a classical scholar as well. Rav Yannai may well have known just how problematic the guest's claims were, yet nevertheless chose to attribute *derekh eretz* to him, because Rav Yannai realized in a flash of illumination that the conundrums of the guest, the contradictions and oddities, all amounted to a profound lesson: The guest's true identity is unknowable. Even a compromised manifestation of *derekh eretz* is meaningful, because who can really know what lurks behind the masks he now realized his guest wore?

Another way to think about this is to consider the nature of stereotypes. All human beings approach others with a set of preconceptions. If A dresses with expensive clothing, she is probably wealthy. If B talks with certain grammatical errors, he is probably ill-educated. If C speaks with a southern accent, she is probably from the south and fits certain stereotypes of a southerner. These are common expectations, or stereotypes, and they can be very useful devices which facilitate the negotiation of our complex social worlds. Yet at best they are no more than useful devices. While they sometimes may (or may not) be statistically likely, they are nevertheless no more than statistical likelihoods. They reveal nothing certain about the person in question.

The mysterious guest appeared distinguished, and so Rav Yannai responded to him as such. When he failed to live up to those expectations, however, Rav Yannai was resentful and deeply angered. Yet later, the man appeared far more sophisticated than the ignoramus Rav Yannai thought him to be. Perhaps the central message of the midrash, then, is to warn Rav Yannai, and the reader, about the moral dangers of stereotyping. Let us recall the etymology of the word "prejudice," which derives from the Latin *praejudicium,* and means to pre-judge, exactly what Rav Yannai did, and what so many of us regularly do as well. If we can never penetrate to the truth behind the stereotypes, then we must be deeply cautious about relying upon them when responding to others. Why *derekh eretz*? Because true identity is murky, and expectations and stereotypes are sometimes flawed. We never know who we might be calling a dog, and therefore we must never call anyone a dog. Every person must be treated with *derekh eretz.*

That said, there may be yet an even deeper meaning than this explanation to the claim of the midrash, for consider the multiple disruptions in the text. First, as noted above, the relationship between *derekh eretz* and Torah is disrupted. They emerge not as distinct, but rather as overlapping spheres. Second, consider the scholar and the *am ha'aretz.* Throughout rabbinic literature these are presented as two distinct classes of people who, during certain periods of Jewish history, even despised one another. Yet our midrash disrupts that binary. First, there is Rav Yannai. He is the paradigmatic scholar, yet he comes to recognize his own lack of *derekh eretz* which, as we have argued, is in itself a lack of Torah proper, something that a classical scholar should have known. In this respect, before Rav Yannai's evolution, his scholarship is undercut and questioned. So too, inversely, the guest. He appears to be an ignoramus, based upon Rav Yannai's examination, but he emerges not only as a "scholar" of one dimension of Torah, namely, *derekh eretz,* but perhaps far more scholarly in the classical sense too, as we have suggested. Thus, these categories emerge as beset by deep ambiguities. Who is the scholar and who is not, and are these categories as opposed as they first appear? What do the categories even mean, if they are so ambiguous?

While the text itself certainly does not say so, one possible reading of the theology behind the disruption of categories here is this: When it comes to treating others with respect, categories must be disrupted because they are simply irrelevant. There is only one relevant category, a category that Rav Yannai came to learn can never be disrupted, and that is the category of humanity. Rav Yannai first called the mysterious guest a dog, but then discovered just how wrong he was to do so. The guest was indeed a human being, with all the mysteries that inhere in the human condition illuminated in this brilliantly constructed midrash. Merely by virtue of that humanity he must be treated with *derekh eretz.* On this reading, the reason all human beings must be treated with respect is not only, as I argued above, because we can never know the true status of others, masked as they are. In addition, all human beings must be treated with respect because their very humanity itself demands it. The midrash has demonstrated how all the usual categories and binaries break down. All that remains is the sheer humanity of the "other."

While speculative, as the midrash does not say so, it is possible that this point may also be the deeper meaning of the obligation to assess one's ways, the teaching that begins and ends the midrash, the importance of which Rav Yannai comes to affirm. To rigorously assess oneself is to peel away the masks that each of us wears, to cut to the core of who we are and how we've behaved. But to cut to the core of who we are is to discover that behind all the masks, behind all the compromised behavior and disrupted categories, all that is left is our sheer, irreducible humanity. I may be wise or ignorant or neither, I may be a master of Torah or a failure at *derekh eretz,* but whatever I am, I am still human, still created in the image of God. Merely by virtue of that humanity you must treat me with *derekh eretz.*

This may be one subtle implication of the significance of the midrash's culminating teaching, that twenty-six generations of *derekh eretz* preceded the revelation at Sinai. Those generations began with the creation of Adam and Eve, who were created in the image of God. Creation in the image of God may be a very good reason why Adam and Eve and all their descendants must be treated with *derekh eretz,* for they and their descendants, merely by virtue of their humanity, all bear the image of God. If the Torah subsumed elements of *derekh eretz* in its teachings, why would the Torah not have subsumed the very reason for those teachings, foreshadowed in its very own story of creation?

On the face of it, this midrash tells the sweet tale of a great man who learned a lesson about *derekh eretz.* But more careful reading suggests that this complex, brilliant midrash subverts itself again and again, revealing ever deeper meanings behind its tale. Rav Yannai's elusive guest beckons all readers to follow along his mysterious path.

Piety, Poverty, and Wealth

Chapter 4

Moral Decision-Making During a Time of Crisis: R. Yehuda HaNasi Struggles with the Mitzva of *Tzedaka*

Bava Batra 8a

INTRODUCTION

In the last chapter, we encountered Rav Yannai, a student of R. Yehuda HaNasi, the great third-century Sage most responsible for compiling the Mishna. In that aggada, a mysterious guest who may (or may not) have been an imposter confronts Rav Yannai and teaches him a crucial lesson. In this aggada, too, a mysterious man confronts Rebbe, and provokes Rebbe to reflect about the responsibilities of a wealthy man toward the poor during a period of famine.

The obligation to give charity is a crucial one in the Jewish tradition, going back to the Torah itself.[1] One enduring question, however, is what the criteria should be for recipients of charity, given limited charity resources. Does every poor person deserve charity? What about a Jewish apostate? Or a person infamous for cruelty to others? Our aggada takes up one facet of this important question.

The main protagonist of this aggada, R. Yehuda HaNasi, was a man of considerable wealth. He lived in the Land of Israel during the second century CE, and was the formal leader of the Jewish community – hence the title "*Nasi*," meaning "prince," a title that came to be associated with heads of the Sanhedrin, the Jewish high court. According to many talmudic sources, he was on very close terms with Antoninus, a Roman emperor, and rivaled him in wealth.[2] His most commonly used moniker was "Rebbe," meaning "My Master" – the master *par excellence* – and this is because his leadership centered around his encyclopedic knowledge of Torah. Rebbe (the name I use in this volume) played a pivotal role in gathering and organizing the vast traditions of Oral Law, thereby compiling the Mishna, the first authoritative compilation of Jewish Law in history, upon which the whole Talmud is based. This was an achievement of monumental proportions, and Rebbe is one of the most adulated figures in rabbinic Judaism. For this reason alone, his struggle to define the limits of charity takes on extra significance.

This aggada invites the reader into its understanding of both Rebbe's heart and his mind. Rebbe first places a sharp limitation on who deserves his largesse, but when confronted with the reality of that limitation in the person of an indigent man seeking food, he embarks upon a sinuous moral journey with multiple stops along the way until he finally resolves his dilemma. This struggle illuminates the remarkable modesty that was a hallmark of Rebbe's character, his openness to reconsidering his convictions in light of new information, and new moral insight.

רַבִּי פָּתַח אוֹצָרוֹת בִּשְׁנֵי בַצּוֹרֶת, אָמַר: יִכָּנְסוּ בַּעֲלֵי מִקְרָא, בַּעֲלֵי מִשְׁנָה, בַּעֲלֵי תַלְמוּד, בַּעֲלֵי הֲלָכָה, בַּעֲלֵי הַגָּדָה; אֲבָל עַמֵּי הָאָרֶץ אַל יִכָּנְסוּ. דָּחַק

1. Deuteronomy 15:7.
2. See sources cited in chapter 6 below, pp. 68 n. 2.

רַבִּי יוֹנָתָן בֶּן עַמְרָם וְנִכְנַס. אָמַר לוֹ: "רַבִּי, פַּרְנְסֵנִי!" אָמַר לוֹ: "בְּנִי, קָרִיתָ?" אָמַר לוֹ: "לָאו". "שָׁנִיתָ?" אָמַר לוֹ: "לָאו". "אִם כֵּן, בַּמָּה אֲפַרְנְסֶךָ?" [אָמַר לוֹ:] "פַּרְנְסֵנִי כְּכֶלֶב וּכְעוֹרֵב". פַּרְנְסֵיהּ. בָּתַר דִּנְפַק יָתֵיב רַבִּי וְקָא מִצְטַעֵר, וְאָמַר: אוֹי לִי שֶׁנָּתַתִּי פִּתִּי לְעַם הָאָרֶץ! אָמַר לְפָנָיו רַבִּי שִׁמְעוֹן בַּר רַבִּי: שֶׁמָּא יוֹנָתָן בֶּן עַמְרָם תַּלְמִידְךָ הוּא, שֶׁאֵינוֹ רוֹצֶה לֵיהָנוֹת מִכְּבוֹד תּוֹרָה מִיָּמָיו? בָּדְקוּ וְאַשְׁכַּח. אָמַר רַבִּי: יִכָּנְסוּ הַכֹּל.

It is related that **Rabbi** Yehuda HaNasi once **opened** his **storehouses** to distribute food **during years of drought. He said: Masters of Bible, masters of Mishna, masters of Talmud, masters of** ***halakha*****, masters of aggada may enter** and receive food from me, **but ignoramuses should not enter. Rabbi Yonatan ben Amram,** whom Rabbi Yehuda HaNasi did not know, **pushed** his way in, **and entered,** and **said to him: Rabbi** Yehuda HaNasi, **sustain me.** Rabbi Yehuda HaNasi **said to him: My son, have you read** the Bible? Rabbi Yonatan ben Amram **said to him,** out of modesty: **No.** Rabbi Yehuda HaNasi continued: **Have you studied** Mishna? Once again, Rabbi Yonatan ben Amram **said to him: No.** Rabbi Yehuda HaNasi then asked him: **If so, by what** merit **should I sustain you?** Rabbi Yonatan ben Amram **said to him: Sustain me like a dog and like a raven,** who are given food even though they have not learned anything. Rabbi Yehuda HaNasi was moved by his words and **fed him. After** Rabbi Yonatan **left, Rabbi** Yehuda HaNasi **sat, and was distressed, and said: Woe is me, that I have given my bread to an ignoramus.** His son, **Rabbi Shimon bar Rabbi** Yehuda HaNasi, **said to him: Perhaps he was your disciple Yonatan ben Amram, who never in his life wanted to** materially **benefit from the honor** shown to the **Torah? They investigated** the matter **and found** that such was the case. **Rabbi** Yehuda HaNasi then **said: Let everyone enter.**

R. YONATAN PUSHES HIS WAY INTO THE STOREHOUSE

A famine afflicted the Land of Israel, and Rebbe, wealthy man that he was, and also leader of the Jewish community, opened his storehouses to provide food for the needy. This was surely an act of great generosity.

Nevertheless, Rebbe placed a crucial restriction upon those eligible for support. While he welcomed those who were masters of various Torah disciplines, from Bible to Mishna, to Talmud, to halakha, to aggada, those who were *amei ha'aretz,* ignoramuses, were prohibited by him from seeking food.

The first point to make about this passage is the social stratification it implies. It is interesting to note that there are diverse specialties within Torah scholarship. For example, one can be expert in halakha but not aggada, or Mishna but not Talmud. In part, this is a matter of level of advancement in Torah studies. Thus, a master of Mishna is more advanced than a master of Bible, since knowledge of Mishna presupposes knowledge of the Bible, and a master of Talmud is likely to be more advanced than a master of Mishna, since knowledge of Talmud presupposes knowledge of Mishna. Yet a hierarchy of knowledge is not all there is to this classification, for it is hardly apparent that a master of aggada must likewise be a master of halakha.[3] There seems to be an element of specialization as well. Due to variations in individual talent and personal interests, Jews throughout the ages have focused their special attention on different dimensions of the Jewish intellectual tradition. Kabbalists were not necessarily masters of halakha, masters of halakha were not necessarily expert in the Prophets, and so on, although true masters of each no doubt possessed basic knowledge of the other.

It is also interesting to note that there is no category between any of the "masters" depicted above and the ignoramus. Either one is a master of some domain of Torah study, or one is a sheer ignoramus. But surely there are Jews who, while not master of any of these disciplines, possessed some knowledge of each, or even some knowledge of just one. The dichotomy here seems acute indeed.

Of course, it is possible that the aggada uses the term "master" loosely. One needn't be a true master to elevate oneself above the status

3. For a discussion of the role of masters of aggada during this time period, see David Levine, "Masters, Preachers and Aggadists: An Aspect of Jewish Culture in Third and Fourth Century Palestine," in *"Follow the Wise": Studies in Jewish History and Culture in Honor of Lee Levine,* ed. Z. Weiss, O. Irshal, and J. Magnes (NY, 2010), 275–296.

of an ignoramus. It is also possible that the aggada reflects its perspective on a certain historical reality. That is, perhaps the author of the aggada meant to suggest that in his time and place Jews either possessed some real knowledge of one of the disciplines of Torah study, or they were total ignoramuses, and indeed there were very few Jews in between. Both of these interpretive strategies might be correct. But in either case, our aggada casts a spotlight on an ancient rabbinic tension between ignoramuses on the one hand, and the Rabbis and their followers on the other, and that is the most important point.

Elsewhere the Talmud dwells extensively on this tension, which in fact was severe indeed. The *locus classicus* is Pesaḥim 49b, where a number of teachings are cited. For example, R. Meir taught that anyone who marries his daughter to an *am ha'aretz* is considered as though he binds her and places her before a lion. Likewise, R. Elazar taught that one may not travel in the company of an *am ha'aretz*. Not surprisingly, this antipathy was reciprocated by *amei ha'aretz* toward the Rabbis. Thus, R. Akiva taught that when he himself was an *am ha'aretz* in his youth, he would have bitten a Torah scholar like a donkey, whose bite is particularly dangerous. In short, key members of the community of scholars and their adherents regarded *amei ha'aretz* as uncouth ignoramuses, boorish, and not careful about halakha, especially laws of purity and impurity, and certain agricultural laws as well. For their part, at least some *amei ha'aretz* regarded Torah scholars and their adherents as supercilious, clannish, and arrogant.[4] Given this background, and especially these rabbinic attitudes toward *amei ha'aretz,* Rebbe's position on charity is more understandable.[5]

That said, it is still rather surprising, to say the least, that Rebbe could condemn *amei ha'aretz* to starvation. While many might have been boorish opponents of the Rabbis and all that the Rabbis stood for, they were still not only human beings but also Jews. As the Maharsha points

4. There is extensive scholarly literature on this subject. For a recent survey and discussion, see Y. Furstenberg, "*Am Ha'Aretz* in Tannaitic Literature and Its Social Context," *Zion* (2013): 287–319 (Heb.),

5. Note too a later, amoraic teaching in the name of R. Ami: "Anyone without knowledge, it is forbidden to have compassion upon him" (Berakhot 33a).

out, an undisputed teaching of the Tosefta requires that even gentiles receive Jewish communal support during times of need.[6] Therefore, it would follow that members of the Jewish community proper should certainly be supported. How then could Rebbe block their access to food during a famine?

This question, not surprisingly, troubled the classical commentators. The thirteenth-fourteenth century authority R. Yom Tov ben Avraham Asevilli, popularly called the Ritva, addressed this issue in his commentary. He suggested that Rebbe assumed that *amei ha'aretz* could and would successfully seek sustenance elsewhere, for there were many charitable Jews and Jewish communities. Otherwise, Rebbe would certainly have opened his storehouse to all. He chose not to do so because he believed they were in no danger of starvation.[7]

In any case, while this restrictive policy may have been Rebbe's initial position, it is one he eventually comes to regret. His change of heart is precipitated by the arrival of one R. Yonatan the son of Amram, who pushed his way into the storehouse, asking for food. Rebbe responds with a term of endearment, calling this petitioner "my son." He asks him whether or not he has read the Bible. R. Yonatan responds that he has not. Once again Rebbe inquires, this time whether or not he has read Mishna. Once again, R. Yonatan responds in the negative. Rebbe then asks, "If so, by what merit should I sustain you?" Before examining R. Yonatan's response to this question, several points should be made about the exchange so far.

First, why did R. Yonatan push himself into the storehouse? Why did he not enter like any other destitute person seeking help from the wealthy Rebbe? One answer might be that R. Yonatan was desperate

6. Gittin 3:18; also cited in Gittin 61a.

7. Ad loc. *Beit Yosef* in the commentary to Tur *Yoreh De'ah* 251 cites another version of the Ritva, according to which Rebbe excluded *amei ha'aretz* because he believed there were insufficient resources for all, and if he were to permit *amei ha'aretz,* scholars would starve. Were there enough resources for all, he would not have barred anyone. This positon finds its way into the *Shuḥan Arukh* 251:11. For a discussion, see footnote 21 on page 8 of the 1998 edition of the Ritva published in New York by Moshe Blau. The Maharsha on our aggada proposes yet another explanation.

for food, and despaired over his poverty.[8] This might also explain why Rebbe responds by calling him "my son," for it seems unlikely that every visitor to the storehouse would be greeted in this fashion. This reading would suggest a picture of Rebbe as compassionate and highly sensitive to the nuances in the behavior and needs of others, a picture reinforced by the nature of Rebbe's inquiries. Note that, surprisingly, Rebbe does not ask R. Yonatan if he was a "master of Bible" or a "master of Mishna," the criteria he himself had set out. Rather, he lowers the bar, and asks merely if R. Yonatan had "read" Bible or Mishna. Why the change in criteria? Perhaps because Rebbe sensed the man's desperation, and wanted any excuse to provide him with sustenance.

This reading is reinforced by Rebbe's response to R. Yonatan's confessions of ignorance: "If so, by what merit should I sustain you?" One detects a kind of despair on Rebbe's part too, as if he meant to say, "My son, I'd love to help you, but I need at least some justification for doing so, even a justification that would not meet my normal standards. Just work with me a little, let's together try to come up with some basis that would permit me to help you as I wish I could."

We might say, then, that Rebbe was already struggling with the moral cost of the restrictions that he himself had set for the distribution of his resources. While he still adheres to them, when confronted face to face with a suffering and desperate human being, he weakens, lowers the bar for charity, and expresses frustration when, by virtue of those restrictions, he could not provide for this impoverished man. His moral principles cause his moral pain. While Rebbe is not yet ready to abandon those principles, he deeply feels their cost.

"FEED ME LIKE A DOG OR A RAVEN"

R. Yonatan's response to Rebbe is stark and powerful. He asks Rebbe to feed him like one might feed a dog or raven. The reference here is to God, who provides food even for such lowly creatures. If God can provide food for the likes of dogs and ravens, surely Rebbe can provide for

8. An additional explanation will emerge later in this chapter.

a human being, learned or not.[9] God sets no standards in providing for His creatures, nor should Rebbe. This is likely an appeal to the principle of *imitatio dei,* the obligation, in the language of the Torah, to "go in His ways" (Deuteronomy 28:9), upon which the *Sifrei* (Deuteronomy, *Ekev*: 49) comments: "Just as God is called merciful and compassionate, so too should you be merciful and compassionate." Thus, just as God is merciful toward all His creatures, including stray dogs and unattractive ravens, so too should Rebbe be merciful and provide food even for ignoramuses.[10]

Rebbe acquiesces to R. Yonatan's heartfelt plea, changes his mind, and offers him food. Surprisingly, however, immediately after R. Yonatan leaves the storehouse, no doubt laden with food, Rebbe changes his mind once again. He expresses great distress at having offered R. Yonatan food, and exclaims, "Woe is me that I have given my bread to an *am ha'aretz.*" We must ask ourselves what happened here. If Rebbe was persuaded that the right thing to do was to give R. Yonatan food, why does he immediately regret it, a regret both powerfully expressed and deeply felt? Is Rebbe so mercurial that he can't make up his mind, and changes it from moment to moment? Surely this is unlikely in a man of Rebbe's stature, accomplishments, and senior leadership position.[11]

Perhaps the best way to read this is as a struggle between moral emotions and moral principle.[12] For example, some people give charity because they are moved by feelings of compassion for the impoverished.

9. See Rashi, ad loc., who comments that the reference is to God, and also explains why R. Yonatan chose these two creatures specifically.
10. See comments of *Iyun Yaakov* in the standard editions of the *Ein Yaakov,* ad loc., who adds that ravens are scavengers who do not feed their own young, but God nevertheless provides for them.
11. The *Iyun Yaakov,* ibid., suggests that he regretted giving him quality food based upon the phrase "my bread." This interpretation, at least to this reader, seems a less than straightforward reading of the text.
12. Two extreme positions that exemplify these perspectives are those of David Hume, the eighteenth-century Scottish philosopher, and Immanuel Kant, of the same century in Germany. Hume argued that all moral behavior is ultimately driven by what he called "sentiment," whereas Kant maintained that no choice is moral unless it is driven by principle, which he called the Categorical Imperative. See Humes' *An Inquiry Concerning the Principles of Morals* (Chicago, 1930) and Kant's *Foundations of the Metaphysics of Morals,* tr. L. W. Beck (NY, 1959).

Others give charity because they are committed to the principle that those blessed with resources must share them with those in need. Of course, motives for giving charity can also be mixed, and some might give both because they feel overwhelmed by compassion and also because they believe it is the right thing to do. However, the difference between these two kinds of motives for moral behavior should be kept clear, for sometimes moral emotions conflict with moral principle. That is exactly the case with Rebbe and R. Yonatan.

Rebbe's principles drove him to exclude *amei ha'aretz* from his largesse, yet his compassion for a human being suffering in front of him drove Rebbe to change his mind and provide R. Yonatan food. The emotion of compassion overrode his principles. However, as soon as that emotion lost its intensity, because the poor man was out of sight and well-provided for, Rebbe regretted that he had allowed his emotions to overcome his principles in a moment of weakness. Rebbe might well have believed that all human beings, and perhaps leaders especially, should always follow their convictions, not their passing emotions, which can lead reason astray. This is why Rebbe regretted his change of mind. Emotions, even those that some might characterize as moral, like compassion, should never drive decisions, for they contaminate the rational decision-making process.[13]

Two parallels to this in rabbinic literature are worth highlighting. First, there is King Saul's failure to completely fulfill the obligation to wipe out the Amalekites. R. Mani is quoted as teaching:

13. This is exactly Maimonides' position in *The Guide for the Perplexed* I:54(Chicago, 1963), trans. S. Pines, 123–127. It is hardly without interest that the Talmud records numerous dialogues between Rebbe and Antoninus, a Roman emperor. While the exact identity of Antoninus has been the subject of much debate amongst historians, some identify him with the great general and Stoic philosopher Marcus Aurelius, who like all Stoics maintained that emotions should never serve as the basis for choice. Even if that identification is false, however, these ideas were current amongst the circle of Roman leaders in which Antoninus would have been situated, and given the close relationship the Talmud describes between him and Rebbe, it is surely fascinating that these very ideas which are central to Stoic moral philosophy would have engaged Rebbe as well.

> When the Holy One, Blessed be He, said: "Go and attack Amalek" [a command which included women, children, infants, and animals], Saul said: "Now if on account of one life [that is taken in a case where a slain person's body is found and the murderer is unknown], the Torah said to bring a heifer whose neck is broken [in an atonement ritual described in Deuteronomy 6:1–9], all the more so must I have pity and not take all these Amalekite lives. And if the men have sinned, in what way have the animals sinned, in what way have the children sinned?" A Divine Voice then came forth and said to him: "Do not be overly righteous" (Ecclesiastes 7:16).[14]

God issued a command to completely annihilate the Amalekites and their animal possessions, and religious principle requires Saul to obey God's command. However, according to R. Mani, Saul expresses compassion for those who were to be killed and refuses to carry out the command. On this reading, Saul's moral emotion, compassion, conflicts with the principle that one must obey God's command. Saul loses his kingship over this failure to follow principle, and R. Mani criticizes him for excess "righteousness," for misplaced compassion. The midrash quotes this teaching, too, and concludes with a piquant comment of Reish Lakish: "Whoever becomes merciful when he should be cruel, becomes cruel when he should be merciful."[15] Moral emotions unguided by right reason will lead to wrong behavior. Only principle may drive choice.

A second example in rabbinic literature of the conflict between principle and moral emotions is especially illuminating, because it derives from Rebbe's own life. Rebbe suffered from a serious and very painful illness, and the Talmud takes up the question of why this was so. Did Rebbe ever behave in such a fashion as to warrant such draconian divine punishment? Here is the Talmud's account of the cause of his illness, and its cure:

14. Yoma 22b.
15. Ecclesiastes Rabba 7:16 (translation mine).

> [This suffering] came upon Rebbe due to an incident, and left him due to another incident. What was that incident? There was a certain calf that was being led to slaughter. The calf went and hung its head on the corner of Rebbe's garment, and was weeping. Rebbe said to it: Go, as you were created for this purpose. It was said [in heaven]: Since he was not compassionate, let afflictions come upon him. And [this suffering] left him due to an incident. One day the maidservant of Rebbe was sweeping his house. There were young weasels lying about and she was in the process of sweeping them out. Rebbe said to her: Let them be, as it is written: "His mercies are over all His creatures" (Psalms 145:9). Since he was compassionate, we shall be compassionate on him [and he was relieved of his suffering].[16]

In this story, Rebbe first affirmed a basic theological principle: Each creature possesses its own role in the divine ecology of the world. Rebbe, who was obviously not a vegetarian, believed that the role of cows was to be slaughtered for food. According to Rebbe, this is God's plan, which cows must accept without complaint. There was no room in this principled and rational picture of the world for Rebbe to feel compassion for the weeping cow. His moral feelings were entirely the product of his reason, and reason concluded that cows must be led to slaughter. Yet the Talmud maintains that this was wrong, and that even if the cow was rightfully led to slaughter, Rebbe should have felt sorry for it and didn't, a failure which caused his own suffering.[17]

The cure for Rebbe's ailment was the compassion he felt and expressed toward weasels. Reason does not require that he maintain the weasels in his own home. They can surely find another place to roost. Yet he felt enough compassion for them – citing the verse that God has mercy on all His creatures – that he chose to keep them in his home.

16. Bava Metzia 85a.
17. See chapter 5 of Moshe Sokol, *The Snake at the Mouth of the Cave: Exploring Talmudic Narratives* (Jerusalem, 2021), 66–67, for a fuller discussion of this theme, and Martha Nussbaum, *The Fragility of Goodness* (Cambridge, 1986), ch. 2, 3, commenting on several Greek tragedies.

His newfound compassion prohibited for him what reason would have permitted, thereby demonstrating that he had found a role for moral sentiment in the decision-making process.[18] Rebbe was a new man, and his illness was cured.

The themes of the story which is the focus of this chapter and the stories about the cow and the weasels overlap. In both, Rebbe struggles with the question of the role of pure compassion in a life regulated by rational principles. Should Rebbe's compassion for the suffering of an *am ha'aretz* overcome his principled opposition to sustaining them? Should Rebbe feel compassion for a cow brought to slaughter if God's plan for the world included bringing cows to slaughter? The denouement of the story about the weasels suggests that there must always be a role for compassion. That said, compassion for weasels does not clash directly with any norm or principle, and even the new Rebbe would probably endorse the slaughter of the cow. The main difference between the new Rebbe and the old one is that the new Rebbe would feel pain over permitting a weeping cow to go to slaughter, even if that pain does not drive choice, whereas the old Rebbe felt no pain at all.

What Rebbe learned is that just as God's mercy extends over all His creatures, Rebbe's own mercy should as well. He should always feel compassion for every creature, animal or human. That said, God, whose mercies extend over all creatures, still permits the slaughter of cows, and sometimes even mandates it, for mitzva purposes such as sacrifices in the Temple, or food for the holidays. God may feel compassion for cows, but compassion is not a sufficient driver of His choice, and indeed sometimes God makes choices contrary to His own mercy. Rebbe too may sometimes choose principle over compassion, as was the case in the position Rebbe first took, excluding the *am ha'aretz* from his storehouse

18. Of course, this case is different from the stories about the ignoramus and about Saul, because in those cases principle required a course of action which was contrary to the course of action that compassion would initiate. Here, reason does not mandate eliminating the weasels or sending the cow to slaughter, but only permits such behavior. Nevertheless, in all cases there is a tension between principle and moral emotions, even if there is no contradiction. In all the stories about Rebbe, he seems to struggle with the same issue: How much weight should he give to moral feeling in making a moral choice? For more about this, see below.

during the famine. And sometimes Rebbe may choose compassion even if not required to do so by principle, as was the case with the weasels. While admittedly we cannot know with any certainty when in Rebbe's life the story which is the focus of this chapter took place in relation to the stories told about the cow and the weasels, several possibilities suggest themselves.[19] What seems clear is that in both these stories, Rebbe is struggling with overlapping moral questions.

That said, can we trace the development of Rebbe's attitude to this question within our own aggada? To gain a clearer picture of this, it will be helpful to distinguish a number of phases through which Rebbe passed during the course of the story. First there is Rebbe One, who forbids ignoramuses from deriving benefit from his food. There is no evidence that Rebbe felt conflicted or bad about this decision at that phase in his moral evolution, much like Rebbe did not feel pain over the weeping cow. Then, R. Yonatan, a desperate man, pushes his way into the storehouse seeking food, for which Rebbe can provide no justification if he adheres to his principles. Yet, as I argued above, the text suggests that Rebbe felt pained by the limitations of his principles, even as he affirmed them. Let's call this phase in Rebbe's development Rebbe Two.

Next, R. Yonatan makes the argument that he should be fed by God, no less than dogs or ravens are fed. As a result, Rebbe succumbs to the compassion this argument evokes in him, he relents, and provides R. Yonatan food. This is Rebbe Three. After R. Yonatan leaves, Rebbe regrets that he succumbed to emotion, re-affirming his conviction that choice must always and only be driven by principle, not feelings. This

19. The story about the *am ha'aretz* may have taken place during Rebbe's illness, during which time he had not yet resolved the challenge of compassion versus principle. Our aggada is a picture of Rebbe along the way to his final stage, of compassion for even animals. It may also have taken place after Rebbe's cure. Although Rebbe learned to have compassion for all creatures, such compassion is not limitless, as I noted in the body of the chapter, and in his view, *amei ha'aretz* may deserve ill treatment. On this reading, what he is struggling with would be what emotions are appropriate to human beings who fall so far short of what God demands, and to what extent those emotions should drive choice. While one might argue that more mercy should be shown to starving human beings than to weasels, if those human beings are *amei ha'aretz*, that conclusion may not hold.

then is Rebbe Four.[20] Whether or not Rebbe feels pain over his treatment of *amei ha'aretz* thus depends upon which Rebbe we are speaking of.

At this point it is surely worth remarking upon a very impressive quality that Rebbe demonstrates in our aggada. His views are not set in stone. He is a man open to change, to reconsidering his views, to reflection and compassion. Many people are highly dogmatic and stubborn. Despite Rebbe's vast learning, power, and station in life, he emerges here as open-minded, as someone willing to humbly reconsider and revise his views, so far no less than four times. As we shall see in the next chapter of this volume as well, this vividly exemplifies the mishna's teaching, that with Rebbe's death, modesty died as well.[21]

REBBE OPENS THE STOREHOUSES TO ALL

Thus far we have traced Rebbe's evolution from Rebbe One to Rebbe Four. However, in point of fact, Rebbe's evolution does not end with Rebbe Four, for the aggada continues, and records a remarkable, even astonishing development. Rebbe's son, R. Shimon, now appears, and suggests to his father that R. Yonatan might possibly be one of Rebbe's own students. Why then did R. Yonatan not tell Rebbe the truth about his own learning when Rebbe interrogated him after he pushed his way into the storehouse? After all, if he was a student of Rebbe, surely he fit one of the categories which would justify securing provisions. R. Shimon himself proposes an answer to that very question: R. Yonatan might have chosen not to benefit from his knowledge of Torah. To justify accepting charity on grounds of a person's Torah is to make the Torah a means to the end of personal gratification. However, the Torah is of

---

20. It is unclear if Rebbe Four is the equivalent of Rebbe Two. It is possible that he reverted back to exactly that phase in his moral evolution. It is also possible that as a result of the error he now believes he made, he would want to suppress some of the moral emotions he felt then, since they led him astray, even if he did not want to eliminate them entirely, as was the case in Rebbe One. In other words, Rebbe Four may be an intermediary position between Rebbe One and Rebbe Two. I tend to favor the latter reading, with each phase marking out a different station in Rebbe's evolution, but both seem legitimate.
21. See chapter 2 for discussion and sources.

such incomparable value that it is always and only an end in itself, and may never serve as a means to anything other than itself.

This was Hillel's teaching in *Pirkei Avot*: "One who makes worldly use of the crown of Torah shall fade away." The mishna continues: "From this you learn that one who seeks personal benefit from the words of Torah risks destroying his life." It is, in the piquant language of the same mishna, to make the Torah "a spade with which to dig."[22] Rebbe's son thus suggested that R. Yonatan might have followed exactly this teaching, choosing to hide his true identity as a man of learning in order to gain access to Rebbe's storehouse.

The aggada next reports that an investigation revealed the truth of R. Shimon's suggestion: R. Yonatan was indeed a student of Rebbe. Why then did Rebbe not recognize him? Either Rebbe had many students and he did not know them all, or, perhaps more likely, R. Yonatan shrouded himself when entering the storehouse, and was therefore unrecognizable. In short, R. Yonatan was an imposter. He fabricated a false identity for himself to gain access to food. Why? We have only R. Shimon's conjecture, so that he would not use his Torah knowledge for personal pecuniary benefit. It is in fact likely that R. Shimon at least suspected, if not knew of, R. Yonatan's true identity all along, for otherwise why make the suggestion at all? But if so, why then did R. Shimon pose the suggestion only as a possibility, introducing it with the word "perhaps"? Could he not have conducted a full investigation and then informed his father of the results, of the unvarnished truth, at the very outset? The probable answer is that as a young man and dutiful son he would not want to confront his father directly. It is far more respectful and diplomatic for a son to pose a suggestion to a father than to directly assert that he was mistaken. This would be consistent with the teaching of an early midrash on the Torah, which forbids a child from contradicting his parent.[23]

What further complicates this picture is its intergenerational framework. Rebbe, the venerated master, takes one position. R. Yonatan, as his student, and thus a member of the next generation, opposes this

22. *Pirkei Avot* 4:7.

23. *Torat Kohanim on Leviticus, Parashat Kedoshim,* 19:3, cited in Kiddushin 31b.

position, at least for himself, and engages in subterfuge in order to receive what is really his due. Next, R. Shimon, likewise of the younger generation, supports R. Yonatan's action. It emerges then that the two who question Rebbe's position are members of a younger generation and Rebbe is their elder. This might have been a point of great sensitivity for Rebbe, and would therefore require extra sensitivity on the part of both R. Yonatan and R. Shimon. In this aggada, the younger generation possessed a certain wisdom that the older generation did not. In a great inversion, Rebbe, the revered master (and the very meaning of his name!), became in this one respect their student, and they his master. They saw something he did not see.

This observation brings us back to the previous chapter, about Rav Yannai, who was duped by an imposter to teach Rav Yannai a crucial moral lesson. The theme recapitulates itself exactly, and this time the duped party was Rav Yannai's own teacher, Rebbe. In both cases, a learned man disguises himself as an ignoramus to further refine the moral qualities of two great men: a teacher, Rebbe, and his mature student, Rav Yannai.

What makes this parallel even more intriguing is that the identity of the disguised student who instructs Rebbe is R. Yonatan ben Amram. We know very little about R. Yonatan ben Amram, but it is interesting that the Talmud reports that a teacher of Rav Yannai was a Rav Natan ben Amram.[24] Binyamin Lau argues that since the name Yonatan ben Amram appears nowhere else in rabbinic literature, and since in some variants of the Talmud Yerushalmi the name appears as Rav Natan ben Amram, it is likely that in our aggada the man who pushed his way into the storehouse is really R. Natan ben Amram.[25] Thus, Rav Yannai became a student of the very man who disguised himself in order to teach a moral lesson to his own master, Rebbe.

In short, Rav Yannai was not only a disciple of an imposter, but also a disciple of the very man who used his impostering to instruct his other master, the great Rebbe. In the aggada which is the subject of this chapter, the same cycle repeats itself. In both aggadot, obscuring

24. Avoda Zara 36b.

25. Lau, *The Sages, Vol. IV*, 87–89.

the identity of the moral instructor makes instruction possible. Why would that be?

While I shall argue that there is more to it than this, we can begin to answer this question by observing that it is far more difficult to improve yourself if the reprover is someone you know. The baggage of that relationship can make it especially challenging to change one's ways. Shame, defensiveness, personal relationship to authority, and relative difference in social standing are all factors which may complicate the task of accepting rebuke. For example, it would surely be more difficult for a teacher to accept rebuke from a student than from the head of the school. Similarly, if an adolescent is rebelling against a parent, accepting rebuke from a parent might be far more difficult than accepting rebuke from a peer. If the identity of the rebuker is obscured, the subject of that rebuke possesses a kind of *tabula rasa,* which may be the key to personal transformation. This murkiness of identity will continue to richly resonate as a theme of this aggada, as we shall see.

In any case, let us return to the narrative. Rebbe, true to form, acknowledges exactly that his son and R. Yonatan saw what he did not, and he recants. Remarkably enough, we now arrive at Rebbe Five. Yet his reversal is perplexing. For he could have admitted his error about R. Yonatan and allowed him permanent entrée into the storehouse, on account of R. Yonatan's true identity as a member of the class of scholars. But that is not what Rebbe does. Rather, he reverses himself completely, and rejects the very foundational distinction he drew between scholars and ignoramuses. Now, everyone without exception may receive support from Rebbe's wealth, for Rebbe eliminated all class distinctions. It seems fair to ask why Rebbe rejects the very fundamental principle he first so confidently affirmed.

One obvious answer to that question is that it derives from the suggestion R. Shimon himself made to explain R. Yonatan's impostering: He refused to derive benefit from his Torah learning. But the problem of deriving benefit from Torah learning is not R. Yonatan's alone. Its logic is impeccable and derives from no less an authority than the great Hillel, as recorded in the mishna in *Pirkei Avot,* which Rebbe himself would eventually canonize. If only scholars could have access to Rebbe's storehouse during a famine, then every scholar who seeks that access must justify it on grounds of his Torah learning. But that is to violate the teaching of Hillel. Rebbe came to see this, and therefore recanted his original stipulation.[26] Rebbe changed his mind, not his heart, and acted on the basis of principle, not on the basis of pure moral sentiment. It is even possible that R. Yonatan pushed himself into the storehouse to make this point exactly, and not merely to ask for food.

Yet this approach, as sound as it first appears, does raise a problem. Surely Rebbe knew of Hillel's teaching; indeed, he himself recorded it in the Mishna he compiled.[27] But if Rebbe knew that Torah must never be exploited for personal gain, why then did he insist in the first place on limiting access to the storehouse only to those learned in Torah? Surely it should have been obvious to him that such a limitation would force supplicants to profess their Torah knowledge to justify entrée, thereby violating Hillel's teaching. What then was Rebbe thinking?

Presumably, that the wrong of supporting an *am ha'aretz* overrides the wrong of using Torah knowledge for personal gain. Rebbe could not sidestep violating one of these two principles, for they came into unavoidable conflict during a famine. Either Rebbe allows *amei ha'aretz* to benefit from his provisions – thereby violating the principle that such individuals should not be supported – or he allows only the learned in – thereby violating Hillel's teaching. Given this inescapable clash of principles, Rebbe originally chose to violate the Hillel principle rather than violate the *am ha'aretz* principle. This was clearly a conscious choice on Rebbe's part. But what changed when he discovered R. Yonatan's true identity? Why should that discovery have led him to reject the value choice he had initially made? This seems to me to be a serious problem with the interpretation of the text cited above.

For this reason, I would like to propose another reading of the text. It begins with the simple suggestion that Rebbe might have lost confidence in his ability to ascertain who was deserving and who was not.

---

26. See too Shmuel Faust, *Aggadeta* (Or Yehuda, 2011) (Heb.), 281–282, and for a brief but generally valuable discussion of this aggada.
27. Even if the story told in this aggada took place before this mishna was compiled by Rebbe, it is extremely unlikely that Rebbe did not know of this teaching by the great Hillel.

Perhaps other scholars would also feign ignorance, for whatever reason, and be denied the food they deserved, and perhaps ignoramuses would feign knowledge to seek sustenance for which in point of fact they were not eligible. Therefore, Rebbe chose to allow everyone in. But taking this suggestion to a deeper level, what Rebbe really might have learned when he discovered that R. Yonatan was an imposter, was that all human beings may be imposters. That is, just like R. Yonatan was masked, so too all human beings may be masked as well. Rebbe was unable to penetrate to the true identity of a man who, it turns out, was his very own student. Now if he could not penetrate to the identity of his very own student, whose identity could he ever really know?

As many tests as Rebbe might pose to those who seek entrée into his storehouse, Rebbe learned that he could never be confident that he had ascertained the true mettle of his interlocutor. All human beings are fundamentally masked. Those who appear ignorant, like R. Yonatan, may be truly knowledgeable. Those who appear knowledgeable may be masking a profound ignorance. Those who appear happy may be masking a deep sadness, and those who appear morose may be content with their lives. Those who appear self-confident may be masking deep anxieties, and those who appear diffident may be self-confident after all. Those who appear humble may be masking arrogance, and those who appear arrogant may be masking extreme self-criticism. These masks may be consciously adopted, or they may be unconscious defense mechanisms, but masks they certainly are.

On this reading, Rebbe learned a deep truth about the human condition: It is impossible to penetrate with any certainty beneath the many masks that people wear. It will be recalled that I suggested above that one reason Rebbe did not recognize his own student is because R. Yonatan shrouded himself before entering the storehouse. That physical shroud then would be a trope for the shrouding that constitutes the human condition.

In order for people to function successfully in society, they must make judgments about others. Is he someone I should do business with? Is she someone I can trust with a confidence? Such judgments are inescapable. Yet while they are inescapable, those who make them must remain ever-conscious of their tentativeness, for who really knows what that person is truly like? Indeed, this insight may partly lie behind the mishna's teaching in *Pirkei Avot*: "Give everyone the benefit of the doubt."[28] But why should everyone be given the benefit of the doubt? Why not rely on appearances of wrongdoing? Because, as Rebbe discovered through the impostering R. Yonatan, appearances often mask the truth.

If these themes sound familiar, they should, because they emerged in the previous chapter as well. It will be recalled that Rav Yannai encounters a mysterious guest, and in so doing, like Rebbe, he encounters the mysteries of the human condition.

If we compare the two, Rav Yannai's transformation described in that chapter may well have been even broader than Rebbe's, described here. Rebbe's was challenged by crisis, by a famine, and his newfound openness may have obtained only during such exigent times. Indeed, one way to frame the overall theme of our aggada is confronting moral dilemmas during crises. However, the overall theme of the aggada in the chapter on Rav Yannai is moral growth, Rav Yannai's newfound assessment of his ways, telegraphed by the opening and concluding verse of the midrash analyzed there. This moral growth took place not during a time of crisis, but following an everyday encounter with a man on the street. The theme of elusive identities recurs again and again in that midrash, in many complex ways, because, as I suggested, it is at the very core of its teaching.

Both Rebbe and Rav Yannai, teacher and student, demonstrate remarkable and enviable openness to self-criticism and to change, and these qualities are amongst the hallmarks of their moral greatness. These individuals rise to the challenges that life presents them, re-assess their ways, and ever seek to make the morally best choices they can. Both must travel a tortuous and sinuous route to moral change. Rebbe adopted many differing positions during his journey, as we have seen, while Rav Yannai's journey involved less changes of mind than changes of heart. But both had the self-confidence and moral character to admit that they must change, and each grew to a new moral plateau.

---

28. *Pirkei Avot* 1:6.

To return to our narrative, Rebbe first relied upon his judgment as to whether the person seeking food was an *am ha'aretz*. In ancient times that was a crucial category, for it played a role in determining whether or not for halakhic reasons a learned man could eat together with someone else, whether or not his daughter could marry into that person's family, and so on. Given the animosity between the learned and the *amei ha'aretz*, Rebbe did need to make a judgment about who was an *am ha'aretz* and who was not, much as he and all his colleagues always did. This is what people do all the time when interacting with others.

However, famine gripped the land, and the lives of human beings were at stake. While in normal times we must sometimes rely on certain superficial judgments in order to function in society, can we make such judgments in moments of crisis when so much is at stake? Rebbe learned from the impostering R. Yonatan that at least during a famine everyone – not only the learned – must be fed from his storehouse. Just as R. Yonatan wore a mask, so too all human beings are masked. Can we really ever know for sure who is an ignoramus and who is learned? Rebbe learned that the tentative judgments we traditionally make to function in society must be abandoned in times of crisis. All human beings are masked and therefore, in times of crisis, all human beings must equally be invited to the table.

This then is Rebbe Five, the final Rebbe that we encounter in our aggada. The decision he makes at the last stage in his development is driven by principle, not by emotion. For his decision is made on intellectual grounds. He now possesses a deepened understanding of the human condition, that all human beings are ultimately masked in enigma. But what then about moral emotions? May they also play a role in moral decision-making? What stance would Rebbe take about this vexing question? Based upon this aggada alone, we cannot answer that question with any certainty, for it is indeed possible that Rebbe Five would eschew all moral emotions in decision-making. His regret over succumbing to compassion over principle in allowing R. Yonatan to take food may have remained with him and may have been absolute.[29] However, the aggada about the cow and the weasels certainly suggests

29. This depends upon how we read Rebbe Four. See n. 20, above.

that compassion does indeed play a role for Rebbe in moral decision-making. While that is true, however, it is nevertheless true only in a limited way. For in those cases compassion does not directly contradict the choices made on the basis of principle. Having compassion for cows does not mean that the cow should not be sent to slaughter, but only that in so doing, one should feel pain over the anguish of another living creature. Thus, while we can infer that compassion does play a role in moral decision-making for Rebbe, we can infer only that it does so in some contexts, but not always.

We might then ask how we are to define the limits of compassion. If compassion indeed plays a role in the decision-making process, might it not get out of hand, and drive the decision when it should not? That is exactly how Rebbe felt when he first encountered R. Yonatan and succumbed to compassion over principle, and that remains an enduring problem. What then are the limits to morally good emotions? When, and to what intensity, may they be productively felt? Compassion may be a virtuous emotion, but even virtuous emotions have a way of leaping beyond their legitimate borders, as the Talmud observes in the case of King Saul and the Amalekites. Our aggada leaves these questions open, much like Socrates left so many philosophical questions open in the Platonic dialogues. Not all questions may be easily answered. Yet our aggada, unlike Socrates, provides a crisp halakhic response in the case at hand. Rebbe makes a principled and very concrete decision to open the doors of his storehouses to all. While philosophical questions may be left open, life demands practical decisions too, and Rebbe, great halakhist that he was, made the decision that he believed was right in the circumstances at hand.

Rebbe's journey was a long and sinuous one, as he struggled with profound questions about moral decision-making and the impenetrability of the human condition. If Rebbe learned much from his encounter with the mysterious and shrouded R. Yonatan, so too do we the readers.

Chapter 5

R. Ḥanina ben Dosa, His Wife, and the Smoke-Filled Kitchen

Ta'anit 24b–25a

INTRODUCTION

Our image of the leading figures of the Mishna and Talmud is that of distinguished scholars who spent their days and nights mastering the intricacies of God's Torah. Yet that is not altogether accurate, as some were distinguished less by their vast knowledge and studiousness than by their personal piety. Of course, this is not to say that they were not also scholars, for they may well have been, but their hallmark, their distinctive path in the service of God, was located elsewhere.

One outstanding model of this phenomenon was R. Ḥanina ben Dosa, a contemporary of R. Yoḥanan ben Zakkai who lived in the Land of Israel following the destruction of the Second Temple. Much like his predecessor Ḥoni HaMe'agel,[1] R. Ḥanina was a man of exemplary piety,

1. See Sokol, *The Snake at the Mouth of the Cave*, ch. 8, for a discussion of Ḥoni's life,

a miracle worker to whose potent prayers God paid special attention. A long series of stories about his spiritual prowess and supernatural abilities appears in the Talmud,[2] from which the aggada in this chapter is drawn. One element of R. Ḥanina's piety was his asceticism: He lived in abject poverty, with no more food in the house, even for Shabbat, than some carobs. While I shall have more to say about R. Ḥanina in the course of this chapter, our attention will be drawn especially to his wife. This story leads us into the heart and mind of his wife, who lived in the same poverty that R. Ḥanina did. No doubt his wife believed deeply in the life her saintly husband chose, for we have no record of her voicing any complaint about it, until the latter part of the aggada, which is the focus of this study.

No doubt, too, she derived much spiritual satisfaction in her marriage to a man of R. Ḥanina's stature and in the elevated life they led together. Nevertheless, there is also some cost to living with a holy man like R. Ḥanina, as we shall see, and one wonders how his wife bore that cost. How did she cope with her life of poverty? Did this cause a strain in their marriage? How did R. Ḥanina respond to his wife's needs? Any life devoted to greatness, spiritual or intellectual or artistic, to mention just a few examples, requires commensurately great personal sacrifice. What of the spouse of such a person, husband or wife? This chapter will examine the extreme challenge of marriage to extreme greatness; here, the supreme greatness of a life besotted by God.

אָמַר רַב יְהוּדָה אָמַר רַב בְּכׇל יוֹם וְיוֹם בַּת קוֹל יוֹצֵאת וְאוֹמֶרֶת כׇּל הָעוֹלָם כּוּלּוֹ נִיזּוֹן בִּשְׁבִיל חֲנִינָא בְּנִי וַחֲנִינָא בְּנִי דַּיּוֹ בְּקַב חָרוּבִים מֵעֶרֶב שַׁבָּת לְעֶרֶב שַׁבָּת הֲוָה רְגִילָא דְּבֵיתְהוּ לְמֵיחֲמָא תַּנּוּרָא כׇּל מַעֲלֵי דְשַׁבְּתָא וְשָׁדְיָיא אַקְטַרְתָּא

The Gemara continues to discuss the righteous Rabbi Ḥanina ben Dosa and the wonders he performed. **Rav Yehuda said** that **Rav said: Each and every day a Divine Voice emerges** from Mount Horeb **and says: The entire world is sustained by** the

---

spirituality, and times. See also the very valuable discussion of both these figures in B. Lau, *The Sages, Volume I: The Second Temple Period* (Jerusalem, 2007), 57–83.

2. Ta'anit 24b–25a.

merit of **My son Ḥanina** ben Dosa, **and** yet for **Ḥanina, My son, a *kav* of carobs,** a very small amount of inferior food, **is sufficient** to sustain him for an entire week, **from** one **Shabbat eve to** the next **Shabbat eve.** The Gemara relates: Rabbi Ḥanina ben Dosa's **wife would heat the oven every Shabbat eve and create** a great amount of **smoke,**

מִשּׁוּם כִּיסּוּפָא הֲוָה לַהּ הָךְ שִׁיבָבְתָּא בִּישְׁתָּא אֲמַרָה מִכְּדֵי יָדַעְנָא דְּלֵית לְהוּ וְלָא מִידֵּי מַאי כּוּלֵּי הַאי אֲזָלָא וּטְרָפָא אַבָּבָא אִיכַּסְפָא וַעֲיַילָא לְאִינְדְּרוֹנָא

due to embarrassment, to make it appear that she was baking, despite the fact that there was no bread in her house. **She had a certain evil neighbor** who **said** to herself: **Now, I know that they have nothing. What,** then, **is all this** smoke? **She went and knocked on the door** to find out what was in the oven. Rabbi Ḥanina ben Dosa's wife was **embarrassed, and she ascended to an inner room** [*inderona*].

אִיתְעֲבִיד לַהּ נִסָּא דְּחָזְיָא לְתַנּוּרָא מְלֵא לַחְמָא וְאַגָּנָא מְלֵא לֵישָׁא אֲמַרָה לַהּ פְּלָנִיתָא פְּלָנִיתָא אַיְיתַי מָסָא דְּקָא חָרִיךְ לַחְמִיךְ אֲמַרָה לָהּ אַף אֲנָא לְהָכִי עֲיַילִי תָּנָא אַף הִיא לְהָבִיא מַרְדֶּה נִכְנְסָה מִפְּנֵי שֶׁמְּלוּמֶּדֶת בְּנִסִּים

A miracle was performed for Rabbi Ḥanina ben Dosa's wife, **as** her neighbor **saw the oven filled with bread and the kneading basin filled with dough. She said to** Rabbi Ḥanina's wife, calling her by name: **So-and-so, so-and-so, bring a shovel, as your bread is burning. She said to** her neighbor: **I too went inside for that** very purpose. A *Tanna* **taught: She too had entered** the inner room **to bring a shovel, because** she was **accustomed to miracles** and anticipated that one would occur to spare her embarrassment.

אֲמַרָה לֵיהּ דְּבֵיתְהוּ עַד אֵימַת נֵיזִיל וְנִצְטַעַר כּוּלֵּי הַאי אֲמַר לַהּ מַאי נַעֲבֵיד בְּעִי רַחֲמֵי דְּנִיתְבוּ לָךְ מִידֵּי בְּעָא רַחֲמֵי יָצְתָה כְּמִין פִּיסַּת יָד וִיהַבוּ לֵיהּ חַד כַּרְעָא דְּפָתוּרָא דְּדַהֲבָא חָזְיָא בְּחֶלְמָא עֲתִידִי צַדִּיקֵי דְּאָכְלִי אַפָּתוּרָא דְּדַהֲבָא דְּאִית לֵיהּ תְּלָת כַּרְעֵי וְאִיהוּ אַפָּתוּרָא דִּתְרֵי כַּרְעֵי

The Gemara further relates: Rabbi Ḥanina's **wife said to him: Until when will we continue to suffer this** poverty? **He said to her: What can we do?** She responded: **Pray for mercy that something will be given to you** from Heaven. **He prayed for mercy** and something **like** the **palm of a hand emerged and gave him one leg of a golden table. That night, his wife saw in a dream** that in **the future,** i.e., in the World to Come, **the righteous will eat at a golden table that has three legs, but** she will be eating **on a table that has two legs.**

אֲמַר לַהּ נִיחָא לָךְ דְּמֵיכָל אָכְלִי כּוּלֵּי עָלְמָא אַפָּתוֹרָא דְּמַשְׁלַם וַאֲנַן אַפָּתוֹרָא דִּמְחַסַּר אֲמַרָה לֵיהּ וּמַאי נַעֲבֵיד בְּעִי רַחֲמֵי דְּנִשְׁקְלִינְהוּ מִינָּךְ בָּעֵי רַחֲמֵי וְשַׁקְלוּהוּ תָּנָא גָּדוֹל הָיָה נֵס אַחֲרוֹן יוֹתֵר מִן הָרִאשׁוֹן דִּגְמִירִי דְּמֵיהָב יָהֲבִי מִישְׁקָל לָא שָׁקְלִי

When she told her husband this story, **he said to her: Are you content that everyone will eat at a complete table and we** will eat **at a defective table? She said to him: But what can we do? Pray for mercy, that** the leg of the golden table should **be taken from you. He prayed for mercy, and it was taken** from him. A *Tanna* **taught** in a *baraita*: **The last miracle was greater than the first, as** it **is learned** as a tradition that Heaven gives but **does not take back.**

SOME BACKGROUND ABOUT R. ḤANINA BEN DOSA

The story told in the aggada begins with a preface, a teaching of Rav Yehuda derived from Rav: A heavenly voice taught that the sustenance on which the whole world depends for survival derives from the merits of R. Ḥanina, but all R. Ḥanina himself required for his own sustenance was a measure of carobs for the week. Clearly, this is the very height of irony. The world's living creatures require vast, virtually unquantifiable amounts of food for their survival and flourishing, yet what makes all that food possible is a lone individual whose only needs are mere carobs. But like all ironies, this one too forces the reader to ponder what lies behind it. Just *why* is it the case, irony of ironies, that R. Ḥanina makes all that food possible? Is there any causal link between his remarkably limited need for food on the one hand, and the vast amount of food his limited needs make possible, on the other?

One answer to this question may begin with this observation: If the world can produce the likes of R. Ḥanina, then God would find the very existence of the world worthwhile, despite the many enduring failures of the human beings who inhabit it. The Torah relates in Genesis that God regretted creating human beings when He saw just how evil they were (6:5–6). But, our aggada may be implying, if only God had then found the likes of R. Ḥanina, then He would never have harbored such doubts. People of the stature of R. Ḥanina make the whole human project worthwhile. There are echoes here, too, of Abraham bargaining with God over the survival of the city of Sodom: Even ten righteous people would have justified the continued existence of Sodom (Genesis 18:32).

That said, we still lack an explanation for the specific role played by R. Ḥanina's asceticism. Why was it his asceticism in particular that uniquely provided for the sustenance of the world? This question in turn leads to another: Why does R. Ḥanina require so little food? Why doesn't he seek at least some bread for Shabbat, or food for the Shabbat meals? Rav, the author of this teaching, does not say, but several answers suggest themselves, and they begin with one of R. Ḥanina's few formal teachings recorded in talmudic literature.

> R. Ḥanina ben Dosa said: For one who puts fear of sin before wisdom, wisdom endures. For one who puts wisdom before fear of sin, wisdom does not endure. He also used to say: For one whose good deeds exceed his wisdom, wisdom endures. For one whose wisdom exceeds his good deeds, wisdom does not endure.[3]

R. Ḥanina here valorizes good deeds and fear of sin over pure wisdom. Without good deeds and fear of sin, wisdom is doomed to failure; good deeds and fear of sin make wisdom possible. No doubt he saw in his own days how purveyors of wisdom, perhaps even those learned in Torah, could become corrupted if they did not possess fear of heaven, and if

3. *Pirkei Avot* 3:11–12.

they stressed wisdom at the expense of actually doing what wisdom required. Every generation has been witness to these failures. Surely R. Ḥanina in his own life exemplified the virtues of great fear of heaven, and of good deeds, which were constitutive of his unusual piety.

A story told in Berakhot 34b enriches the talmudic picture of R. Ḥanina, who, it is reported, had gone to study under R. Yoḥanan ben Zakkai, the great teacher and leader of Jewish life following the destruction of the Second Temple. After R. Ḥanina's arrival, R. Yoḥanan ben Zakkai's son took severely ill, at which point R. Yoḥanan asked his student to pray on his son's behalf. R. Ḥanina was a virtuosic prayer, as is evident from the many stories told about him in talmudic literature. He put his head between his knees, sought mercy on R. Yoḥanan's son, and his prayers were answered. The child survived. R. Yoḥanan comments that if he himself had prayed for his son all day it would have been for naught. R. Yoḥanan's wife then speaks up and challenges her husband: "Is Ḥanina greater than you?" R. Yoḥanan responds that Ḥanina is like a servant before his master, God, whereas he, R. Yoḥanan, is like a minister before his master.

Rashi's reading of this rejoinder is telling. A servant possesses a certain intimacy with a king, despite his lowly status, because he is frequently about, tending to the king's needs. This contrasts with the minister, who despite his prestige and authority, possesses less intimacy because he sees the king far less frequently, only at necessary and far more formal meetings.[4] R. Yoḥanan, due to his great stature as a Torah authority and leader, is like the minister, whereas R. Ḥanina, despite his lesser stature as a mere servant, possesses a certain intimacy with God, for which reason his prayers are answered.

The image that emerges of R. Ḥanina is that of a loyal, humble, and submissive servant of God, whose life is shaped by intense fear of sin and the quest for good deeds. His piety is not that of a powerful prince of God, confident of his authority as a distinguished Torah scholar, God's very minister. His piety is much simpler, modest and less heady, as he is possessed by fear of sin and by diligently performing whatever

4. For a contemporary discussion of this idea, see James Kugel, *The Kingly Sanctuary* (2013), ch. 6.

good deeds he could muster. The Mishna in Sota[5] taught that when R. Ḥanina died, men of action passed from the world. The spirituality of R. Ḥanina could not have been more different than that of his great master R. Yoḥanan ben Zakkai.

This in turn may shed light on R. Ḥanina's asceticism, on why he never sought more food than the carobs that barely graced his table. He simply wasn't interested in more food. What mattered to him more than anything else, as a simple, pious servant of God, was to avoid sin and perform good deeds. Nothing else mattered at all. Why bother with food if his heart, spirit, and mind were focused entirely on God? This exemplary life made the sustenance of all humankind worthwhile.

Moreover – and as we shall see, this is a theme that emerges later in the story itself – material well-being in this world stands in inverse relation to well-being in the World to Come. The more material well-being there is in this world, the less well-being there will be in the World to Come, and the more well-being in the World to Come, the less material well-being in the present world. This perspective is at the heart of the asceticism that has found its expression in many religious traditions over time. Material well-being distracts from spiritual pursuits, and is at odds with a life devoted to God, the most perfectly spiritual of all beings.[6] A person can live with God or with material well-being, but not with both simultaneously. R. Ḥanina chose God, and so abandoned material well-being. His life was consumed by fear of sin and good deeds, by God and nothing else, and all of humankind survived on his account. This then provides a richer understanding of why R. Ḥanina's asceticism provides for the sustenance of the entire universe.

Interestingly, elsewhere the Talmud records the story of another Sage who survived on carobs, the great R. Shimon bar Yoḥai, who lived in a cave for thirteen years together with his son, while escaping the persecution of the Romans.[7] After the twelfth year he was liberated, but when he saw people plowing and planting he exclaimed, "How could people leave eternal life and spend time on life that is only temporary?"

5. Mishna Sota, 9:16..
6. For a fuller discussion of this issue, see Sokol, *Judaism Examined,* ch. 4.
7. Shabbat 33b.

So angry was he at this perversion of values that whatever he gazed upon burned to a crisp. A heavenly voice emerged, accused him of attempting to destroy the world, and sent him back into the cave for another year.

The themes in these two stories, and the theology they advocate, are parallel: This world and the World to Come are inversely related. Focusing on life in this temporary material world comes at the cost of eternal life in the World to Come, and life in the World to Come requires abandonment of the pleasures and distractions of life in this world. Both Sages lived on carobs, embodying in their own lives the antithetical relationship between the two worlds.

Yet it is not without interest that R. Shimon bar Yoḥai subsisted on carobs for thirteen years, whereas R. Ḥanina subsisted on carobs, so far as we know, for much of his adult life. Moreover, when R. Shimon bar Yoḥai subsisted on carobs he lived in a cave, segregated entirely from the distractions of the world. What better place could there be for focusing one's energies on God alone? Presumably, too, while trapped in the cave he had little choice of cuisine. All this contrasts sharply with R. Ḥanina, who lived not in a cave but in the world, with all of its distractions and blandishments, a married man at home in the neighborhood. Surely, the parallels between these two stories are striking: R. Shimon bar Yoḥai's thirteen years in a cave are in at least some ways the spiritual equivalent of R. Ḥanina's adult life in the world. Both subsisted on carobs. Yet the difference is no less striking: R. Shimon bar Yoḥai burns the world in anger at everyone's failure to abandon this world for a purely spiritual life focused on the World to Come. No such anger is ever reported about R. Ḥanina, whose life was devoted to good deeds and to helping others, not burning them.

Thus, despite the parallels between the theology held by these two great men, their inner lives could not have been more different. R. Ḥanina was the pious man of good deeds, helping those in need, modest, unassuming, and full of fear of sin. R. Shimon bar Yoḥai possessed an Elijah-like fiery passion for God, and could brook no compromises with the absolute and total devotion his vision of God demanded.

Finally, we come to yet another perspective on the questions posed above about the inner logic of Rav's teaching. R. Ḥanina taught humankind, by personal example, the true significance of food. The life he lived vividly demonstrated that food beyond what is necessary for survival has no value, that the whole point of food is to enable humans to exist so that they can live a life in fear of sin and in performing good deeds. He made the sustenance of the world possible by modeling to the world the value of that sustenance, which consists of no more nor less than enabling fear of sin and good deeds.

R. ḤANINA BEN DOSA'S WIFE AND THE SMOKING KITCHEN

With this background, we can now enter into the story itself, which, tellingly, begins not with R. Ḥanina, but with his wife. The aggada reports that she had an unusual habit every Friday: She would heat the oven and create a great amount of smoke. Why? Because, as the omniscient narrator of the story relates, she was embarrassed. The houses of all her friends and neighbors would be redolent with the succulent smell of bread and other foods cooking for Shabbat. But R. Ḥanina's house was empty, save for some carobs, with nothing to cook. So his wife simulated cooking by creating smoke, which she hoped her neighbors would take to be a sign that she had something to cook, that she was not so impoverished that she could not properly prepare for Shabbat.

Let us step back and consider this for a moment. Was R. Ḥanina himself embarrassed? The aggada does not report that he was, and indeed, given the portrait of him that emerges from our analysis above, it would be astonishing if he were. Given his theology, and his inner spiritual life, why would he be? But what of his wife? On the one hand, she is not yet depicted as complaining about their poverty. This occurs only later, after the episode with the nasty neighbor. But until then, she is silent and uncomplaining. Why? Probably because, as a loyal wife to R. Ḥanina, she affirmed the principles to which he had devoted his life. He was a holy man, a miracle worker, as she – and everyone else around them – knew.

We do not know how long they had been married when this episode took place, nor do we know what R. Ḥanina was like when she married him. But even if he wasn't yet the preeminent man he became, it is likely that even then he was special, if not yet holy, then on the path to holiness; if not yet the miracle worker, then on the path to miracle working. The Talmud contains no report that he underwent a conversion to this status. Rather, it seems likely that he evolved toward it over time, that she knew the man she was marrying, and chose to live the life of holiness and asceticism that were already, or were about to become, his defining qualities. The reason she did not complain is probably because she herself believed in the principles that defined R. Ḥanina's life.

But why then was she embarrassed? If she believed in those principles, like R. Ḥanina did, then why was she, but not he, embarrassed? Part of the answer, no doubt, is that she lived with her neighbors, but he lived in a spiritual universe of his own creation. She took care of the household and did the cooking, unlike her husband. Therefore, she more than he would have been tested by shame. But that said, even if it had been R. Ḥanina who took care of the household and she did not, it is hard to imagine that he would have been embarrassed as she was.

I believe the crucial factor here is the dissonance between belief and emotion. While she may cognitively have affirmed the absolute value of the ascetic life that R. Ḥanina chose, emotions do not always march in lockstep with beliefs. Thus, someone may be convinced that the eerie sounds he hears near the house in the middle of the night are just from the neighborhood cat, but that doesn't mean that he still won't feel some fear or anxiety. This is very obviously the case with action. Knowing something is true doesn't always lead to acting like it is: I may know that the right thing to do is to get up early in the morning to exercise, but that doesn't mean I'll actually do so. The same dissonance can be true with emotion as well.

R. Ḥanina himself had so completely identified with his theology, with his ideals, that he felt them too, but his wife may not yet have achieved that complete identification, and so felt ashamed by her poverty, even if she had never complained about it to her husband. To make the point even clearer, let us consider a possible example of this phenomenon from contemporary Jewish life. What about the wife of a student committed to long-term Torah study in a *kollel*? This may entail financial deprivation, and extra work outside the house by the wife to support a large family. This *kollel* wife may indeed be fully committed to the supreme value of Torah study on the part of her husband, and may even have been attracted to him precisely because of those lofty ideals. Nevertheless, does that commitment capture all her feelings? Might some such women, perhaps not many but some, feel frustration too, despite their ideals, like the wife of R. Ḥanina ben Dosa?

The story continues with a particularly nasty neighbor of R. Ḥanina and his wife, who knew of their poverty, and wanted to call the wife out on her dissimulation. She banged on the door, and the wife was so mortified by this that she escaped to an inner chamber of the house. The neighbor is extremely nasty, and the wife is extremely embarrassed. What might lie behind the neighbor's motivations, and what might lie behind the wife's escape to an inner chamber of the house?

Of course, the neighbor could have simply been a plain old villain. Unfortunately, there are people like that in the world, and she may well have been one of them. But another explanation seems plausible too. Is it not possible that the neighbor may have been shamed herself, by the lofty values of her neighbors, by their lives of holiness and asceticism? After all, she lives the good life, and cooks what she wishes for Shabbat, but her neighbors, they aspire to far more. Does she feel guilt at her own bourgeois life in comparison to her neighbors' remarkable self-sacrificial devotion to God? And does she wish to expiate that guilt by taking her holy neighbor down a notch or two, by demonstrating her dishonesty and even hypocrisy? Just like there are villains in the world, there are also people who are not villains but who may sometimes act that way, to compensate for unresolved feelings of guilt and shame.

What about the wife's escape to the inner chamber of the house? Here too, this may entirely capture what actually happened: Intensely ashamed, she did not want to confront her accusatory neighbor, and therefore hid herself in avoidance. Yet the phrase "inner chamber" is evocative, and one wonders if there was more to her escape than its most literal meaning. Note that the shame she now feels is acute. One might ask what she feels about that feeling of shame. On the one hand, she is mortified by her neighbor's aggressive pounding on the door. On the other hand, assuming that she shares her husband's principles and aspirations, how could she not also feel shame over her shame? For she would know that if she had fully integrated those principles like her husband had, she would have felt no embarrassment at all, just as R. Ḥanina himself presumably felt no embarrassment. Why feel shame over doing the right thing? This is a kind of meta-shame, shame over feeling ashamed, feelings of guilt about having those very feelings of embarrassment. Perhaps the inner chamber to which she escapes is not only a literal one, from her neighbor, but a figurative one too, from herself.

The Talmud next reports that a miracle was performed for her, and that the neighbor, who must have peeked inside the house, saw an oven full of bread and a basket full of dough. The neighbor yells out to the lady of the house, "So-and-so [like Mrs.], bring a shovel, as your bread is burning!" She responds that, indeed, that was exactly her intent when she left the kitchen, to run and fetch the shovel used for removing baked bread from the oven. At this point, a parenthetical teaching is interpolated into the story, not part of the original narrative, which affirms the truth of her response, and which asserts that the reason she left to get the shovel was that she was accustomed to miracles, and simply assumed that one would transpire.

Now let us consider again the motivation of R. Ḥanina's wife in entering the inner chamber. The aggada itself reports that she did so to escape the embarrassment of encountering her nasty neighbor, behavior which we analyzed above. On this reading, confirmed by the text of the aggada itself, her answer to the neighbor turns out to be less than honest. She did not go inside to fetch the shovel, as she said, but to avoid embarrassment, as the omniscient narrator of the aggada says. Yet this later interpolation to the narrative reads her motivation quite differently: She was motivated not by shame, but by the expectation that a miracle would be performed, for which reason she went inside to fetch the shovel. Apparently, the author of the interpolation was not comfortable portraying the wife of R. Ḥanina as telling a white lie, or as even needing to tell a white lie. No lies were necessary, because she was expecting exactly that miracle that took place. And the reason the miracle took place was that both R. Ḥanina and his wife lived miraculous lives, so holy were they. In short, the difference between the original aggada and the interpolation is over the true religious stature of R. Ḥanina's wife. While the former sees her as capable of a white lie, and therefore in that respect flawed, the latter rejects this picture.

Now it must first be observed that even on the first reading, that R. Ḥanina's wife was embarrassed and was less than perfectly truthful, the aggada insists that a miracle was still performed "for her." Indeed, she had never requested a miracle before, during their years of poverty, nor did she request one now, at the moment of her most acute shame. Indeed, one might argue that the reason she merited a miracle was precisely because she had not then, nor had she ever, requested one. She was a pious woman and faithful wife, aspiring to holiness, and never demanded or asked for more than what she possessed. She modeled one kind of a righteous woman, for which reason she merited a miracle. But of course, even righteous people may not achieve the very highest levels of their aspirations. R. Ḥanina's wife was authentic, she felt shame and did not mask or repress what she felt, even escaped because of that shame, and told a white lie as a consequence. Even imperfect people can achieve greatness and merit miracles. Piety comes in shades of gray, and miracles may be performed even for the gray-shaded pious.

Thus is the reading of the text of the aggada as we have it. But the interpolator could not agree. He refused to accept that R. Ḥanina's wife was capable of shame and of telling white lies.[8] She and her husband were so holy that they were awash in miracles throughout their lives.[9] Her piety does not come in shades of gray. Perhaps what is really at stake here between these two readings, then, is not primarily over the true religious stature of R. Ḥanina's wife. Rather, at a deeper level, the key difference may be what level of religious stature is necessary for the supernatural to intervene. Is gray-shaded piety enough?

It is important to observe here that the interpolator's reading stands in tension with the story as a whole. For why would R. Ḥanina's wife fill her house with smoke if she felt no shame? Moreover, if the couple were so awash in miracles, why was their poverty so abject? Put differently, why perform a miracle now, just because of a nasty neighbor who caused no shame to R. Ḥanina's wife, and not before, despite their

---

8. Talmudic sources themselves justify white lies under certain circumstances. See, for example, Ketubot 16b–17a and Yevamot 65b.
9. B. Lau, *The Sages*, Volume I, 76–79, argues that this interpolation, and the many stories about R. Ḥanina as miracle worker are all later traditions. However, in the aggada as we have it, which Lau maintains is early, R. Ḥanina performs a miracle too.

need?[10] Thus the interpolation seems to be an addition that does not fully cohere with the aggada itself, even as it seeks to elevate R. Ḥanina's wife to the level of piety its (anonymous) author thinks must be necessary for the miracle that transpired.

According to both the aggada as we have it and to the interpolation, R. Ḥanina's wife is passive. She does not proactively request anything, neither bread nor a miracle to bring bread. She fills the house with smoke, but only in reaction to her shame; she takes no steps to ameliorate the very conditions which brought about that shame. Moreover, she is given no name. She is always referred to as the wife of R. Ḥanina, and she seems to live in the orbit of his holy star. Even her nasty neighbor does not call her by any name: She is merely "so-and-so," *plonita* in the original Aramaic. Yet this passive posture is reversed immediately after the episode with the neighbor and the miraculous bread. She finally finds her own voice.

THE HEAVENLY TABLE WITH THE MISSING LEG

R. Ḥanina's wife now speaks to her husband for the first time in this aggada, and we get our first glimpse of them as husband and wife. What can we learn about their relationship and the impact upon it of their poverty, and her shame? Moreover, we get our first glimpse of R. Ḥanina the man, who had heretofore been an absent figure, looming in the background of the story. Note that even when he appears, he does so as the object of his wife's request, not as the initiator of the exchange. R. Ḥanina's wife is the proactive one, a critical turning point in her persona, and in the aggada as a whole.

---

10. Of course, it is possible that for the interpolator, R. Ḥanina's wife felt only mild but not acute shame, for which reason she filled the house with smoke, but still would never have sought to escape the encounter with her neighbor. This renders her better than she appears in the first reading, although still imperfect. And it is possible that no food was miraculously provided to R. Ḥanina and his wife because none was desired. That said, the interpolation still seems to be an addition that does not fully cohere with the story itself, even as it seeks to elevate R. Ḥanina's wife to the level of piety its anonymous author thinks is requisite for the miracle that transpired.

After all this time living in abject poverty, R. Ḥanina's wife challenges her husband: "Until when will we continue to suffer this poverty?" This is not only a challenge, but an acknowledgment of the grounds for the challenge, that they are suffering. She puts this in the plural, not the singular, to include him in the suffering she now overtly reveals that she feels. How did she evolve from a wife who lives in harmony with her husband to a wife who challenges her husband? What precipitated this radical change in her posture?

The likely answer is her experience with her nasty neighbor and, at least according to the aggada as we have it (and not that of the interpolator), the acute shame she felt. She could tolerate that shame no longer. Recall the reading we offered of the "inner chamber" which she entered, the inner chamber of the intense shame over the shame she felt, her meta-shame, her feelings of guilt over even feeling shame. These experiences proved to be the tipping point. She could remain silent no longer.

At this stage in the aggada, we finally hear from the great R. Ḥanina himself. His response to the challenge is a question: "What can we do?" How can we address the problem? This response is fascinating, on several counts. First, R. Ḥanina responds not with an answer, but with a question. He provokes his wife to take some responsibility for their well-being, and not to place the burden on him alone. She is the proactive one in this dialogue and, following her lead, he insists on yet even more proactivity from her, perhaps more than she bargained for. Moreover, he wants her to partner with him in arriving at a solution. If she comes up with a solution, then she bears responsibility not only for its success, if it does succeed, but for its failure too, if it fails. This is a brilliant pedagogical move because, as we shall see, the solution she proposes is one she ultimately comes to reject. In other words, R. Ḥanina leads his wife to see for herself the justification for the life they have chosen, the ultimate value of the poverty in which they live. He does not preach to her, nor dogmatically insist that she endure poverty. He enables her to discover on her own the preeminent value of the life he has chosen to lead.

Not only is this a brilliant pedagogical move, it is also deeply respectful of his wife's humanity. R. Ḥanina does not criticize her for questioning their poverty, nor does he assert his husbandly or rabbinic authority over her, which he could easily have done. Rather, he responds to her challenge with respect, and encourages her to be his partner, he, the exalted R. Ḥanina, in resolving their difficulties. "What shall *we* do," you and I, husband and wife together, to make our lives better?

She responds to his question with a request, "Pray for mercy that something will be given to you." Not surprisingly, she asks him to unleash his considerable powers of prayer, which have helped so many others, to help them as well. But notice that she says the prayer is for something to be given to him, in the singular. She does not say to be given to us, in the plural, as she first said, when posing the challenge to him, "Until when will *we* continue to suffer?" Why the change? No doubt because she recognizes that if miracles are indeed to be performed, they will be performed only in the merit of R. Ḥanina's greatness, not her own. Of course, she may also mean that as male breadwinner of the family he bears ultimate responsibility, in traditional societies such as theirs, for bringing food to the table. If their food is insufficient, and a miracle brings them food, then the miracle absolves him of his responsibilities. So the gift would be to him more than to her.

R. Ḥanina accedes to her request, and prays. Not surprisingly, his prayers are answered, but their answer comes in an unexpected form: The palm of a hand emerges from heaven, and gives him one leg of a golden table. Their table which had been empty of bread may now be filled with bread through the leg of another table, a golden one. R. Ḥanina can sell the golden leg of the heavenly table and fill the empty earthly table with bread. In an inversion of the usual processes of alchemy, heavenly gold can be transmuted to earthly bread. But what is the origin of this mysterious golden leg? Why is it severed from the table?

The aggada does not leave these questions unanswered, for their answer appears in a dream. The first question, though, is who does the dreaming? This is unclear, and the text of the Talmud comes in two variants. According to the variant recorded in Rashi, R. Ḥanina's wife dreams, and according to another variant of the text recorded in *Dikdukei Soferim*[11] (and this may be the most straightforward reading of the text

11. Ad loc. See also the marginal notes of the *Mesoret HaShas* and *Hagahot HaBaḥ*, ad loc.

as we have it in the standard editions of the Talmud Bavli), R. Ḥanina himself does the dreaming. Let us examine each variant separately, starting with R. Ḥanina as the dreamer. What he sees in his dream is that in the World to Come the righteous will be eating at a golden table with three legs, but he and his wife will be eating at a table with only two legs. He reports the dream to his wife, then asks her if she is content that the two of them will eat at a defective table of only two legs in the World to Come, while all the other righteous eat at a table with the full complement of three legs.

What R. Ḥanina is doing is challenging his wife to rethink her request for miraculous intervention. He does not tell her that it is wrong for them to make the request, that it is wrong for them to abandon their ascetic life of poverty, but only reports to her his dream. Then he poses a question to her, asking her if she is content to eat at a defective table in the World to Come. He thus leaves it to her to think the matter through, and come to her own conclusions. This is consistent with his first response to her request, when he asks her what should be done. His strategy throughout has been to respect his wife and empower her to come to identify on her own with the sublime value of the life they have chosen to lead. The choice now, finally, becomes her own choice too, not merely her husband's choice to which she acquiesces.

This she expresses by asking her husband what options they have. She regrets requesting the miracle, autonomously chooses their lives of extreme poverty, and no longer wants that golden leg, which sits uncomfortably before her. What she does is ask if the miracle is reversible. This reflects a deep evolution in the inner life of R. Ḥanina's wife. Whereas she originally had acquiesced to their poverty, she still felt shame over it, because her identification with it had not been complete. She married into those values, but had never made them her own. Now, finally, her identification with a life of poverty is complete.

The first step in this evolution was her proactivity. She could never make those values her own until she stepped out of the shadow of her pious and holy husband enough to question them, for sometimes religious growth comes only by questioning religious assumptions. R. Ḥanina's wife first had to confront her own discomfort, then take personal action to ameliorate it by seeking miraculous intervention through her husband. This assertion of self was an essential step in her development as a fully mature, self-actualized religious woman.

Next, her husband sensitively and respectfully creates the circumstances which enable her to identify on her own, as a mature, autonomous woman, with the piety that was the hallmark of his own life. Now she finally could, and did, choose that piety for herself. The table they would both eat at in the World to Come would be three-, not two-legged.[12] I would venture to suggest that the shame she once felt would no longer endure. With this great step her emotions merged into her beliefs.

Let us now examine Rashi's variant of the text, according to which the dreamer was not R. Ḥanina, but his wife. We might well understand why R. Ḥanina would see these visions in his dream, holy man that he was. But what about his wife?

One possible answer is that the proximate cause of her dream was less her holiness than her mental state. She had finally emerged from her concealed inner chamber, and proactively sought to improve their family circumstances by challenging her husband to bring food to the table. This was a dramatic about-face. Yet how would she feel about rejecting their pious and sacred past? How would she feel about challenging her holy husband and the life he was leading? Might she not have felt ambivalent, troubled, even guilty about such provocative behavior, even if at the same time she felt it justified? Perhaps her dream gives expression to that guilt and ambivalence, by portraying their new life of this-worldly relative comfort as leading to a deformed life in the eternal World to Come. She dreamt exactly what she feared.[13]

On this reading, R. Ḥanina's wife discovers within herself her deepest identification with the life they led together. Her disturbing dream teaches her that deep down, from within the inner chamber of her heart, it turns out she feels all along that R. Ḥanina was right, and

---

12. Note that in some variants of the text he reports to her that he eats at a table of two legs, but then asks her if she is content with them *both* eating at a table of two legs. He shifts from singular to plural, inviting her into the inner sanctum of those righteous who eat at tables with three legs, if and only if she chooses the life of poverty.
13. See the teaching of R. Shmuel in the name of R. Yonatan in Berakhot 55b, that a person is shown in a dream "only what he thinks about in his heart."

that to question his life of asceticism was to violate something she herself in fact held dear. She could make this discovery only after challenging her husband, for that very challenge enabled her to discover what her deepest beliefs were, via the vivid medium of a troubling dream. By discovering this from within herself, she could finally identify wholeheartedly with their life of asceticism, which she had never done before, because now it could emanate from her, not from him.

Note that the verb "see" (in Aramaic, *ḥaza*) appears twice in the story, first when the nasty neighbor sees the miracle in the kitchen, and second when, according to Rashi, R. Ḥanina's wife sees the dream. I would venture to suggest that the first vision elicited the second vision. The neighbor's vision of the kitchen miraculously filled with bread triggered the request by R. Ḥanina's wife to ask for more miracles, so that their table could permanently be graced with bread. That request in turn triggered her vision of the deformed table, which led her autonomously to choose a kitchen empty of bread. Two visions spin the circle back to its very beginnings.

It is worth stressing that according to both these variant readings, the fundamental arc of the aggada is the same: It traces the religious evolution of R. Ḥanina's wife over time, from reactive to proactive, from follower to instigator, from an ambivalent to a self-actualized, autonomous, and wholehearted affirmation of their lives of poverty. R. Ḥanina remains the same, a pious, miracle-working, understanding, and respectful husband. This posture made her transformation possible.

We must now turn to the symbolism of the three-legged table. First, it is worth noting that this otherworldly table missing a leg is a vivid metaphor for the theological underpinnings of that teaching which, it will be recalled, served as a prelude to the story: The sustenance of the world is a consequence of the merits of a man who himself subsists on no more than carobs. As discussed above, this teaching suggests an inverted relationship between well-being in this world and well-being in the next. The more well-being for a person in one world, the less well-being for that person in the other. Put differently and more broadly, the material and the spiritual stand in antithetical relationship with one another.

The table with the missing leg embodies that inverted relationship, for if R. Ḥanina and his wife use the golden leg for sustenance in this world, their table in the World to Come will be missing a leg. Conversely, if they do not use the leg for sustenance and continue to live lives of poverty in this world, then their table in the World to Come will be fully equipped with legs. Thus, the teaching which serves as a prelude to the story provides a perfect account of the mysterious symbolism which comes at the story's end, revealing a deep theoretical unity within the overall aggada from its beginning to its conclusion.

We might now ask why all those other righteous people deserved to sit at a table with three legs in the World to Come, but R. Ḥanina and his wife would not have deserved such a table unless they had relinquished the golden leg and reverted to their life of poverty. Does the aggada mean to teach that all righteous people who merit such a table must live in the same poverty as R. Ḥanina and his wife? If that were the case, then R. Ḥanina's asceticism would not be remarkable at all, for countless other righteous people must have lived lives as ascetic as his, for they had merited the full table. Why then does the aggada stress only in R. Ḥanina's case, but not for others, that the whole world is sustained on his impoverished merit?

Perhaps the aggada means to suggest that each righteous person must find his or her own path to the World to Come. R. Ḥanina's path was one of asceticism and self-denial, of simple piety, of fear of sin, and of good deeds. Were he to abandon his mode of divine service, and sell the golden leg for food, he could never have merited his own table in heaven, because that would be to abandon his own distinctive path to the World to Come. However, the path for other righteous persons might have been quite different. For some it may have been vast knowledge of Torah, for others the teaching of Torah, and for others heroic acts of service to those in need. None of these paths in themselves may require a life of asceticism. The table each person merits in the World to Come depends upon realizing his or her own path to God, not upon realizing the path of another. Different models of religious aspiration call upon different perfections. R. Ḥanina's called upon a life of poverty, but the religious aspirations of others did not. For this reason, R. Ḥanina, but not other righteous persons, was called upon to renounce the golden leg in order to secure his complete table in the World to Come.[14]

We can now turn to the symbolism of the table's legs. One question leaps out at the reader: Why a table with three legs rather than four? As it turns out, in ancient Greece and Rome, most tables did indeed have three legs.[15] That said, it still seems fair to ask if the number is symbolic beyond the reality upon which it is based, for the story could have chosen other symbols of a defective table. Thus, the dream could have depicted other righteous individuals sitting at a large table, and R. Ḥanina and his wife at a very small, rickety one, with the hand from heaven providing them golden utensils from the table for R. Ḥanina's use, such as bowls and plates, rather than the table's leg. We must still ask why the legs of the table were used to convey the story's message. To fully unpack the story, then, we must still focus on the legs and their number.

Many of the classic commentators struggle with the significance of the number three. The Maharsha (ad loc.) proposes that it represents the three pillars upon which the world is based (following the teaching of the Mishna in *Pirkei Avot* 1:2): Torah, divine service, and acts of kindness. If R. Ḥanina were to pray for miracles for himself, he would be misusing the ideal of pure service of God, and only two of these pillars – "legs" – would remain to him. In his commentary to *Pirkei Avot* (ad loc.) entitled *Ruaḥ Ḥayim,* the nineteenth-century founder of the Volozhin Yeshiva, R. Ḥayim of Volozhin, suggested, similarly, that one of these three pillars would be missing, but for him it was the pillar of acts of kindness. If R. Ḥanina were to pray for miracles for himself, then that would divert divine forces for good from others to satisfy his own personal needs. For both of these interpretations, the use of the metaphor of legs makes sense: The table of their good life would be destabilized in the absence of one of the legs upon which the world rests.

While these are valuable suggestions, they do not inhere in the themes of the aggada itself, and therefore may seem to some readers almost artificially imported from the outside to make sense of symbolism

14. See chapter 2 for a fuller discussion of this point.
15. G. M. A Richter, *The Furniture of the Greeks, Etruscans and Romans* (London, 1966), 66, and Roger Ulrich, *Roman Woodworking* (New Haven, 2007), 225.

on the inside. I would like to propose yet another reading of the three legs of the table, which follows upon one of the central themes of the aggada as interpreted in this chapter. Crucial here, in our reading, has been the marital relationship between R. Ḥanina and his wife, and the extent to which they shared at the deepest level a common conception of the highest ideals of Jewish life.

What then sustains a marriage? While not a contemporary of R. Ḥanina himself, R. Akiva taught the following: "A man and wife, if they merit, the Divine Presence rests between them. If they do not merit, then fire consumes them."[16] One way to understand this teaching (and there are others) is that an ideal marriage consists of three parties: husband, wife, and God. If God is present in a marriage it will flourish around a shared commitment by both husband and wife to the same lofty ideals. If God is absent from a marriage, then the marriage will be consumed by the flames of selfish needs and passions. Now even if R. Ḥanina himself had not heard this teaching, it would have been self-evident to a talmudic Jew. For a marriage to flourish it must be founded upon a shared relationship with God.

The three "legs" of a good marriage then are husband, wife, and God. The crucial question our aggada raises is the extent to which R. Ḥanina and his wife shared a common conception of what God wanted of them. In this sense it could be asked whether R. Ḥanina's God was the same as hers. If not, then their marriage was lacking the "Divine Presence" for support, for they could not unite around what each thought their God wanted of them. In other words, it was lacking a "leg."

When R. Ḥanina's wife challenged R. Ḥanina to provide food for them, she was demonstrating that they did not share a common conception of what God wanted from them, and so their ideal table lost its divine .leg, which broke away from their heavenly table and entered their home. Their marriage was unstable. When she requested that the leg be restored to the heavenly table, she was affirming a now deepened commitment to the life of piety and asceticism of her husband. She found the same God as he, their marriage stabilized, and their heavenly table was restored. The striking image of the hand descending from heaven with

16. Sota 17a.

the table leg adds texture to this analysis. The great divine hand extends itself in loving support of a husband and wife, or retracts that loving support from them, depending upon whether or not that husband and wife worship the very same God and strive for shared devotional ideals.

Thus, the narrative of the story concludes. Yet, surprisingly, the overall aggada does not conclude here, for its last line records yet another interpolation. The interpolator asserts that the miracle of returning the golden leg to heaven was greater than the miracle of bringing it down from heaven to earth in the first place. Once again, the interpolator insists on the miracle-working gifts of R. Ḥanina and the supernatural aura of his household, which resonate in the reader's ears as the aggada comes to its final conclusion.

Yet it is difficult, for at least this reader, not to hear in these last words a secondary layer of meaning as well. For consider a central theme of the aggada as it emerges in the analysis offered here: the trajectory of R. Ḥanina's wife as she evolves over time into a self-actualized person who comes autonomously and deeply to affirm the lofty values of a life of piety and self-denial. What is the symbol of that evolution? The return of the golden leg to heaven. Perhaps, then, the editor of our aggada chose to include this final interpolation into the text because he also meant to teach this: The greatest miracle of all is the mysterious process of human development. Can we ever really understand how a person evolves and grows to choose a life of the most abject poverty in the service of a transcendent God?

Chapter 6

R. Shimon ben Ḥalafta, His Wife, and the Miraculous Jewel from Heaven

Ruth Rabba 3:4

INTRODUCTION

This aggada parallels in many important ways the aggada to which the last chapter was devoted, for which reason a comparison between the two illuminates each. In both stories, a husband and wife live in extreme poverty, as a result of which the husband seeks the intervention of heaven to ameliorate their lot. In both stories a hand descends from heaven and miraculously provides an object of considerable value, which can be sold for ample food. Finally, in both stories, the wife objects to this arrangement on the grounds that benefits in this world come at the expense of their fullest reward in the World to Come. As a result, a hand miraculously appears from heaven to scoop up the valuable object once given.

The main protagonist in the aggada which is the subject of this chapter was a contemporary of R. Yehuda HaNasi, the primary compiler of the Mishna, while the main protagonist of the aggada discussed in the previous chapter, R. Ḥanina ben Dosa, lived some one hundred years earlier, during the period following the destruction of the Temple. Nevertheless, it is not clear when these two aggadot were committed to writing, and which one might have drawn upon the other. Both may have been circulating for some time before they were recorded. In any case, the parallels are striking and can hardly be coincidental.

While the similarities between the two aggadot are evident, careful study reveals that the differences between them are no less significant than the similarities. What led each of these two pious men to choose a life of poverty? What were their respective wives like, and what was their relationship with them? In this aggada about R. Shimon ben Ḥalafta, his great teacher, R. Yehuda HaNasi, the central figure in chapter 4 of this volume, plays a pivotal role here as well. Does he change as a result of his encounter with R. Shimon ben Ḥalafta's wife, and why? Finally, what deep principles give rise to the choice of a life of abject poverty and what is the relationship between those principles and the personalities of those who affirm them? What portrait might the author of this text want us to draw of the man – and woman – behind the ideology?

דִּילְמָא רַבִּי חִיָּא רַבָּה וְרַבִּי שִׁמְעוֹן בֶּן חֲלַפְתָּא הֲווֹ יָתְבִין לָעֲיִין בְּאוֹרָיְיתָא בַּהֲדֵין בֵּית מִדְרָשָׁא רַבָּא דְּטִבֶּרְיָא בַּעֲרוּבַת פִּסְחָא, וְאִית דְּאָמְרֵי בַּעֲרוּבַת צוֹמָא רַבָּא, וּשְׁמַעֵי קָלְהוֹן דִּבְרִיָּיאתָא בָּיְיבִין, אֲמַר לֵיהּ אִילֵּין בִּרְיָיתָא מָה עִסְקוֹן, אֲמַר דְּאִית לֵיהּ זָבַן וּדְלֵית לֵיהּ אָזֵיל לְגַבֵּי מָרֵי עֲבִדְתֵּיהּ וְהוּא יָהֵיב לֵיהּ. אֲמַר לֵיהּ אִם כֵּן הוּא אַף אֲנָא אֵיזֵיל גַּבֵּי מָרֵי עֲבִדְתִּי וְהוּא יָהֵב לִי, נְפַק וְצַלֵּי בַּהֲדָא אִילוּסִיס דְּטִבֶּרְיָא, וַחֲזָא חַד יְדָא מוֹשְׁטָא לֵיהּ חֲדָא מַרְגָּלִיתָא, אֲזַל טָעִין גַּבֵּי רַבֵּנוּ, אֲמַר לֵיהּ הָדָא מְנָא אִית לָךְ, הָדָא מִילָּא דְּאִיסְטוּפִיטָא הִיא, אֶלָּא הֵא לָךְ תְּלָתָא דִּינָרִין, וַאֲזַל וַעֲבֵד לִיקָרָא דְּיוֹמָא, וּבָתַר יוֹמָא טָבָא אֲנַן שָׁטְחִין קָלֵיהּ וּמָה דְּהוּא עָבֵיד טִימִיתַהּ תִּיסַב. נְסַב תְּלָתָא דִּינָרִין וַאֲזֵיל זְבַן זְבוּנִין וְעָל לְבֵיתֵיהּ,

Here is an illustration. Rabbi Ḥiyya the elder and Rabbi Shimon the son of Ḥalafta were studying Torah in this great house of study in Tiberias on the eve of Passover, but there are those who say on the eve of the great Fast [Yom Kippur], when they heard the noise of a crowd making a ruckus. And he said on the outer benches: "What's the commotion?" He said: "He who has something buys, and he who does not have something is going to the master of his servitude and he is making him give to him." And he said: "If this is so, I will go to the master of my servitude and make him give to me." He went and he prayed at the Eleusis of Tiberias, and he saw a hand holding out to him an expensive pearl, and he went to take it to his master, our Rabbi [Yehuda]. He said to him: "How did this come to be yours? It is priceless! So now, here are three dinars for you. Go and get your needs for the festival and after the festival we will go and announce it, and whatever price we get for it you will have." So he took the three dinars and went and bought his purchases and went home.

אָמְרָה לֵיהּ דְּבֵיתְהוּ שִׁמְעוֹן שָׁרֵית גָּנֵיב, כָּל פָּעֳלָךְ לֵית הִיא אֶלָּא מְאָה מָנֶה וְאִילֵּין זְבִינָתָה מָה אִינוּן, מִיָּד תַּנֵּי לָהּ עוֹבָדָא. אָמְרָה לֵיהּ מַאי אַתְּ בָּעֵי תְּהֵי גְּנוּנָךְ חָסֵר מִן דְּחַבְרָא מַרְגָּלִיתָא לְעַלְמָא דְּאָתֵי. אֲמַר לָהּ וּמָה נַעֲבֵד, אָמְרָה לֵיהּ זִיל תַּחֲזוֹר זְבִינָתָא לְמָרֵיהוֹן וְדִינָרַיָּא לְמָרֵיהוֹן וּמַרְגָּלִיתָא לְמָרָא.

And his wife said to him at home: "Shimon, are you a thief? The whole estate that is yours, it is only worth one hundred *maneh* and with what did you make these purchases? He told her the whole matter. She said to him: "What is your desire? Would you lessen your bridal chamber from your companion by one pearl in the World to Come?" He said to her: "What should be done?" She said to him: "Go and return the purchases to their masters and the dinars to their master and the pearl to its master."

כַּד שָׁמַע רַבֵּינוּ מִצְטָעֵר, שְׁלַח וְאַיְתְיַהּ, אֲמַר לָהּ כָּל הָדֵין צַעְרָא צַעַרְתְּ לְהָדֵין צַדִּיקָא. אָמְרָה לֵיהּ מָה אַתְּ בָּעֵי דִּיהֵא גְּנוּנֵיהּ חָסֵר מִדִּידְכוֹן חֲדָא מַרְגָּלִיתָא לְעַלְמָא דְּאָתֵי. אֲמַר לָהּ וְאִין הֲוָה חָסֵר לֵית בָּן מְמַלְיָיה יָתֵיהּ. אָמְרָה לֵיהּ רַבִּי בְּהָדֵין עַלְמָא זְכֵינַן מֶחֱמֵי אַפָּךְ, וְלֹא אֲמַר רֵישׁ לָקִישׁ כָּל צַדִּיק וְצַדִּיק יֵשׁ לוֹ מָדוֹר בִּפְנֵי עַצְמוֹ, וְהוֹדָה לָהּ. וְלֹא עוֹד אֶלָּא שֶׁדַּרְכָּן שֶׁל עֶלְיוֹנִים לִתֵּן וְאֵין דַּרְכָּן לִטֹּל, הַנֵּס הָאַחֲרוֹן קָשֶׁה מִן הָרִאשׁוֹן, מִנְסֵיב לֵיהּ הֲוָת יְדָא אַרְעַיָּא [למטה], וּמִי מוֹשְׁטָא לֵיהּ הֲוָה יְדָא עִילָּאָה, כְּאִינִישׁ דְּמוֹזִיף לְחַבְרֵיהּ

When our Rabbi [Yehuda] heard, he was distressed. He sent and had her come, and he said to her: "All this distress you have

> distressed this righteous man!" She said to him: "What is your desire? Would you lessen your bridal chamber from your companion by one pearl in the World to Come?" He said to her: "And if it is lessened, can it not be replaced?" She said to him: "Rabbi, in this world we are worthy to look upon your face, but did not Reish Lakish say: 'For every righteous man there is a righteous chamber all to himself'?" And he yielded to her. [She continued] "And further, is it not the way of those in the upper world to give and their way is not to receive?" The later miracle was weightier than the previous. Receiving it, his [Shimon's] hand was toward the earth and giving it back, his hand was facing toward the sky, like a man who lends to his friend!

R. SHIMON BEN ḤALAFTA CONFRONTS HIS POVERTY

The aggada opens with R. Shimon ben Ḥalafta and his study partner R. Ḥiyya, studying together in the large *beit midrash* in Tiberias. The time was either the day before Passover or Yom Kippur, hardly common occasions for study. After all, there is an obligation to eat on the day before Yom Kippur and people are generally busy preparing for the holy day of prayer and fasting. Likewise, before Passover there is always much to do in preparation for the holiday and the Seder night. Yet the two of them were in the *beit midrash*, a testimony to their remarkable devotion to Torah study. One wonders how many other students were present alongside them.

While they were isolated in space they were not isolated in sound, for they heard a tumult of voices outside. R. Shimon asked his study partner what all those noisy creatures were up to. R. Ḥiyya responded that they were people either making purchases for the holiday or, if they lacked the resources for such purchases, they were approaching their employers for funds, which in turn were granted.

Several questions beg themselves about this dialogue. First, how could R. Shimon not have known what these noisy voices were? The holiday was about to commence, and of course people would be busy preparing for its many needs. Apparently the *beit midrash* was near enough to the marketplace for its noises to be heard. How could this have escaped R. Shimon's attention? R. Shimon's use of the term "creatures" is also unexpected. Clearly the voices were those of people, not cows or dogs. Why then did he not ask about the noise of "people," rather than "creatures"?

What this suggests is a certain obliviousness, a profound if simple piety on R. Shimon's part. His was the world of the study hall, of intense inner spirituality. The world of buying and selling, the world of material goods and its pleasures, was simply not his. He did not willfully ignore the mercantile; he was simply oblivious to it. The voices he heard were undifferentiated, neither human nor animal. This is not because he didn't know they were people, but because when it came to the world outside the study hall, outside his inner citadel of spirituality, they were all one big mass, all creatures of God. The average person was as different from him as were cows and dogs, for all are enmeshed in the world of flesh. And R. Shimon was enmeshed only in the world of spirit, of Torah study in the *beit midrash*.

R. Ḥiyya's response is interesting, especially its second point. Why does R. Ḥiyya add that those who do not possess the resources to purchase food for the holiday turn to their employers? R. Shimon had asked what the noise was all about, and a sufficient answer to that question would have been the first point R. Ḥiyya made, that everyone was busy buying food. After all, what percentage of the tumult in the marketplace could really be attributed to those seeking out their employers, who may well not have been in the marketplace anyway, but off in the fields?

It is difficult to avoid the conclusion that R. Ḥiyya was subtly hinting to R. Shimon that he too should be taking concrete action to provide for the fast-approaching holiday. Study in the *beit midrash* is all very well and good, but food for the holiday is a mitzva too. Let us now recall that there is a history to R. Ḥiyya, a person of some means, and R. Shimon, who lived in perennial poverty. According to one midrash, R. Ḥiyya provided R. Shimon with a field in which he could work as a sharecropper to support his family.[1] We cannot know for certain whether

1. Ruth Rabba 5:12. Note that there was conflict between them over the amount which the field should have provided.

the episode recounted in our source took place before or after the offer of the field, although it is perhaps more likely that it took place afterward. For if it had taken place before, and R. Shimon had retained the field, then he would have derived income from it, and would not have been as impoverished as described here. In either case, however, R. Ḥiyya's hint to R. Shimon here about taking action to address his poverty is clearly similar to the event described there, whether it preceded it or not. R. Ḥiyya rejects the pure otherworldliness of his study partner and expects practical action of R. Shimon.

R. Shimon does indeed pick up on R. Ḥiyya's hint and takes action, but not the action one might expect. He does not seek a human employer, but he seeks his ultimate employer, God Himself, to request wages due. R. Shimon leaves the *beit midrash* to pray outside the town, in the caves of Tiberias. He moves from one segregated place – the study hall – to another segregated place, a cave. He remains outside the world of commerce, of buying and selling, of food for the holiday, now tucked within a cave to pray. Ironically, he seeks sustenance for his outside world, for his household, but never enters that outside world to do so. R. Shimon never leaves his inner sanctum of spirituality.

We might ask ourselves why this is so. Was this a very deliberate choice on R. Shimon's part? Or was it mostly a consequence of his otherworldly persona? Might it have been both? Most of us have encountered people who live in the clouds, who can't be bothered with the mundane, and in a religious context this personifies a certain saintly, almost otherworldly type. As the text unfolds, I believe we will see that this picture of R. Shimon is closest to the truth.

In the event, his prayer was efficacious, and a hand miraculously appears with a precious jewel. The similarity to the aggada about Ḥanina ben Dosa analyzed in the previous chapter is surely striking. But note that here a jewel is granted to R. Shimon, unlike the leg of a table granted to R. Ḥanina. What is the significance of this difference? For a possible answer to this question, we must proceed with the tale.

R. Shimon immediately takes this miraculous jewel to his great teacher R. Yehuda HaNasi, often called Rebbe. Why does he do so? Would it not have been more natural to first bring it home to his wife? As it turns out, his wife was quite upset about the jewel, which he may have anticipated, and therefore first sought the imprimatur of Rebbe before heading home. It is also possible that in his otherworldly simplicity, poverty, and piety, he simply didn't know what to make of a jewel, and, perhaps feeling insecure, sought advice. Recall that R. Ḥanina ben Dosa did not seek advice about the value of the golden leg. R. Ḥanina emerges from the aggada discussed in the previous chapter as a man of quiet confidence, who knows what he wants and knows how to get there. He brilliantly and with self-effacing confidence enables his wife to see the world as he does. R. Shimon emerges from this aggada as a very different type indeed.

It is not accidental that the advice he sought was from Rebbe, for not only was Rebbe his teacher, as well as the leading rabbi of his generation, he was also a man of great wealth, as noted in chapter 4.[2] Surely Rebbe will know what to do with this jewel, and indeed he does. He remarks upon its great value, and encourages R. Shimon to wait until after the holiday to sell it for its maximum value, in the interim offering him a sum of money to provide for the holiday. Rebbe wants R. Shimon to keep the jewel, and to maximize his profits therefrom. This is because Rebbe was not only amongst the greatest Torah scholars of his generation, but amongst the wealthiest and most powerful as well.[3]

Rebbe thus rejected the view of R. Ḥanina ben Dosa, discussed at length in the previous chapter, that this-worldly wealth and otherworldly stature are antithetical. Perhaps this is because Rebbe maintained that wealth enables one to study Torah unhindered by this-worldly worries over survival. More likely, given his own stature, he maintained that this-worldly success provides one with the social capital to make a religious difference in the world. Rebbe's own power, wealth, cultural sophistication, and prestige enabled him to develop a meaningful relationship with the Roman leadership and helped him acquire their respect. Rebbe used that respect, as leader of the Jewish community in the Land of Israel, to

2. Berakhot 57b; Bava Batra 8a and elsewhere.

3. Gittin 59a records the teaching that no one from Moses to Rebbe achieved the same level of both Torah and worldly greatness. Rashi, ad loc., takes this to be a reference not only to worldly power but wealth, unsurprisingly, given the many sources that attest to Rebbe's great riches.

compile the Mishna and to issue edicts for the benefit of the Jewish people.[4] As we shall see, Rebbe's role in the aggada as it unfolds is crucial indeed, and we shall soon analyze in greater detail his views on this issue.

R. SHIMON BEN ḤALAFTA CONFRONTS HIS WIFE

R. Shimon does as he was told, buys provisions for the festival with the funds laid out by Rebbe and returns home laden with goods. One might think that his long-suffering wife would be overjoyed. However, the reverse is the case and his wife, upon seeing those goods, lashes out at him. "Have you begun to steal?" she charges. It is unlikely that she suspected that her pious husband had actually become a thief. Rather, this may have been no more than a rhetorical flourish. Even more likely, however, is that she intended a deeper critique, that R. Shimon had stolen their invaluable portion in the World to Come, merely to provide for their this-worldly holiday meals. Let us recall that R. Shimon's wife had devoted herself with much self-sacrifice to their shared otherworldly ideals. She was not ready to abandon her deepest commitments for mere material gain.

R. Shimon's wife wants to know where R. Shimon acquired the money to make these purchases. R. Shimon, ever-agreeable, immediately tells her the tale. With his otherworldly simplicity, he cannot stand up to the *force majeure* of his wife. She immediately asks him if he wants his heavenly canopy to be short a jewel in the World to Come. The jewel he received, she maintained, came at the cost of a jewel in heaven. R. Shimon agrees with alacrity to her objection, and responds, simply, "What shall we do?" Of course, R. Shimon's wife knows exactly what to do, and tells him in no uncertain terms: Return what you bought to

4. This receives further discussion later in this chapter. There is considerable literature on Rebbe and his life and times. See, for example, A. Oppenheimer, *R. Judah the Prince* (Jerusalem, 2007) (Heb.), and the discussion in Binyamin Lau, *The Sages, Volume III: The Galilean Period* (Jerusalem, 2013), 309–385. See too the recent biography of Rebbe, Dov Zakheim, *The Prince and the Emperors* (Jerusalem, 2021), for an extensive discussion, including an analysis of Rebbe's stature amongst the Romans, and the emperors with whom he had a relationship.

its owners, return the money you received from Rebbe, and return the jewel to its owners.

At this point in the story, it is worth comparing this episode with the episode involving R. Ḥanina ben Dosa. First, there is a gender reversal. At least according to one variant in the text, R. Ḥanina ben Dosa is not happy with his wife's request for food, and creates a set of circumstances which enables his wife to come around on her own to his own view about the value of poverty. In the R. Shimon story, the husband is amenable to a life of greater comfort, but his wife strenuously objects. While in the first story, R. Ḥanina is the ideologue and his wife the more pliant one, in the second story, R. Shimon is the more pliant one, and his wife is the ideologue. People do sometimes bend to the will of their spouses. Sometimes the more dominant spouse is the husband, and sometimes it is the wife.

Moreover, consider how different the response of R. Shimon's wife to R. Shimon was, compared to the response of R. Ḥanina ben Dosa to his wife. R. Shimon's wife bowls him over with her objections. While she too poses a question about whether or not he wants his heavenly lot to be shortchanged, the question is really more of a statement, and she tells R. Shimon exactly what he must do to make amends, a course of action to which he does not object. R. Shimon bends to his wife's will. Not so with R. Ḥanina, who empathetically and artfully leads his wife to acknowledge on her own the values he espouses.

While the wives of R. Ḥanina and R. Shimon both believe that a life of this-worldly success is antithetical to maximal success in the World to Come, their relationship with their spouses and the means they use to bring them over to their convictions could not have been more different. No doubt this is because their personalities were also different. But not only were the personalities of the two dominant spouses different, the personalities of the pliant spouses were different as well. R. Ḥanina's wife grew and evolved over time, to adopt a mature and autonomous affirmation of values with which she had never fully identified in the past. R. Shimon does not evolve over time. His views change according to the most dominant party in the three relationships in which he finds himself. When R. Ḥiyya implicitly encourages him to take action, he does. When Rebbe encourages him to sell the jewel, he agrees. When his wife insists that keeping the jewel is wrong, he agrees. This is consistent with his saintliness, his simple yet profound piety, his obliviousness to practical matters, and his exclusive passion to live a life apart, in the world of the *beit midrash*. There is no real conflict between R. Shimon ben Ḥalafta and his wife. As we shall see, the only conflict this midrash depicts is between R. Shimon's wife and Rebbe, the two most powerful figures in the story.

We must now turn to the metaphor of the canopy lacking a jewel, very different from the metaphor of the table missing a leg. What is the significance of this change of metaphors?[5] Consider a three-legged table missing one leg and now down to just two legs. The table would barely stand, if it could at all. This suggests that in the Ḥanina ben Dosa aggada, accepting material comfort in this world would have had profoundly destabilizing, perhaps even altogether destructive, consequences for eternal life in the World to Come. Comfort in this world and success in the World to Come are simply mutually exclusive. This is an extreme view, one which virtually mandates radical poverty for Ḥanina ben Dosa. How could he even entertain the loss of a stable place in the eternal World to Come merely for the transitory pleasures of bread and chicken?

This characterization is not true for the metaphor of the canopy missing a jewel. First, the canopy still stands. God and R. Shimon would still share intimate space under its enclosure. Moreover, the metaphor used by R. Shimon's wife nowhere suggests that the canopy will be stripped of all jewels. Rather, it states merely that the canopy will be missing the one jewel which descended from heaven to sustain R. Shimon. However, this does not imply that no jewels at all would be left. Since it is hard to imagine a full-fledged canopy with only one jewel atop it, which would get lost in the large expanse of a canopy, the likeliest reading of the text is that the canopy was bedecked with many jewels, with one and only one now missing for use by R. Shimon below.

This in turn suggests a more moderate understanding of the relationship between material goods in this world and spiritual status in the

5. The text itself portrays an actual miracle. The chapters in this volume all take the text as it appears, but seek a symbolic or metaphoric reading where doing so illuminates its multiple meanings.

World to Come. While material goods in this world do come at some cost to spiritual status in the World to Come, the cost is far from destabilizing or destructive. The canopy still stands and can enclose God and R. Shimon, and many jewels still remain atop it. To be sure, the canopy is missing a jewel, and that means that R. Shimon's ideal status with God is compromised. He could not reach the very highest level of intimacy and glory due him. But he hasn't fallen all that short, for after all, he is missing only one jewel.

Thus we see that the difference between the metaphors of the canopy and the table is of considerable importance, because it suggests a profound theological difference between the two aggadot. The Ḥanina ben Dosa aggada advocates an extremist position. For someone like him, the choice is radical indeed: *ḥallot* for Shabbat or a secure place in the World to Come, but not both. Anyone like R. Ḥanina who aspires to an eternal and secure relationship with God must forgo all this-worldly goods. This is a radical position, one not shared by the more moderate R. Shimon aggada.

It is likely that this difference is at least in part grounded in the social and historical circumstances of these two great men. Let us first recall that R. Ḥanina lived at the time of R. Yoḥanan ben Zakkai, not long after the destruction of the Temple. Jews had lost their primary vehicle for worshipping God, the Temple, and had lost all its glorious splendor too, including the surrounding palatial homes of the wealthy. Jerusalem was in ruins, autonomy lost, its inhabitants dead or exiled, and the remaining Jewish community often mired in poverty. Not surprisingly, a *baraita* reports that this catastrophe led many to adopt an ascetic lifestyle.[6] R. Ḥanina lived in the aftermath of the destruction, and may well have been influenced by the asceticism it provoked. While R. Ḥanina's was not a theology of mourning, his overall Weltanschauung may have been influenced by the times. For what does the good life in this world amount to? Distraction from God, sin and temptation, ashes and despair. All that really matters is an enduring relationship with God which can only be achieved by abandoning a world which in truth had abandoned the Jews.

---

6. Bava Batra 60b.

R. Shimon lived almost a century later in the north of the Land of Israel, during a period of rapprochement with the Romans due in no small measure to the relationship between Rebbe, the head of the Jewish community in the Land of Israel, and the Roman leadership. Rebbe's wealth, sophistication, and wisdom endeared him to his Roman overlord, and the Talmud records numerous conversations between them.[7] The impulse toward asceticism would have been blunted, not only because of the relative peace of the Jewish community at that time, but also because Rebbe's own life hardly exemplified such behavior. Indeed, he used his great wealth to help others in need.[8] R. Shimon was part of the circle of scholars around Rebbe, which would therefore likely have moderated his views and those of his wife and others as well.

Of course, this raises the question of exactly what Rebbe's views were on the question. Was he really as moderate as his wealth would suggest? The Talmud does record that at his death Rebbe lifted up his ten fingers and exclaimed that not one of his fingers derived pleasure from this world.[9] Similarly, the Talmud states that he was called "Our Master the Holy One" because he never looked at his genitals or, according to another explanation recorded in that passage, because he never touched himself below his belt.[10] How do we reconcile the lavish lifestyle Rebbe lived with these sources? I think the most likely explanation is that they reflect different dimensions of the very same person. While Rebbe may have eaten from all that sumptuous food at his table, let us recall that eating does not entail pleasure on the part of the eater. So elevated was Rebbe, the Talmud may be teaching, that food did not matter to him. If someone doesn't care about the food he eats, then his meal can consist of the greatest delicacies the world has to offer, but he or she will still derive no pleasure from them.[11]

---

7. See Zakheim, ibid., ch. 6, for an extensive discussion of these interactions and their historicity.
8. Eiruvin 73a; Bava Batra 8a, and elsewhere.
9. Ketubot 104a.
10. Shabbat 118b.
11. Commentators have offered a variety of explanations for his tension, in all likelihood a Rorschach for their attitudes toward asceticism generally. Thus, *Tosafot* on Avoda Zara 11a (s.v. *Tznon)* suggests that Rebbe himself did not indulge in any of

In short, on this reading there was a dichotomy between Rebbe's outer and inner worlds. His outer world, the one visible to all, consisted of riches, but his inner world, by his own testimony, was elevated far beyond the siren call of those very riches he possessed. Rebbe did not advocate an overtly ascetic life, and most of those around him with means did not live ascetically. But he did believe that the material goods one possesses should ideally be no source of pleasure. However, we might ask, why then possess them?

Rebbe might have maintained that the vast majority of people need them to live a full life, without constant worry over putting food on the table which, if nothing else, can impede one's ability to study Torah. Recall that Rebbe taught in *Pirkei Avot* that the ideal path for a person to choose is one that is "honorable to the one who chooses it and honorable in the eyes of others."[12] The Hebrew word translated here as "honorable" – *tiferet* – has the connotation of beauty and harmony as well. Rebbe may be understood to have advocated a harmonious and balanced life, and one that would be perceived as such by observers. A life of asceticism would hardly be perceived by most observers as

---

the delicacies on his table, only his many dependents did. A number of the classic commentators on Shabbat 104a reprinted in the *Ein Yaakov* ad loc. likewise maintain that Rebbe himself led an ascetic life. However, other commentaries there disagree, e.g., the *Iyun Yaakov*, s.v. *Amar*, and the *Eitz Yosef*, s.v. *Velo*. R. Eliyahu Dessler, a leading Mussar movement thinker, likewise explained that while Rebbe may have indulged in these delicacies, he derived no personal pleasure from them, for his goal in so doing was only for elevated, sacred purposes. (See vol. I of *Mikhtav MeEliyahu* [Bnei Brak, 1965], 6.) The account I offer falls overall within this second school of interpretation, although it differs from them as well. Some may also read the source about Rebbe's asceticism as an attempt by some to blunt what might otherwise appear to be an excessively sybaritic lifestyle on Rebbe's part. That said, the interpretation I favor is the one I offer in the body of the text, and is consistent with Rebbe's attitude toward emotions, discussed in chapter 4. See note 13 there, which places this approach in the Stoic school of thought. What applies to emotions may well apply to pleasure as well. For a general overview and discussion of asceticism in rabbinic Judaism, see Eliezer Diamond, *Holy Men and Hunger Artists: Fasting and Asceticism in Rabbinic Culture* (Oxford, 2003). See also Moshe Sokol, "Attitudes Toward Pleasure in Jewish Thought: A Typological Proposal," in *Judaism Examined* (Brighton, MA, 2013): 83–111.

12. *Pirkei Avot* 2:1.

honorable, balanced, or harmonious. The despair of poverty, of constant scrounging for food, is hardly honorable and harmonious, nor is it conducive to Torah study, a supreme value. Moreover, extreme poverty could undermine the possibility of helping the broader community, which, as leader of the Jewish community, Rebbe valued. Rebbe's asceticism was internal, not external, part of his inner life but not a public practice. This view led to the more moderate attitude of the aggada about R. Shimon. It is possible to possess enough food for Shabbat and still merit all the jewels one might want in the World to Come.

That said, consider the position of R. Shimon's wife. While it was she who deployed the more moderate metaphor of the jewel, at the very same time, she insisted on a life of abject poverty. Why? If her theology was more moderate – witness the jewel metaphor – why then does she advocate the extreme position of R. Ḥanina? While the extreme theology of R. Ḥanina should indeed lead to extreme practice, why should the moderate theology of R. Shimon's wife also lead to the same extreme practice?

While we cannot be certain, since there is no clear evidence from the text, this conjecture seems plausible: Rebbe's own position, a likely source of that generation's theological moderation, is in tension with itself. The very dichotomy between inner and outer in Rebbe's life undercuts the force of his moderation. If down deep Rebbe saw no value to pleasure, then surely some of his followers may have been inspired to adopt a life that possesses no capacity for pleasure at all. First, how many can live the esoteric/exoteric gap that Rebbe lived? How many people can live with the accoutrements of the pleasurable life, yet feel no pleasure in them? Perhaps the great "Holy Master" could, but mere mortals, could they? Moreover, Rebbe's negative view of pleasure per se may logically give rise to a suspicion about all pleasurable activities. Not all his followers may have succeeded in theologically integrating the honorable life with the ascetic one. One can indeed be influenced by Rebbe's practical moderation, and see the cost of a life with material goods as only one jewel in the canopy. Yet one may at the same time yearn for more. And that is exactly what R. Shimon's wife did.

R. Ḥanina understood asceticism to be a crucial value, mandatory for him in order to achieve the fullness of the World to Come. R. Shimon ben Ḥalafta's wife may have understood asceticism not as mandatory for achieving the fullness of the World to Come, but as supererogatory behavior, which brings its own exceptional merit, that one extra jewel in the canopy. The inner logic of Rebbe's theology thus may have led some of his followers down the path of the maximalist, even if their premises were not maximalist but moderate. Such is often the way of life of the intensely religious. The supererogatory becomes the new norm.

R. SHIMON BEN ḤALAFTA'S WIFE CONFRONTS REBBE

Rebbe learned that R. Shimon's wife had insisted upon the return of the jewel. This pained Rebbe and he summoned her to his quarters.[13] Rebbe challenged her: "How could you cause such pain to a righteous man like your husband?" The word for the pain Rebbe felt at her actions is the same Aramaic word he used to describe the pain she had caused her husband, as if to say Rebbe's pain and her husband's pain are one.

It is surely of interest to note that Rebbe does not directly challenge her theology. He does not assert that she is simply wrong about her demand that R. Shimon return the jewel. Rather, he accuses her of being a disloyal wife by causing her husband pain, and by implying that she does not fully appreciate just how righteous is the man she married. Rebbe speaks the language of spousal relationships, not the language of rabbinic dispute. Perhaps this is because he assumed that as a woman and wife, such is exactly the kind of discourse she would likely understand. In so doing, he demonstrated considerable emotional intelligence and wisdom.

That said, the text makes clear that Rebbe could not have been more wrong in his initial assessment of just who R. Shimon's wife really was. First, she refuses this gambit, and chooses not to respond defensively, but to counterattack. It is Rebbe, she charges, who is causing pain to this great righteous man, for he is denying R. Shimon the same

13. Note that Rebbe was in conflict about his wealth with another great man of his era, R. Pinḥas ben Yair, a man like R. Shimon ben Ḥalafta of extraordinary piety. See Ḥullin 7a and the discussion in Lau, *The Sages, Vol. III*, 327–333.

jewel-bedecked canopy in the World to Come as Rebbe himself. Why should Rebbe lead Shimon to a fate inferior to his own? This is accusatory and aggressive. Let us recall that she was speaking to Rebbe, the *Nasi*, the leader of the entire Jewish community and one of its leading scholars. Surely the typical woman of that era would respond with deference, if not awe. That R. Shimon's wife could speak as she did is nothing less than astonishing, and reflects her toughness of mind and spirit.

Rebbe responds that he possesses the power to restore any jewels missing in R. Shimon's next-worldly canopy. There is no need to worry, he tells her. He is not harming R. Shimon in the World to Come, but is merely providing him the added benefit of a more comfortable life in this world. While R. Shimon's wife responds to Rebbe's charges against her not defensively but offensively, Rebbe responds to the charges against him defensively but not offensively. The framework of the dialogue remains in the sphere of human relationships, not in the sphere of theology. Rebbe had charged her with not caring for her husband. She in turn charged Rebbe with failure to care for R. Shimon. Rebbe then responds that he does indeed care, and will himself see to R. Shimon's otherworldly well-being.

Interestingly, it is not the great rabbi who now shifts the dialogue from the relational to the theological, but R. Shimon's wife: The gender reversals so characteristic of this midrash continue. She attacks Rebbe once again, now on theological grounds. "How can you replace a jewel missing from my husband's canopy in the World to Come?" she argues. "Is there not a tradition that every righteous person inhabits his own dwelling place there, and no one can access the dwelling place of another?"[14] Upon hearing her argument, Rebbe concedes that she is right.

Before analyzing the meaning of their exchange, it is important to note that Rebbe concedes that his theology is wrong, and that the

---

14. The text of the midrash as we have it has R. Shimon's wife citing the teaching of Reish Lakish to this effect. However, as the commentators to the midrash point out, this is anachronistic. Reish Lakish lived in the generation following that of Rebbe, and therefore could not have been cited as a source by R. Shimon's wife, even if later he is quoted as teaching this tradition, in Shabbat 152a. Apparently, this was a tradition that preceded Reish Lakish, about which R. Shimon's wife knew. The

woman who challenges him is right. Given the times in which they lived, this is nothing short of remarkable, and reflects Rebbe's extraordinary humility, recalling the teaching of the mishna that with Rebbe's death, humility and fear of heaven died too.[15] What better example could there be of Rebbe's humility than this? This exactly mirrors the Rebbe we encountered in chapter 4 of this volume.

That said, let us return to substance. First, why did Rebbe think he had the power to replace a missing jewel in the World to Come? Was he so convinced of the rectitude of his position that he was confident he could convince the heavenly authorities to return the jewel? Or, was he so convinced he was right that he was certain that R. Shimon's canopy would in fact never even be lacking jewels, and would therefore never even need replacing? We cannot be sure. But we do know that he believed initially that he could have access to R. Shimon's canopy, and it was R. Shimon's wife who convinced him otherwise. What exactly is the issue here, and how does it relate to the content of the aggada?

What then does it mean that each righteous person possesses his or her own dwelling place in the World to Come, to which no other righteous person has access? Perhaps it means that the religious achievements of each human being are unique to him or her. Every person has his or her own personal history, personality, innate gifts or deficits, and religious tests and challenges. For some, the challenge might be controlling one's desires, for others it might be controlling one's temper, for another it might be the struggle with arrogance, and for others it might be the struggle to study Torah. Moreover, every person, given his or her unique past history, personality, and innate gifts, will struggle differently with each of these challenges. Thus, the pious person who merits a portion in the World to Come will inherit a portion that is absolutely unique to him or her. No one may have access to another person's portion in the World to Come. How can anyone else truly understand the challenges and successes of another if they are so different from his or her own?

later editors of the midrash, who knew of Reish Lakish's teaching, put the citation anachronistically in her mouth. It is indeed possible that the entire midrash is a later re-working of the narrative.

15. Sota 9:16.

Furthermore, it follows from this perspective that each person must find his or her own unique path to the World to Come as well. If we are all religiously different, our paths to religious redemption will be different too. For some, the primary vehicle for achieving a portion in the World to Come will be Torah study, for others acts of compassion, and for others a life of self-denial. There is no one monolithic way to achieve redemption; rather there are as many different ways to achieve redemption as there are different people in the world.

R. Shimon's wife meant to argue that Rebbe's view about a life of piety, namely that it does not require ascetic self-denial, may be the right path for Rebbe, but is not necessarily the best life for a man like R. Shimon or, for that matter, for a woman like his wife. Rebbe could not have access to R. Shimon's dwelling place in the World to Come, for Rebbe's religious perfection was not the religious perfection of R. Shimon. In short, R. Shimon's wife was a religious pluralist. She believed that there were multiple models for religious perfection corresponding to the complexities of the human condition.

However, Rebbe took a monistic, not pluralist, view. He maintained that there is indeed one ideal model of Jewish life, although no doubt there might be many nuances within it. This is exactly what he taught in *Pirkei Avot,* cited above: "What is the path a person should choose? The path that is honorable to the one who chooses it, and honorable in the eyes of others."[16] There is one path that people should choose, not many paths, and that one path is the path of "honor," of "harmony." If there is only one path, then every righteous person can understand the righteousness of his colleague, and can see into his dwelling place in the World to Come, for they all share the very same path.

Rebbe was convinced that piety does not require poverty. He did not share the pluralism of R. Shimon's wife, and insisted that R. Shimon too can have a portion in this world without sacrificing his portion in the World to Come. Rebbe thus made two claims, that he could peek into R. Shimon's dwelling place and also that R. Shimon could live a comfortable life in this world. On this analysis, both these positions are two sides of the very same theological coin, a theology which embraces a monistic

16. *Pirkei Avot* 2:1.

rather than pluralistic picture of religious life and values, according to which piety does not require poverty. On the monistic view of the ideal religious life, Rebbe could have access to R. Shimon's dwelling in the World to Come, and he could likewise maintain that for everyone, piety does not preclude comfort in this world.

Yet remarkably enough, Rebbe came to retract this position. He reversed himself, and accepted the pluralism of R. Shimon's wife. He admitted that she was right, and that he could not provide for R. Shimon in the World to Come, because he could have no access to R. Shimon's distinctive path in the service of God. This means that he acknowledged that there are multiple legitimate paths to God, not all of them his own. R. Shimon's path of poverty was right for R. Shimon. Rebbe's path of material well-being was right for Rebbe, and that is as it should be. But we must still ask what led Rebbe to reverse himself, and acknowledge that R. Shimon's wife was correct.

The text itself provides no clear answer. Of course, he might simply have been persuaded by the force of her argument, although that seems unlikely. What could R. Shimon's wife add to Rebbe's vast storehouse of knowledge? More likely, I believe, is that he was persuaded less by the force of her argument than by the passion and conviction with which she conveyed it. He might have heard in her voice so sincere and intense a commitment to her husband's way of life that it could only emerge from a deeply authentic spirituality. Rebbe could not deny that authenticity, and chose to acknowledge its legitimacy. In the end, Rebbe learned from this anonymous woman that the paths to divine service are much richer and more complex than even he, the greatest of masters, could suspect. In a dramatic inversion, Rebbe, the great teacher whose very name means "my master," became the humble student of R. Shimon ben Ḥalafta's wife. This is an extraordinary testimony to Rebbe's humility, as it is an extraordinary testimony to the character and stature of R. Shimon's wife.[17]

---

17. An even more minimalist reading of Rebbe's admission might be that he did not concede the legitimacy of her position, but only that he did not want to debate her any further. However, that is unlikely, since the midrash explicitly asserts that he "admitted to her."

In an echo of the R. Ḥanina ben Dosa aggada, the midrash likewise concludes with a reversal of the original miracle, and the heavenly jewel is now returned to heaven. This, the midrash asserts, is a greater miracle than the first. The vehicle for this return, like the vehicle for the initial gift, is a hand which both provides the jewel and also takes it away. In our midrash, the significance of this image of the hand is paramount.

Initially, asserts the midrash, the hand of the recipient, "those who reside below," was beneath the hand of the donor, "those who reside above." That is the symbolic norm: recipients stoop beneath donors. Yet this image is reversed when the jewel is returned by "those who reside below" to "those who reside above." Now the hand of those who reside below is above the hand of those who reside above. What a striking image! A mere human being, R. Shimon, stands above God (or His agents), extending Him a hand. God is, as it were, the humble recipient of R. Shimon's gift.

This is a powerful evocation of the exceptional piety of R. Shimon, who gives God the self-sacrificial gift of himself, the gift of a life of comfort in favor of a life of abject poverty. And God, in His wisdom and love, humbly accepts R. Shimon's gift, lowering His hand below that of R. Shimon's.

The first humble reversal in the midrash was Rebbe's. The second, far greater, humble reversal is that of God Himself, which echoes and magnifies the first. None can stand before R. Shimon's otherworldly, modest, and profound piety, personally affirmed and dramatically defended by his anonymous wife. All the greats change. Rebbe reverses himself, and even God (or His agents) humbly places His hand below R. Shimon's. Ironically, those who *prima facie* place lower in the hierarchy are proven right, and those who *prima facie* place higher in the hierarchy conform to the convictions of those below them. R. Shimon's wife, a woman interacting with the male rabbinical leader of the whole generation remains steadfast throughout in her convictions, unlike the others. The midrash thus undercuts the very hierarchy itself.

It is worth recalling here an episode recorded in several places in the Talmud about Yosef the son of R. Yehoshua who experienced death but then was revived. When asked what he saw during his brief sojourn in the next world, he reported that "I saw an upside-down world, with those above situated below, and those below situated above."[18] As the commentators understand it, what Yosef saw was an inversion. Those who had achieved wealth and prestige in this world – those who were at the top of the socioeconomic hierarchy – were situated at the very bottom of the next world's hierarchy, and those who were impoverished and poorly valued in this world were situated at the very top of the hierarchy in the World to Come. R. Shimon ben Ḥalafta's life is a brilliant example of this radical inversion.

Consider now who changes over the course of the events described in this midrash. R. Shimon's wife is simply immutable, an indomitable force before all her interlocutors. Rebbe, of course, evolves. What of R. Shimon himself? While he does change superficially to accommodate the stronger will of those around him, that change is no more than a reflection of his enduring otherworldliness. Whether Rebbe tells him to keep the jewel and he complies, or whether his wife tells him to return the jewel and he complies, it is ultimately all the same to R. Shimon. At the deepest level, he remains oblivious to the material world. R. Shimon's soul is at home not in this world but in the next. R. Shimon lives only "amongst those who reside above."[19]

18. Bava Batra 10b; Pesaḥim 50a. See Rashi, ad loc.

19. Another version of this midrash appears in Exodus Rabba 52, in which a very different picture of R. Shimon emerges than what it described in the midrash that is the subject of this chapter. In Exodus Rabba, R. Shimon is portrayed as a far more decisive and proactive man, with a very different relationship to his wife. Rebbe plays a more secondary role in that midrash, unlike here. It is surely not without interest how different midrashim convey very different pictures of the man, and of the dynamic amongst all three figures.

Confronting the Past and Future

Chapter 7

Why Did R. Yoḥanan ben Zakkai Cry?

Berakhot 28b

INTRODUCTION

R. Yoḥanan ben Zakkai, the central figure in this aggada, was the person most responsible for the survival of Judaism and the Jewish people following the destruction of the Second Temple in 70 CE. According to the Talmud, he managed to persuade the Romans to permit him and his students to escape the siege of Jerusalem, and establish a center for Torah study and Jewish life in Yavneh. Despite the devastation that soon followed with the sacking of Jerusalem, he continued to teach Torah to his elect students, and established a Jewish communal structure and de facto replacement for the Sanhedrin which he headed, and from which he courageously and brilliantly led the surviving remnants of the Jewish community. For all these reasons he was amongst the most important Rabbis in all of Jewish history.

This aggada transports the reader to R. Yoḥanan ben Zakkai's deathbed, and his final encounter with his students. When his students come to visit him he immediately breaks down in tears, expressing overwhelming anxiety at his fate in the World to Come. Why does R. Yoḥanan ben Zakkai cry? For a man who almost singlehandedly enabled Judaism to survive the cataclysm of the Temple's destruction and the mass murder and exile of so many of Jerusalem's inhabitants, he of all people should be confident of his eternal reward. Why the immense trepidation? What advice does he give his students at this critical juncture? Finally, what are his very last words as he leaves this world for the next, and what is their enduring significance?

כְּשֶׁחָלָה רַבִּי יוֹחָנָן בֶּן זַכַּאי נִכְנְסוּ תַּלְמִידָיו לְבַקְּרוֹ. כֵּיוָן שֶׁרָאָה אוֹתָם הִתְחִיל לִבְכּוֹת. אָמְרוּ לוֹ תַּלְמִידָיו: ״נֵר יִשְׂרָאֵל, עַמּוּד הַיְמִינִי, פַּטִּישׁ הֶחָזָק״, מִפְּנֵי מָה אַתָּה בּוֹכֶה?

A similar story is told about Rabbi Eliezer's mentor, Rabban Yoḥanan ben Zakkai: When **Rabbi Yoḥanan ben Zakkai fell ill his students entered to visit him. When he saw them, he began to cry. His students said to him: Lamp of Israel, the right pillar, the mighty hammer,** the man whose life's work is the foundation of the future of the Jewish people, **for what** reason **are you crying?** With a life as complete as yours, what is upsetting you?

אָמַר לָהֶם: אִילּוּ לִפְנֵי מֶלֶךְ בָּשָׂר וָדָם הָיוּ מוֹלִיכִין אוֹתִי, שֶׁהַיּוֹם כָּאן וּמָחָר בַּקֶּבֶר, שֶׁאִם כּוֹעֵס עָלַי אֵין כַּעֲסוֹ כַּעַס עוֹלָם, וְאִם אוֹסְרֵנִי – אֵין אִיסּוּרוֹ אִיסּוּר עוֹלָם, וְאִם מְמִיתֵנִי – אֵין מִיתָתוֹ מִיתַת עוֹלָם, וַאֲנִי יָכוֹל לְפַיְּיסוֹ בִּדְבָרִים וּלְשַׁחֲדוֹ בְּמָמוֹן, אַף עַל פִּי כֵן הָיִיתִי בּוֹכֶה, וְעַכְשָׁיו שֶׁמּוֹלִיכִים אוֹתִי לִפְנֵי מֶלֶךְ מַלְכֵי הַמְּלָכִים הַקָּדוֹשׁ בָּרוּךְ הוּא, שֶׁהוּא חַי וְקַיָּים לְעוֹלָם וּלְעוֹלְמֵי עוֹלָמִים, שֶׁאִם כּוֹעֵס עָלַי – כַּעֲסוֹ כַּעַס עוֹלָם, וְאִם אוֹסְרֵנִי – אִיסּוּרוֹ אִיסּוּר עוֹלָם, וְאִם מְמִיתֵנִי – מִיתָתוֹ מִיתַת עוֹלָם, וְאֵינִי יָכוֹל לְפַיְּיסוֹ בִּדְבָרִים וְלֹא לְשַׁחֲדוֹ בְּמָמוֹן. וְלֹא עוֹד, אֶלָּא שֶׁיֵּשׁ לְפָנַי שְׁנֵי דְרָכִים, אַחַת שֶׁל גַּן עֵדֶן וְאַחַת שֶׁל גֵּיהִנָּם, וְאֵינִי יוֹדֵעַ בְּאֵיזוֹ מוֹלִיכִים אוֹתִי, וְלֹא אֶבְכֶּה?

He said to them: I cry in fear of heavenly judgment, as the judgment of the heavenly court is unlike the judgment of man. **If they were leading me before a flesh and blood king** whose life is temporal, **who is here today and** dead **in the grave tomorrow; if he is angry with me, his anger is not eternal** and, consequently, his punishment is not eternal; **if he incarcerates me, his incarceration is not an eternal incarceration,** as I might maintain my hope that I would ultimately be freed. **If he kills me, his killing is not for eternity,** as there is life after any death that he might decree. Moreover, **I am able to appease him with words and** even **bribe him with money,** and **even so I would cry** when standing before royal judgment. **Now that they are leading me before the supreme King of Kings, the Holy One, Blessed be He, who lives and endures forever and all time; if He is angry with me, His anger is eternal; if He incarcerates me, His incarceration is an eternal incarceration; and if He kills me, His killing is for eternity. I am unable to appease Him with words and bribe him with money. Moreover, but I have two paths before me, one of the Garden of Eden and one of Gehenna, and I do not know on which they are leading me; and will I not cry?**

אָמְרוּ לוֹ: רַבֵּינוּ, בָּרְכֵנוּ. אָמַר לָהֶם: ״יְהִי רָצוֹן שֶׁתְּהֵא מוֹרָא שָׁמַיִם עֲלֵיכֶם כְּמוֹרָא בָּשָׂר וָדָם״. אָמְרוּ לוֹ תַּלְמִידָיו: עַד כָּאן? אָמַר לָהֶם: וּלְוַאי, תֵּדְעוּ כְּשֶׁאָדָם עוֹבֵר עֲבֵירָה אוֹמֵר: ״שֶׁלֹּא יִרְאֵנִי אָדָם״.

His students **said to him: Our teacher, bless us. He said to them: May it be** His **will that the fear of Heaven shall be upon you like the fear of flesh and blood. His students** were puzzled **and said: To that point** and not beyond? Shouldn't one fear God more? **He said to them: Would that** a person achieves that level of fear. **Know that when one commits a transgression, he says** to himself: I hope **that no man will see me.** If one is as concerned about avoiding shame before God as he is before man, he will never sin.

בִּשְׁעַת פְּטִירָתוֹ, אָמַר לָהֶם: פַּנּוּ כֵּלִים מִפְּנֵי הַטּוּמְאָה, וְהָכִינוּ כִּסֵּא לְחִזְקִיָּהוּ מֶלֶךְ יְהוּדָה שֶׁבָּא.

The Gemara relates that **at the time of his death,** immediately beforehand, **he said to them: Remove the vessels** from the house and take them outside **due to the ritual impurity** that will be imparted by my corpse, which they would otherwise contract.

And prepare a chair for Hezekiah, the King of Judea, who is coming from the upper world to accompany me.

R. YOḤANAN BEN ZAKKAI'S STUDENTS PAY HIM A VISIT ON HIS DEATHBED

R. Yoḥanan ben Zakkai is gravely ill, and his students pay him a final visit before he passes away. While these students are not named, they may have included the five listed in *Pirkei Avot* (2:10): R. Eliezer ben Hyrcanus, R. Yehoshua ben Ḥananya, R. Yose the priest, R. Shimon ben Netanel, and R. Eliezer ben Arakh. His immediate reaction upon seeing them is to burst out in tears. This surprises not only the reader, but it clearly surprises his students as well, who find it very troubling. They raise exactly this question, addressing him with three honorific metaphors "lamp of Israel, the right pillar, the mighty hammer." These are metaphors that convey power, and power for them was inconsistent with the weakness expressed by R. Yoḥanan ben Zakkai's tears.

Moreover, these metaphors are precisely chosen, for they speak to R. Yoḥanan ben Zakkai's historic role in the survival of Judaism following the destruction of the Temple and the razing of Jerusalem. R. Yoḥanan ben Zakkai illuminated Jews with the light of Torah by teaching it in Yavneh. He was the pillar of strength that supported Jews, Judaism, and Torah in the turmoil following the destruction of the Temple. And finally, he was the hammer who smashed despair by revitalizing Torah study as the center of Jewish life in a world devoid of the Temple. R. Yoḥanan ben Zakkai's students fail to understand their great teacher's tears, for they knew firsthand the strength and courage he possessed, and what he had accomplished.

R. Yoḥanan ben Zakkai's response is a fascinating one, and it comes in two parts. First, he draws an analogy between a person brought before a mortal king for judgment, and a person such as himself, on the verge of dying, and brought before God for judgment. A person brought before a mortal king for judgment would be crying and terrified, even though a mortal king will himself eventually die; even though the king's anger is not permanent and the incarceration he might decree would not be permanent either; even though if the king decrees the death penalty, it will affect life only in this world but not the next; and finally, even though a mortal king is always subject to appeasement and bribes. However, none of this is true of the King of all Kings, God, for He is immortal; His anger, and the incarceration or death He might decree, would be eternal; and finally, He is not subject to appeasement or bribes. Surely then R. Yoḥanan ben Zakkai too should be crying, terrified as he stands at the doorstep of death, and before not a mortal king's judgment, but the final judgment of the King of Kings.

R. Yoḥanan ben Zakkai's remarks here raise several questions. Why does he use the expression "leading me before a flesh and blood king"? That is an unusual phrase to describe judgment and death. And who exactly is doing the leading? Moreover, the entire simile is puzzling. Does everyone who appears in judgment before a king cry out in desperate tears? Don't many who face judgment retain their composure? Why is it so self-evident to R. Yoḥanan ben Zakkai, courageous man that he was, that such an encounter with a king would yield tears? This question is rendered all the more acute because R. Yoḥanan ben Zakkai himself itemizes in detail the many limitations of a mortal king, in distinguishing him from God. Given all those limitations, why then cry?

Moreover, is it so self-evident that God does not accept appeasement? What about the rituals in the Temple during the Day of Atonement? Might they not be understood as attempts to appease God? And indeed, perhaps all Temple sacrifices could also be understood as attempts to appease Him. And even if the concept of appeasement is inapt in application to God, what about prayer and repentance? God surely reverses Himself sometimes as a consequence of prayer, and surely God accepts the sincere penitent. Are there not other means to secure a reversal of God's decree? Why then does R. Yoḥanan ben Zakkai counterfactually assume otherwise, that God's decree is irreversible?[1]

---

1. The Maharsha in his commentary, ad loc., suggests that while God can be appeased with prayer and bribed with charity in this world, once a person dies, that is impossible. To this reader, however, this interpretation is not altogether satisfying, since this distinction does not apply to a mortal king, and so R. Yoḥanan ben Zakkai's simile would be off the mark.

Finally, the aggada asserts that R. Yoḥanan ben Zakkai broke down in tears the moment he saw his students, yet the explanation he provides for his tears does not bear whatsoever on their arrival, and is therefore a *non sequitur*. The simile he draws between a mortal and immortal king to explain his tears has nothing to do with his students. According to its logic, he should have been crying before his students ever arrived, as he prepares himself for God's inescapable judgment. The reader is thus left pondering just why R. Yoḥanan ben Zakkai bursts into tears only upon the arrival of his students.

Before attempting to answer these questions, let us proceed with the aggada. R. Yoḥanan ben Zakkai next adds another crucial and especially puzzling point. He tells his students that two paths stand before him, one leading to the Garden of Eden, and the other to Gehenna. He confesses that he does not know which path God will take him down. How then could he not cry? The key question, of course, is why R. Yoḥanan ben Zakkai was beset by such doubts. If he was the hero of Jewish life following the destruction, why then would he fear that he might end up in Gehenna of all places? This seems to make no sense at all.[2]

This question is rendered even more acute if we consider the Talmud's description of R. Yoḥanan ben Zakkai:

> The Sages **said about Rabban Yoḥanan ben Zakkai,** the teacher of Rabbi Eliezer: **In** all **his days he never engaged in idle conversation; and he never walked four cubits without** engaging in **Torah** study **and without** donning **phylacteries; and no person ever preceded him into the study hall; and he never slept in the study hall, neither substantial sleep nor a brief nap; and he never contemplated** matters of Torah **in alleyways filthy** with human excrement, as doing so is a display of contempt for the Torah; **and he never left anyone in the study hall and exited; and no person ever found him sitting and silent,** i.e., inactive; **rather, he** was always **sitting and studying; and only he opened the door for his students,** disregarding his own eminent

2. The classic commentators struggle with this question. See, for example, the Rif and *Eitz Yosef* commentaries in the *Ein Yaakov*.

standing; **and he never said anything that he did not hear from his teacher; and he never said** to his students that **the time has arrived to arise** and leave **the study hall except on Passover eves,** when they were obligated to sacrifice the Paschal lamb, and **Yom Kippur eves,** when there is a mitzva to eat and drink abundantly. **And Rabbi Eliezer, his student, accustomed** himself to model his conduct **after his** example.

While a careful analysis of this remarkable passage would be of great value, for our purposes now, suffice it to say that the portrait that emerges of R. Yoḥanan ben Zakkai is of a man with the most intense devotion to Torah study. Life, for him, was Torah, Torah, and more Torah: never an idle conversation, never walking four cubits without Torah study, no one ever preceding him to the study hall early in the morning or leaving after him late at night. Yet despite this intimate relationship with Torah, he nevertheless respected the Torah so much, kept it in such elevated regard, that he never would think of Torah in filthy places. According to this talmudic tradition, R. Yoḥanan ben Zakkai was a man of extraordinary stature, quite apart from his achievements in Yavneh. As humble as he may have been, how then could he of all people have feared Gehenna?

While there is no explicit evidence from the text itself, there can be very little doubt that R. Yoḥanan ben Zakkai's fears harken back to a momentous decision that he made many years before, as recounted in the Talmud.[3] During a dialogue between R. Yoḥanan ben Zakkai and the besieging Roman general Vespasian, in which R. Yoḥanan ben Zakkai correctly predicts Vespasian's appointment as emperor, Vespasian invites R. Yoḥanan ben Zakkai to make of him a request which he would grant:

> Vespasian then **said to** Rabban Yoḥanan ben Zakkai: **I will be going** to Rome to accept my new position, **and I will send someone else** in my place to continue besieging the city and waging

3. Gittin 56b. B. Lau makes this point as well, in *The Sages, Volume II: From Yavneh to the Bar Kokhba Revolt* (Jerusalem, 2011), 49.

> war against it. **But** before I leave, **ask something of me that I can give you.** Rabban Yoḥanan ben Zakkai **said to him: Give me Yavneh and its Sages** and do not destroy it, **and** spare **the dynasty of Rabban Gamliel** and do not kill them as if they were rebels, **and** lastly give me **doctors to heal Rabbi Tzadok. Rav Yosef read** the following verse **about him, and some say** that it was **Rabbi Akiva** who applied the verse to Rabban Yoḥanan ben Zakkai: "I am the Lord... **who turns wise men backward and makes their knowledge foolish"** (**Isaiah 44:25**), as **he should have said to him to leave** the Jews alone **this time. And** why didn't Rabban Yoḥanan ben Zakkai make this request? **He maintained** that Vespasian **might not do that much** for him, **and there would not be even a small** amount of **salvation.** Therefore, he made only a modest request, in the hope that he would receive at least that much.

R. Yoḥanan ben Zakkai is depicted here as facing a choice of the greatest possible consequences for the Jewish people. Should he request the salvation of Jerusalem and the Temple, or should he request permission to re-establish some semblance of Jewish national and religious life in Yavneh? The first option would yield the best possible result, for what can compare to Jerusalem with its Temple and Sanhedrin? Yet that choice is fraught with risk, for if Vespasian denies it – and well he might – then Judaism would have no future. Is it not then better to choose the inferior option, since it is far more likely to succeed? Judaism would at least survive, even if profoundly diminished.

What a terrifying decision to make! R. Yoḥanan ben Zakkai had no time to deliberate, to reflect fully on its long-term implications. Vespasian waited for an answer, and it turns out that all of Jewish history would come to rest on that critical choice. R. Yoḥanan ben Zakkai took the conservative option: better something than nothing at all. Yet he was criticized, and, according to one tradition recorded in the Talmud, by none other than the great R. Akiva. Moreover, it was not only R. Akiva who might have opposed that decision. The formal rabbinic leader of the Jewish community in Jerusalem, R. Shimon ben Gamliel, remained in Jerusalem during the siege, seemed to have thrown in his lot with the

Zealots, and was eventually killed by the Romans.[4] While R. Yoḥanan ben Zakkai took the initiative and left with some of his students, we have no record of the departure of any of his rabbinic peers. They all stayed in Jerusalem, unlike R. Yoḥanan ben Zakkai.

Let us now reflect on the implication of this decision for R. Yoḥanan ben Zakkai himself. He is at his deathbed, about to meet God in judgment. Is it at all surprising that he would feel haunted by the decision that he had made so long ago? Yes, he had heroically saved Judaism following the destruction of Jerusalem, for the logic behind that effort nourished Judaism throughout the ages. Yes, he had succeeded in demonstrating that the Temple was not the only vehicle to mediate God's relationship with the Jewish people. The Torah could too, its study, a life lived according to its teachings, a life that modeled the Torah's emphasis on care for others. God did not require the Temple to sustain His relationship with the Jews, nor did the Jews require the Temple to sustain their relationship with God. The Torah was all that was necessary, anytime and anyplace, in Jerusalem or in Yavneh, and indeed in Rhineland, Cordoba, Vilna, or New York. This teaching enabled Judaism to flourish throughout the millennia in exile.

Yet as monumental as that achievement was, we must nevertheless ask if it could compare to God's vivid presence in the Temple. Could R. Yoḥanan ben Zakkai have succeeded in saving Jerusalem once and for all? Did his fateful choice deny the Jews the Temple until the arrival of the Messiah, for whom Jews still wait, two millennia later? Did R. Yoḥanan ben Zakkai make an error far more monumental than his achievement? Indeed, that was the opinion of R. Akiva (or Rav Yosef), and no doubt many others as well. His decision was clearly a controversial one.

R. Yoḥanan ben Zakkai stood at the doorstep of death. Is it surprising that he would reprise that choice, and fear it was the wrong one, as R. Akiva and others had maintained? Two paths awaited him, the

4. There is no scholarly consensus on whether or not R. Shimon ben Gamliel did indeed join the Zealots. I am following here the opinion of those who take this position, e.g., Lau, *The Sages*, Vol. I, 355–358. Even according to those who maintain otherwise, so far as we know, R. Yoḥanan ben Zakkai was still the only leading rabbi to attempt an escape, which sets him apart from his colleagues.

Garden of Eden and Gehenna. Which would be his? Did he make the right decision, and will he head to the Garden of Eden? Or did he make the frightfully wrong choice, and will he head to Gehenna? R. Yoḥanan ben Zakkai faced his future, and he could do so only if he first faced up to his past, for successful dying requires an honest confrontation with whatever the past holds. The future is always a child of the past, even if that future is born in death itself.

This perspective on R. Yoḥanan ben Zakkai illuminates our aggada in many ways. First, of course, it explains his intense fear about his ultimate destiny. But consider this as well. Just prior to the talmudic passage cited above which tells the story of R. Yoḥanan ben Zakkai's encounter with Vespasian, the Talmud relates how R. Yoḥanan ben Zakkai initially sought to escape the siege, which required deception of the Zealots who refused to make peace with the Romans and to permit Jews to leave the city despite the siege. R. Yoḥanan ben Zakkai appealed to his nephew, a leader of the Zealots himself, who suggested that R. Yoḥanan ben Zakkai simulate death, and that his students take him out in a coffin for burial outside the city. The Zealot guards at the gates wanted to pierce the coffin with swords to ensure his death, but R. Yoḥanan ben Zakkai's nephew persuaded them otherwise, and they eventually permitted the coffin carried by his two students, R. Eliezer and R. Yehoshua, to leave the city gates. Shortly afterward he met up with Vespasian and a dialogue ensued, culminating in the passage cited above.

Surely the escape from Jerusalem in a coffin simulating death, interrupted by threats to pierce the coffin with swords, was a harrowing experience, and one which led directly to his encounter and fateful dialogue with Vespasian. Would it be surprising then, that when R. Yoḥanan ben Zakkai actually faced death, he relived that experience in which he simulated death, in the coffin? Would it be surprising that R. Yoḥanan ben Zakkai would use the words "leading me" to describe his experience at death, which recapitulates exactly what transpired so many years ago, in the coffin? There too he had been led, carried in the coffin, to an eventual encounter with a king, exactly the trope in R. Yoḥanan ben Zakkai's simile. Indeed, the word used in the original text of our aggada to describe the passage to judgment is *molikhin,* which can be literally translated as "caused me to go." That is exactly what transpired in

Jerusalem. He uses that unexpected verb during his encounter with his students at his death in Yavneh because it exactly recapitulates his death simulation – witnessed by his two students – in Jerusalem. This then is at least part of the explanation for why the arrival of his students caused him to break down in tears. He relived that very moment, surrounded by students, when he escaped Jerusalem only to meet up with Vespasian.

This perspective likewise explains why R. Yoḥanan ben Zakkai assumes that it is natural for a person to cry when brought in judgment before a mortal king. While not everyone loses his composure, R. Yoḥanan ben Zakkai surely projected that he would, because he is reliving his encounter with Vespasian, and re-evaluating the decision he made then. R. Yoḥanan ben Zakkai now fears the awful consequences of that encounter, and therefore for him, especially, encounters with kings are fraught. Moreover, he fears that no appeasement with God is possible, at least for him. Surely others may appease God, through sacrifices or prayer. But R. Yoḥanan ben Zakkai? He, who made the momentous decision not to try to save Jerusalem? For him, the gates of appeasement would be forever shut. In short, R. Yoḥanan ben Zakkai is tormented by a past with which he cannot now fully come to terms.

R. YOḤANAN BEN ZAKKAI BLESSES HIS STUDENTS

R. Yoḥanan ben Zakkai's students now ask him for a blessing before he passes away. What kind of blessing would they have expected from a man of R. Yoḥanan ben Zakkai's stature, from a man whose life was saturated with Torah? They probably expected that he would bless them with mastery of the Torah, or with attaining the Garden of Eden, or with children who would themselves be masters of Torah. But that is not the blessing he offers. He blesses them that their fear of heaven never be less than their fear of another human being.

This blessing astonishes them, and they ask if that is all. Are those the limits of fear of God? Shouldn't one aspire to a fear of God which far exceeds fear of a mere human being? While they do not say so explicitly, we might add that it was R. Yoḥanan ben Zakkai himself who contrasted the limits of a mortal king's judgment with the judgment of God. If a mortal king is so inferior to God, then surely one should fear God far more than one should fear a mortal king. And if the fear of God should exceed the fear of a king, all the more so should it exceed the fear of a simple person of flesh and blood. Thus R. Yoḥanan ben Zakkai's own teaching, with which his encounter with his students began, confounds the very blessing he now offers them.

R. Yoḥanan ben Zakkai offers a provocative answer to his students. He exclaims, "Would that a person fear heaven as much as he fears another person." When a person sins, R. Yoḥanan ben Zakkai teaches, the sinner's primary fear is that someone else might have witnessed his failure. Now it must be observed that this is a fairly dim view of the human condition. While his claim may well be true for the average person, what about for the spiritual elite? Is it fair to say that this is his or her primary fear? Let us remember that R. Yoḥanan ben Zakkai was speaking to his own students, perhaps including the great R. Eliezer and R. Yehoshua who carried him in his coffin out of the gates of Jerusalem, together with the other three-star students listed in the Mishna in *Pirkei Avot* cited above. They were all men of the greatest stature. Is that how they would react to their own sins?

R. Yoḥanan ben Zakkai's answer to this question is "yes," for he does indeed take a dim view of the spiritual possibilities even of the elite. It seems fair to ask, then, on what basis he could make this claim. One possible answer, of course, is that this is what he observed in others during his many years of life. However, this does stretch plausibility, for how could R. Yoḥanan ben Zakkai really know what people think in the recesses of their minds when they sin? They are hardly likely to proclaim publicly the thoughts R. Yoḥanan ben Zakkai attributes to them. A more likely suggestion is that this is what R. Yoḥanan ben Zakkai observed in himself, and if it was true of him, he reasoned, it must be true of anyone else too, given his own spiritual stature. Indeed, R. Yoḥanan ben Zakkai may have reflected on his encounter with Vespasian, and took his reaction to be evidence for this assessment of himself.

Whom did R. Yoḥanan ben Zakkai fear more, Vespasian or God? If he had feared God more, perhaps he would have gambled on Jerusalem, and trusted in God's benevolence. But he didn't. He feared Vespasian more than he feared God, and chose Yavneh over Jerusalem. The same talmudic aggada records another bit of dialogue between R. Yoḥanan ben Zakkai and Vespasian, which starts with a challenge posed by Vespasian to R. Yoḥanan ben Zakkai, as if to say: "Why did you not come to me sooner?" R. Yoḥanan ben Zakkai responds that the Zealots did not permit him to leave the city. Vespasian rejects that excuse, and proffers an allegory:

> Vespasian **said to him: If** there is **a barrel of honey and a snake** [***derakon***] **is wrapped around it, wouldn't they break the barrel in order to** kill **the snake?** In similar fashion, I am forced to destroy the city of Jerusalem in order to kill the Zealots barricaded within it. Rabban Yoḥanan ben Zakkai **was silent** and did not answer. In light of this, **Rav Yosef** later **read** the following verse **about him, and some say** that it was **Rabbi Akiva** who applied the verse to Rabban Yoḥanan ben Zakkai: "I am the Lord… **who turns wise men backward and makes their knowledge foolish**" (**Isaiah 44:25**). As Rabban Yoḥanan ben Zakkai **should have said** the following **to** Vespasian in response: In such a case, **we take tongs, remove the snake, and kill it, and** in this way, **we leave the barrel** intact. So too, you should kill the rebels and leave the city as it is.

Here too, R. Yoḥanan ben Zakkai is criticized by the same R. Yosef or R. Akiva for failure to respond aggressively to Vespasian. In both cases his critics accuse him of a failure of nerve. What now does R. Yoḥanan ben Zakkai think at his deathbed? He fears that he chose conservatively because he was more preoccupied with what Vespasian would think than with what God would think. Or so R. Yoḥanan ben Zakkai, with his ruthless self-criticism, came to believe. I wonder how many other people could achieve R. Yoḥanan ben Zakkai's self-awareness. Most people are masters at self-deception, but at his deathbed, R. Yoḥanan ben Zakkai achieved a clarity of vision which few others achieve.

This then grounds R. Yoḥanan ben Zakkai's dying advice to his students. "Learn from my failures" he meant to teach them. "When I made that fateful choice, at some deep and unconscious level even I feared a mortal more than I feared God. Would that all of you fear God as much as you fear a mortal." He meant to teach his students a profound lesson about the limitations of human nature.

R. YOḤANAN BEN ZAKKAI AND R. AKIVA

I would now like to suggest that there is more to R. Yoḥanan ben Zakkai's conservatism than this, and that his values, and perhaps character and personality too, led to his fateful choice of Yavneh, and not only his probably then unconscious fear of the king. To see why this might be so, it would be helpful to contrast R. Yoḥanan ben Zakkai with R. Akiva, according to one talmudic tradition his great critic, and in many ways his polar opposite.

Let us first return to the Talmud's description of R. Yoḥanan ben Zakkai's many virtues. We have focused so far on his unyielding commitment to Torah study, and to the value he accorded it, factors which are revealing enough. But that passage is revealing in other ways as well for it teaches that R. Yoḥanan ben Zakkai "never said anything that he did not hear from his teacher." R. Yoḥanan ben Zakkai did not seek new insights into Torah, but diligently sought to accumulate, and labored diligently to recollect, everything he could learn from his masters. This reflects a deep intellectual conservatism in a quite straightforward sense, for he sought no more nor less than to conserve the wisdom of the past. Torah was his life, and that meant the preservation of Torah as he had received it from his masters.

R. Yoḥanan ben Zakkai did not valorize the new, did not seek to create fresh readings of the Torah, but rather looked to preserve insights from the past. The old is good, the new dangerous. The old harkens back to Sinai, the new may veer from that which God revealed, and from what one master had heard from another, going all the way back to Sinai.[5] Rabbinic authorities in the mishna cite R. Yoḥanan ben

5. See Sokol, *The Snake at the Mouth of the Cave* (Jerusalem, 2021), chs. 1–3, for an extensive discussion of this theme, especially as it applies to R. Yoḥanan ben Zakkai's great student, R. Eliezer. It is surely interesting that R. Yoḥanan ben Zakkai seems to take the contrary position when encouraging R. Eliezer to teach Torah to the assembled guests as described in chapter 1 of that volume. There he compares the study of Torah not to the preservation of old insights, like water in a well, but to

Zakkai as the source for their views, asserting that "he [R. Yoḥanan ben Zakkai] received [the teaching in question] from his master, and his master from his master, going back to the halakha that Moses received from Sinai."[6] In many ways, this sums up R. Yoḥanan ben Zakkai's conception of Torah study.

If that was a preeminent value for R. Yoḥanan ben Zakkai, then is it surprising that he chose Yavneh over Jerusalem? He would have done so for at least two reasons. First is the general conservatism which found its expression in his approach to Torah study. Second, if he valorized Torah study over all else, was he not likely to believe that Yavneh could serve as a more than adequate replacement for Jerusalem?[7] Of course the Temple was the Temple. But R. Yoḥanan ben Zakkai had devoted his entire life to the preservation and teaching of Torah. He believed that the Torah could replace the Temple as the great mediator between God and His people. If the Torah could do so, then perhaps Yavneh did not look so bad after all. He assumed that he was likely to gain Yavneh, but had great doubts about whether Vespasian would grant him Jerusalem. Given his conservatism, and given his convictions about the role of Torah in Jewish life, was it not more rational for him to choose Yavneh over Jerusalem?

This sheds further light on why R. Yoḥanan ben Zakkai burst out in tears when he saw his students. The simile he drew between a mortal king and God explains why he might cry, but not why the arrival of his

---

the creation of new insights, like the fresh waters of a spring. These two positions seem contrary, and it is possible that they reflected different traditions about the theology R. Yoḥanan ben Zakkai taught. Alternatively, it is possible that R. Yoḥanan ben Zakkai meant only to encourage his student R. Eliezer to think out of his own box, part of his growth as a student and human being.

6. Eduyot 8:3; Yadayim 4:3.

7. Note that one of the most important edicts he issues in Yavneh is that the shofar may be blown there when Rosh HaShana falls on Shabbat, which during Temple times was permitted only in Jerusalem and nowhere else. This suggests that for R. Yoḥanan ben Zakkai, what was crucial about Jerusalem, in this respect at least, was the functioning there of the Sanhedrin, the source of Torah teachings. With the destruction of the Temple, the Sanhedrin relocated to Yavneh, and therefore in Yavneh too the shofar could be sounded on Shabbat. The Torah is portable. Where there is a duly constituted source of Torah authority, there is a new Jerusalem.

students triggered his tears. However, this perspective on R. Yoḥanan ben Zakkai does help answer that question. If his mission in life was to preserve the great oral tradition of the law, if he devoted day and night to its accumulation and memorization, then his students would play a pivotal role in his worldview. They and only they could be the bearers of that tradition into the future.

Note that the Talmud in this passage teaches that R. Yoḥanan ben Zakkai himself would personally get up to open the door for his students. Why would he interrupt his studies to do so? Could he not have deputized one of his assistants or servants to serve as doorman? After all, he was head of the yeshiva. Yet R. Yoḥanan ben Zakkai wanted to teach his students what for him was a crucial message. They and only they are the bearers of Torah into the future. For Judaism to survive, the Oral Torah must survive, for the Torah mediates God to His chosen people. They must carry forward the great chain of Torah transmission from one generation to the next.

If that is their great mission, when R. Yoḥanan ben Zakkai saw them enter to visit him on his deathbed, he could not but reflect about his legacy. What did he leave these students? He left them much Torah, but he also left them with the consequences of that fateful choice he had made long ago. Was he right to choose Torah over Temple? The Temple had been the primary locus of the encounter between God and His people ever since the Tabernacle in the desert. After all, that is how God envisioned His relationship with the Jewish people in the Torah. Of course, Torah is seminal. But can it replace the Temple? What then did he leave his students? When he saw them, he burst out in tears, because he confronted his legacy in their eager faces. And he became terrified that the legacy he had left them was the wrong one. He placed all his hopes for the future in these distinguished men, opened the door for them in the study hall, but he may erroneously have shattered for them, and for all the Jewish people, the future God Himself might have wanted.

Let us now compare R. Yoḥanan ben Zakkai to R. Akiva, in many ways his polar opposite. While R. Akiva lived two generations later than R. Yoḥanan ben Zakkai, they both lived during periods of great Jewish upheaval. R. Yoḥanan ben Zakkai in his maturity experienced the siege of Jerusalem, with its many warring and rebellious Jewish factions, then the destruction of Jerusalem and its aftermath. R. Akiva was born not long before the destruction of the Temple in 70 CE, and in his maturity and especially later years, endured the crushing Hadrianic persecutions of the Jews, and then Bar Kokhba's failed rebellion against Roman rule, which began in 132 CE and ended some two and a half years later. As we have seen, according to one version recorded in the Talmud, it was R. Akiva who criticized R. Yoḥanan ben Zakkai for failing to request of Vespasian the salvation of Jerusalem.

If indeed R. Yoḥanan ben Zakkai's critic was R. Akiva, it should come as no surprise. R. Akiva was the leading rabbinic supporter of Bar Kokhba. Indeed, according to the Talmud, it was he who gave Bar Kokhba that very name, changing it from Bar Koziba to an Aramaic phrase which means "son of a star," a reference to the messianic status R. Akiva believed he possessed.[8] Throughout his adult life, R. Akiva was a vigorous antagonist of the Romans, and during the Hadrianic persecutions he persisted in teaching Torah publicly, despite the ban on doing so. This was seditious behavior from the Roman perspective, and led eventually to his martyrdom. While R. Akiva's brazen public resistance to the Romans was extremely risky and not without its rabbinic detractors,[9] nevertheless, R. Akiva stubbornly insisted it was the right approach to take. When Papus ben Yehuda challenged R. Akiva on the danger of his activities, R. Akiva responded with a now famous parable:

> Rabbi Akiva **answered him: I will relate a parable. To what can this be compared?** It is like **a fox walking along a riverbank when he sees fish gathering** and fleeing **from place to place.**
>
> The fox **said to them: From what are you fleeing? They said to him:** We are fleeing **from the nets that people cast upon us.**

8. Y. Ta'anit 4:7.
9. See Avoda Zara 18b, which records the objection of R. Yose ben Kisma, a leading scholar, to similar activities by R. Ḥanina ben Teradyon.

> **He said to them: Do you wish to come up onto dry land, and we will reside together just as my ancestors resided with your ancestors?**
>
> The fish **said to him: You are the one of whom they say, he is the cleverest of animals? You are not clever; you are a fool. If we are afraid in** the water, **our** natural **habitat** which gives us **life,** then **in a habitat** that causes our **death, all the more so.** The moral is: **So too, we** Jews, **now that we sit and engage in Torah** study, **about which it is written: "For that is your life, and the length of your days"** (**Deuteronomy 30:20**), we fear the empire **to this extent; if we proceed to** sit **idle from its** study, as its abandonment is the habitat that causes our death, **all the more so** will we fear the empire.[10]

The study of Torah, for R. Akiva, was as essential to Jewish life as water is to a fish. Just as a fish faces mortal danger if it leaves its natural habitat, water, so too, Jews face mortal danger if they leave their natural habitat, the study of Torah.

While this passionate if risky commitment to Torah study is a leaf from the pages of R. Yoḥanan ben Zakkai's own book, his approach to Torah study was radically different. R. Yoḥanan ben Zakkai valorized conservative memorization of ancient oral traditions, but R. Akiva prized halakhic creativity, his ability to derive or link new laws to every letter of the Torah, indeed even to how each letter was written. So remarkable was this creativity that the Talmud could claim that even Moses, the man who received the Torah himself at Sinai, failed to grasp it.[11]

Even these few observations illustrate the marked difference between R. Akiva and R. Yoḥanan ben Zakkai. The former was a revolutionary, both in his politics and in his approach to Torah study. R. Yoḥanan ben Zakkai, on the other hand, opposed the rebellious Zealots and sought an accommodation with Rome. Indeed, Yavneh itself was under Roman rule then, and his escape there meant that he was not

10. Berakhot 61b.
11. Menaḥot 29b.

leaving Roman control, but was self-consciously remaining under its protection. As we have seen, this political quietism and conservatism was matched by a conservatism in his approach to Torah study. It is likely that the temperaments of both of these great men were different as well, and it should therefore come as no surprise that R. Akiva would emerge as R. Yoḥanan ben Zakkai's critic.

Contrast now R. Yoḥanan ben Zakkai's message to his students at his death with R. Akiva's message to his students at his death. R. Yoḥanan ben Zakkai's message emerges from a skeptical view of the limitations of the human condition, based upon his rigorous assessment of human psychology. "Would that you fear God as much as you fear human beings!" he taught. R. Yoḥanan ben Zakkai is practical, if nothing else. He chooses Yavneh over certain death in Jerusalem, and is grounded enough to know just what motivates people. As elevated as they may consider themselves, they still fear people more than God. I might add that this deep skepticism finds its echoes in the Mussar movement of the modern era.

R. Akiva could not have been more different. He chose not a life of quiet Torah teaching hidden behind the four walls of a yeshiva, but rather brazen public lecturing before the masses, which finally led to his martyrdom. His gruesome yet awe-inspiring death is described in the Talmud:

> **When they took Rabbi Akiva out to be executed, it was time for the recitation of *Shema*. And they were raking his flesh with iron combs, and he was** reciting *Shema*, thereby **accepting upon himself the yoke of Heaven. His students said to him: Our teacher, even now,** as you suffer, you recite *Shema*? **He said to them: All my days I have been troubled by the verse: With all your soul,** meaning: **Even if God takes your soul. I said** to myself: **When will the** opportunity **be afforded me to fulfill this** verse? **Now that it has been afforded me, shall I not fulfill it? He prolonged** his uttering of the word: **One, until his soul left** his body as he uttered his final word: **One. A voice descended** from heaven **and said: Happy are you, Rabbi Akiva, that your soul left** your body **as** you uttered: **One.**

R. Akiva's students are present around him at the moment of his death, just as were the students of R. Yoḥanan ben Zakkai. They witness his torture, and his heart-wrenching and inspiring recitation of the *Shema*, through which he affirmed his faith in God despite everything. His students cannot comprehend R. Akiva's behavior, and they exclaim, "Our teacher, even now?" The exact meaning of the students' point is unclear, and numerous explanations of it have emerged over the years.[12] One account seems to this reader closest to the truth: The students understood that R. Akiva's faith in God was impeccable, and that whenever he recited the *Shema* he experienced within himself the capacity to martyr himself out of love for God. Nevertheless, they were astonished to see the fervor with which he implemented his convictions in the all too terrifying experience of torture. They simply could not believe that any human being was capable of this. In a way, they were R. Yoḥanan ben Zakkai-ites. They could not imagine that human beings could soar beyond their natural limitations to recite the *Shema* so fervently while flesh was torn from their skin with iron combs.[13]

While they were R. Yoḥanan ben Zakkai-ites, R. Akiva was not. The great and enduring message he taught his students at his death was that there are no limitations to the human spirit. R. Akiva soared above whatever limitations others might possess and affirmed his faith in God despite gruesome torture. And if he could do this then, so too could they. R. Akiva was the revolutionary, not only in his politics, and not only in his approach to Torah study, but in his very spirit. He shattered the boundaries.

In short, R. Akiva was the soaring revolutionary, and R. Yoḥanan ben Zakkai the quietist conservative. These two great men represented radically different models of leadership and spirituality in times of crisis, and, it should be added, even in times of peace as well.

At his death, R. Yoḥanan ben Zakkai does not change his sensibility: "Fear God at least as much as you fear human beings," he taught

12. See the *Metivta* edition of the Talmud, Berakhot, vol. 4, 284–286, for an extensive summary of over twenty explanations.

13. See the commentary of Ben Yehoyada, ad loc. The precise formulation of this idea is my own.

his students. But he now suspected that he himself had failed to live up to that very teaching, which indeed may have been the reason he taught it to his students at his death. Perhaps he had feared a mortal king more than he had feared God, unlike his great successor R. Akiva. Perhaps he had made the wrong choice after all. He now saw that his very practicality, his grounding in the limitations of human nature, both of which had contributed to his quietest conservatism, may ultimately have led him down a path from which there could be no redemption. Unlike a mortal king, God cannot be appeased.

R. YOḤANAN BEN ZAKKAI'S FINAL FEW WORDS

Finally, R. Yoḥanan ben Zakkai utters his very last words before dying, and they are shrouded in enigma. One wonders if he already had one foot in the World to Come, and if he had been fully conscious when he said them.

First, R. Yoḥanan ben Zakkai requests that his students clear the room of vessels, so that they not become impure upon his passing. This is a reference to the laws of ritual purity and impurity. Vessels under the same roof as a corpse become impure, and R. Yoḥanan ben Zakkai wanted the vessels in his home removed to avoid that fate. Second, he asks his students to prepare a chair for the arrival of Hezekiah, the long-deceased king of Judea. What is the meaning of each of these requests?[14]

Probably the best way to understand the first request is that it emerges from R. Yoḥanan ben Zakkai's struggles with his past as he encounters death, the central theme of this chapter. Just what will his legacy be? Will it be a legacy of purity or impurity? Did he make the correct decision during his confrontation with Vespasian? R. Yoḥanan ben Zakkai asked his students to remove all vessels from his home before he dies, so that none will become impure, so that, symbolically, only purity will reign following his departure from the world. It is no accident that he makes this request of his students, for they more than anyone else are the bearers of his legacy. With one foot in this world

14. See the commentaries in the *Ein Yaakov* for various explanations, which this reader, at least, does not find wholly satisfying.

and one foot in the next, he petitions them to ensure that his will be a pure legacy for the eternal future. What a poignant request for the man most responsible for rebuilding Jewish life after the destruction of Jerusalem and the Temple.

Perhaps even more puzzling is his second and final request, that his students prepare a chair for Hezekiah. Why Hezekiah? What is his role? Why a chair? Rashi suggests that Hezekiah will accompany R. Yoḥanan ben Zakkai to the World to Come. But why does R. Yoḥanan ben Zakkai require accompaniment, and why specifically Hezekiah? And if his role is to accompany R. Yoḥanan ben Zakkai, then why does he need a chair?

Hezekiah was famous as one of the greatest kings in Jewish history, about whom the author of the book of Kings asserts: "He trusted in the Lord God of Israel, so that after him was none like him among all the kings of Judah, nor among them that were before him."[15] Hezekiah enacted a series of religious reforms which saved Jews from religious, and therefore national, disaster. R. Yoḥanan ben Zakkai too enacted a series of religious reforms following the destruction of the Temple which saved Jews from religious, and therefore national, disaster. The parallels are obvious. Yet Hezekiah was not the only great religious reformer among the kings: so too was Josiah. Why then does R. Yoḥanan ben Zakkai single out Hezekiah?

One event in Hezekiah's life seems especially relevant to R. Yoḥanan ben Zakkai. Assyria threatened Judea, and captured a number of its fortified cities. Hezekiah sought to appease Assyria and paid a substantial tribute, even stripping gold from the doors of the very Temple to come up with the sum necessary. All this was to no avail, however, because Assyria nevertheless chose to attack. Hezekiah prays to God, the prophet Isaiah predicts that God will miraculously defeat the Assyrian armies, which He eventually does, and the Jews are saved from imminent destruction.

Hezekiah first sought to save his people by appeasement, and even did so at the Temple's expense, stripping gold from its doors, but that attempt at appeasement was a miserable failure. R. Yoḥanan ben

15. II Kings 18:5.

Zakkai too sought to save his people by appeasement, sacrificing the very Temple to do so. Would his appeasement also end in failure? Did he, like Hezekiah, make the wrong decision? Yet here is the crucial point. Despite that failure, Hezekiah, his people, Jerusalem, and the Temple, were eventually saved by miraculous divine intervention. An angel arrives in the dark of night and destroys the Assyrian army encampment, which by morning is a field littered with corpses. God chooses to protect Hezekiah and the Jews, despite Hezekiah's misbegotten plan to appease the enemy.

This then may be why R. Yoḥanan ben Zakkai invited Hezekiah. Hezekiah modeled a failed appeaser whom God nevertheless chose to redeem. R. Yoḥanan ben Zakkai at his deathbed confronted what he feared were his own failures in appeasing the Romans, requesting Yavneh rather than Jerusalem. If Hezekiah could be redeemed, then perhaps, just perhaps, he too could be redeemed as well. He invited Hezekiah to accompany him to the World to Come, because Hezekiah better than anyone else modeled failed, yet eventually redeemed, leadership. Who could better advocate for R. Yoḥanan ben Zakkai as he approached final judgment before God than Hezekiah himself? This, too, is the meaning of the mysterious chair. Hezekiah must first sit, exactly as a king does, on his throne, for Hezekiah remains the great king despite his failures, and he must be seated like one. Hezekiah must first sit and demonstrate that he has been redeemed, before he can take on the task of redeeming another leader who feared for his failure, so many centuries his junior, and who will now face God in the World to Come.

The aggada ends here, but the reader is left to wonder just what transpired following R. Yoḥanan ben Zakkai's death. Did he follow the path to the Garden of Eden, or to Gehenna? The Talmud cites the following teaching about Hezekiah:

> **Rabbi Tanḥum says** that **bar Kappara taught in Tzippori**.... **The Holy One, Blessed be He, sought to designate** King **Hezekiah** as the **Messiah and** to designate **Sennacherib** and Assyria, respectively, as **Gog and Magog,** all from the prophecy of Ezekiel with regard to the end of days (**Ezekiel, chapter 38**), and the confrontation between them would culminate in the final

> redemption. **The attribute of justice said before the Holy One, Blessed be He: Master of the Universe, and if** with regard to **David, king of Israel, who recited several songs and praises before You, You did not designate him** as the **Messiah,** then with regard to **Hezekiah, for whom You performed all these miracles,** delivering him from Sennacherib and healing his illness, **and he did not recite praise before You, will You designate him** as the **Messiah?**[16]

According to Bar Kappara, a third-century scholar and student of R. Yehuda HaNasi, compiler of the Mishna, Hezekiah possessed all the attributes of the Messiah, and with him the Messianic Era would have begun, but for one failure: Hezekiah neglected to sing praises of God for the miracles He had performed for him. Why did Hezekiah fail to sing praises of God? Was it because he felt plagued by guilt over his abject and failed attempt to appease the Assyrians at the cost of stripping the Temple doors of gold and dishonoring God? We cannot know for sure.

In any case, R. Yoḥanan ben Zakkai lived several centuries before Bar Kappara, and even if Bar Kappara's teaching had circulated long before it was attributed to him, there is still no evidence that R. Yoḥanan ben Zakkai himself knew of it, although of course it is possible that he did. In any case, I wish to imagine a denouement to our aggada inspired by Bar Kappara's teaching, an account of that final pathos-filled encounter between Hezekiah and R. Yoḥanan ben Zakkai, and about R. Yoḥanan ben Zakkai's fate following his death. This ahistorical conjecture is not grounded in any evidence from the text itself, and might best be described as a flight of fancy. Yet to this reader it is an apt denouement to R. Yoḥanan ben Zakkai's life, a finale that rings if not of an interpretive truth, then a deeply poetic one.

I imagine the following scene: The souls of Hezekiah and R. Yoḥanan ben Zakkai together approach the heavenly court, Hezekiah a failed messiah, and R. Yoḥanan ben Zakkai beset by fears that he too was a failed messiah. Neither could sing praises of God in life, because each feared they had failed Him. In death, Hezekiah had looked back

16. Sanhedrin 94a.

upon his life with all its great achievements, and had come to affirm those achievements for what they were, compromised, yet nevertheless magnificent. That is why he could, finally, come and sit in the chair – the throne – that R. Yoḥanan ben Zakkai had called him to. R. Yoḥanan ben Zakkai sensed this, which is why he envisioned Hezekiah's presence at his death, in the chair. For it is R. Yoḥanan ben Zakkai's own chair in which Hezekiah sat. R. Yoḥanan ben Zakkai hoped that Hezekiah could, on this final journey, help to heal him, could lead him to a successful divine judgment, could enable him too to sit on a throne, the culmination of a life devoted to the flourishing of the Jewish people following the destruction of the Temple.

On this final journey, Hezekiah does lead R. Yoḥanan ben Zakkai to self-acceptance, and R. Yoḥanan ben Zakkai now comes to terms with the life he led. As they approach the heavenly court, Hezekiah begins to sing the praises of God that eluded him in life, and R. Yoḥanan ben Zakkai joins him, haltingly at first, but then with more and more strength. The two of them on that long-shared journey to heaven join together finally in powerful song, praising the God they had served so faithfully, even if imperfectly, throughout their lives. Redemption at long last is theirs.

Chapter 8

Who Is Responsible for the Breakdown of a Marriage? R. Meir Lectures, a Wife Attends, and a Husband Is Angry

Leviticus Rabba 9:9[1]

INTRODUCTION

Marital relationships are complex indeed, and a third party to that relationship can amplify this complexity beyond all expectations, even if the third party is a distinguished scholar doing no more than delivering a public lecture. The aggada which is the subject of this chapter explores one unhappy marriage, and leads its reader to reflect about who bears responsibility for the failure of that marriage. As with many unhappy marriages there is ample blame to go around, but this aggada subtly

1. Or in some editions, 7:37.

suggests a far broader canvas for the assessment of blame, in surprising and profound ways.

Both the husband and wife are anonymous; we never learn their names or true identities. The only named figure in the aggada is that of R. Meir, the towering second-century *Tanna* whose teachings dominate the Talmud. As we shall see, he plays a pivotal role in the story, and the author's take on R. Meir's role illuminates his challenging theology. The aggada is not found in the Talmud but rather in Leviticus Rabba, an early collection of midrashim compiled during the late amoraic period, approximately 400–650 CE.

Like many midrashim, the story is prefaced by a prologue and concludes with an epilogue, in this case both the same teaching attributed to R. Yishmael: "Great is peace, for regarding the Great Name that was written in holiness, The Holy One, blessed be He, said: 'Let it be erased into the water in order to promote peace between a man and his wife!'" The reference here is to the laws of *sota,* a woman suspected by her husband of adultery. To ascertain her guilt or innocence, the Torah requires the accused wife to drink from a potion consisting of water mixed with the ink derived from erased words of the Torah, words which include God's name. Reconciliation between husband and wife is of such paramount importance that even God's name must be erased to achieve it. This teaching frames the story, whose purpose is to provide a living example of its import.

תָּנֵי רַבִּי יִשְׁמָעֵאל גָּדוֹל שָׁלוֹם שֶׁשֵּׁם הַגָּדוֹל שֶׁנִּכְתַּב בִּקְדֻשָּׁה אָמַר הַקָּדוֹשׁ בָּרוּךְ הוּא יִמָּחֶה בַּמַּיִם כְּדֵי לְהַטִּיל שָׁלוֹם בֵּין אִישׁ לְאִשְׁתּוֹ. רַבִּי מֵאִיר הֲוָה יָתִיב וְדָרִישׁ בְּלֵילֵי שַׁבַּתָּא הֲוָה תַּמָּן חֲדָא אִתְּתָא יַצִּיבָא וְשָׁמְעָה לֵיהּ תָּנְתָא מִדְרָשָׁא, אַמְתִּינַת עַד דִּיחֲסַל מִמִּדְרָשׁ, אָזְלָה לְבֵיתָהּ אַשְׁכְּחָא בּוּצִינָא טָפֵי, אֲמַר לָהּ בַּעְלָהּ אָן הֲוֵית, אָמְרָה לֵיהּ אֲנָא יָתִיבָא וְשָׁמְעָה קָלֵיהּ דָּרוֹשָׁה, אֲמַר לָהּ כֵּן וְכֵן לָא אִעַּיְלַתְּ לְהָכָא עַד דַּאֲזַלְתְּ וְרוֹקַת בְּאַנְפֵּי דָּרוֹשָׁה,

R. Yishmael taught: Great is peace, for regarding the Great Name that was written in holiness, the Holy One, Blessed be He, said: "Let it be erased into water, in order to promote peace between man and his wife!" R. Meir would sit and lecture on Midrash on Friday nights. Once a certain woman was standing there and she was listening to him learning Midrash. She waited until [R. Meir] concluded. [After he had lectured,] she went to her home and she found the candle extinguished due to the lateness of the hour. Her husband asked her, "Where were you?!" She answered him, "I was sitting and listening to the voice of the Midrash-lecturer." He said to her, "Such and such shall happen to me so that you shall not come here (i.e., into my house), until you go and spit in the face of the Midrash-lecturer!"

יְתִיבָא שַׁבַּתָּא קַמַּיְיתָא תִּנְיָנָא וּתְלִיתָא, אֲמָרִין לָהּ מְגֵירָתָא כַּדּוּ אַתּוּן צְהִיבִין, אֲתֵינָן עִמָּךְ לְגַבֵּי דָּרוֹשָׁה, כֵּיוָן דְּחָמֵי יַתְהוֹן רַבִּי מֵאִיר צָפָה בְּרוּחַ הַקֹּדֶשׁ, אֲמַר לְהוֹ אִית מִנְּכוֹן אִתְּתָא דְּחַכִּימָא לְמִלְחַשׁ בְּעֵינָא, אֲמָרִין לָהּ מְגֵירָתָא כַּדּוּ אַתְּ אָזְלַת וְרוֹקַת בְּאַנְפֵּיהּ וְתִשְׁרֵי לְבַעֲלָךְ, כֵּיוָן דְּיָתְבָא קַמֵּי אִידְחִילַת מִינֵּיהּ, אֲמָרָה לֵיהּ רַבִּי לֵית אֲנָא חַכִּימָא לְמִילְחַשׁ עֵינָא, אֲמַר לָהּ אֲפִלּוּ הָכֵי רוֹקִי בְּאַנְפֵּי שְׁבַע זִמְנִין וַאֲנָא מִינְשִׁים, עָבְדָה הָכִין. אֲמַר לָהּ אִיזִילִי אִמְרִי לְבַעֲלִיךְ אַתְּ אֲמַרְתְּ חָדָא זִימְנָא וַאֲנָא רָקִית שְׁבַע זִימְנִין.

So, she sat [outside the house] for a first week, a second week, and a third week. [Eventually,] her neighbors said to her, "You are still in a state of anger with each other?! We will go with you to the Midrash-lecturer." [And so they went to find a solution to her predicament.] When R. Meir saw them, he perceived through the Divine Spirit all that had occurred. He asked them, "Is there a woman among you who is proficient in chanting incantations regarding the eye for one whose eye is ailing?" [The woman's] neighbors said to her, "Now you can go and spit in his face and be permitted to your husband!" And so the woman went and sat before R. Meir in order to recite incantations and spit into his eye. When she sat before him, she became frightened of him. "Rabbi, I am not really proficient in chanting incantations regarding the eye." He responded to her, "Even so, spit in my face seven times and I will be healed." She did so. He said to her, "Go tell your husband, 'You said to spit at the lecturer one time, and I spit seven times!'"

אָמְרוּ לוֹ תַּלְמִידָיו רַבִּי כָּךְ מְבַזִּין אֶת הַתּוֹרָה, לָא הֲוָה לָךְ לְמֵימַר לְחַד מִינָּן לְמִלְחַשׁ לָךְ, אֲמַר לְהוֹ לָא דַּיּוֹ לְמֵאִיר לִהְיוֹת שָׁוֶה לְקוֹנוֹ, דְּתָנֵי רַבִּי יִשְׁמָעֵאל

גָּדוֹל שָׁלוֹם שֶׁשֵּׁם הַגָּדוֹל שֶׁנִּכְתַּב בִּקְדֻשָּׁה אָמַר הַקָּדוֹשׁ בָּרוּךְ הוּא יִמָּחֶה עַל הַמַּיִם בִּשְׁבִיל לְהַטִּיל שָׁלוֹם בֵּין אִישׁ לְאִשְׁתּוֹ.

[R. Meir's] students asked him, "Rebbe, do we disgrace the Torah this way? Should you not have told one of us to chant incantations and spit for you?" He responded to them, "Is it not enough for Meir to be equal to his Creator?! For R Yishmael taught: Great is peace, for regarding the Great Name that was written in holiness, the Holy One, blessed be He, said: 'Let it be erased into the water in order to promote peace between a man and his wife!'"

A MARRIAGE BREAKS DOWN

The story begins by relating that R. Meir delivered a Torah lecture[2] one Friday night, and a woman stood in the audience listening. On the face of it, this is unlikely to have been a common occurrence. After all, how many wives in tannaitic times left home on Friday night to attend a Torah lecture, and one delivered by a towering scholar no less than R. Meir?[3] Why did this particular woman engage is such unusual behavior? In all likelihood, part of the answer is that she was genuinely interested in more Torah knowledge. Yet, as the story unfolds it becomes evident that there was considerable tension between husband and wife. It must be remembered that the lecture took place on a Friday night. Whether or not the

2. The text uses the term "*derasha*," sometimes translated as a sermon, but that has modern connotations the original text would not have had.

3. This has been the long-standing view of the preponderance of scholars, although one recently questioned by Judith Hauptman, in "A New View of Women and Torah Study in the Talmudic Period," JSLI 9 (2010): 249–292. Whatever the merits of her arguments, even the evidence she cites does not include other examples of women attending formal public Torah lectures like we find here. (Of course, R. Meir's own extraordinary wife, Bruriah, might well have done so, but again there is no evidence to that effect.) Note that R. Meir was particularly gifted in the use of parables for his teachings, and his *derashot* typically consisted of one-third halakha, one-third aggada, and one-third parables. It is therefore possible that even the less educated could appreciate the non-halakhic portions of his teachings, which might have included women as well as men. See Sanhedrin 38b and Mishna Sota 9:16. However, to my knowledge, there is no other reference to women attending R. Meir's lectures.

Shabbat meal still awaited, one mitzva surely awaited, and that was the mitzva of *ona,* the obligation upon a husband to have marital relations with his wife, often reserved for Friday night.[4] As the story unfolds, it becomes evident that there was considerable tension between husband and wife. One wonders if the wife consciously or unconsciously sought escape to the study hall from a relationship she did not relish.

Whatever her motivations, she was listening to the lecture, which overextended its usual time.[5] After waiting until R. Meir finished, she eventually returned home, to a darkened house. It was by then so late that the candles she had lit for Shabbat were extinguished. Surely that is an ill omen.

Her husband asks her where she had been all this time. She responds that she had been sitting and listening to the voice of the lecturer. In obvious anger, the husband bans her from their home until she spits in the face of the person who delivered the lecture. The husband in this relationship possesses all the power, not uncharacteristic of the era in which they lived, and his wife submits. Thus, their relationship breaks down. Let us remember that at least according to the Talmud, one reason for the obligation to light candles is to create an atmosphere of peace in the home.[6] The candles were extinguished, and with them, symbolically, peace in the home was extinguished as well.

Of course, the intense anger the husband expresses is not likely to have erupted for the very first time here. Would a husband ban his wife from the home if their relationship had been a good one? Rather, it is probable that their relationship had long been troubled, and that her late night out in the study hall was the final catalyst for its complete

---

4. Ketubot 62b. This is an early amoraic teaching, and refers specifically to scholars. Nevertheless, the logic of the teaching (see, e.g., *Shita Mekubetzet,* ad loc., and Maimonides, *Mishneh Torah, Laws of Shabbat,* 30:14), that enjoying Shabbat is a mitzva and marital relations are enjoyable, would apply to all.
5. While the exact meaning of the text itself is unclear, most commentators, and other variants of the midrash, assume that it means the lecture overextended its usual time. For a summary, see the commentary of the *Eitz Yosef,* ad.loc.
6. Shabbat 25b. Rashi s.v. *Hadlakat Ner Shabbat* explains that people stumble in the dark, hardly a peaceable experience and, according to one textual variant in Rashi, eat in darkness as well, no doubt depressing too. (See *Hagahot HaBaḥ,* ad loc.)

breakdown. Why? We can only conjecture, as the text itself does not say. Perhaps he resented her interest in Torah study, which reflected poorly on his own lack thereof. She who was not obligated in Torah study spent Friday night in the study hall; he who was obligated in Torah study spent the evening at home. Perhaps, too, he impatiently awaited his wife for the marital intimacies recommended for Friday nights.

In any case, two unexpected linguistic turns in the story thus far catch the reader's attention. First, the midrash reports that the wife had stood listening to the lecture, but she herself reports to her husband that she had been sitting and listening to the lecture. Why the shift in posture? Was she sitting or standing? An answer to this question may be reflected in what posture conveys. What is the difference between someone standing at a lecture and someone sitting? One difference may be the extent to which the listener is viewed by herself and others as part of the audience. Imagine someone standing in the back of a lecture hall, versus someone sitting in the middle of the crowd. The person standing is less part of the experience, and less part of the assembled students ensconced in their chairs, fixtures of the study hall. To sit with a group is to be part of the group, whereas to stand while everyone else is sitting is to be isolated, on the way out or in, a transient observer.

On this reading, in reality she was standing, not really part of the group of listeners. This is hardly surprising, since she may well have been the only female in attendance. It would surely have been unseemly in ancient times for a woman to sit amongst the men at a public Torah lecture. But that is not what she reported to her husband. Rather, she wished to convey to him that she really belonged at the lecture, was sitting established, a full member of the audience. In a preemptive strike, she in effect meant to signal to him that she was not a mere dilettante, not someone escaping the home. Just the reverse. She was a serious student, part of the community of serious students. In so doing, she hoped to justify her absence to a husband she correctly expected would be fuming. Clearly, this stratagem was an abject failure. One wonders if it made matters even worse. Perhaps the last thing this husband wanted was a diligent Torah student for a wife, who prioritizes the study hall over the home.

A second linguistic oddity is her claim that she was listening to the "voice of the lecturer." Why the voice? Why not just say she was listening to the lecturer, or to the lecture? What is the significance of his voice? Two answers suggest themselves. First, it is possible that she could not see R. Meir, that she only heard his voice, because she was standing (or sitting) in a location from which her line of sight was blocked. As a woman attending a lecture designed primarily for men, she may have been constrained to locate herself outside the lecture hall proper, or on its very fringes. This reading would undercut the interpretation proposed above, that she wanted to communicate to her husband that she was part of the community of students, not marginalized by them.

A second reading suggests itself as well, one consistent with that interpretation, and one which assumes that her use of the term "voice" was more unconscious than conscious. Let us remember that the lecturer in question was none other than R. Meir, a brilliant, creative scholar of the first order, whose impact on the world of Torah scholarship in that era, and beyond, is incalculable. Moreover, R. Meir was noteworthy for his affirmation of the value of women who become Torah scholars like his remarkable wife Bruriah. No doubt this female student would have known all this. What then was she listening to? To the Torah he taught, or to his voice, a voice that would convey his status, charisma, and respect for deserving women? Put differently, was she attentive to the lecture, or to the lecturer?

Consider, by way of example, the Talmud's comments about Moses, cited separately in the names of R. Yonatan and of Shmuel bar Yitzḥak. These authorities suggest, no doubt hyperbolically, that every man suspected Moses of committing adultery with his wife.[7] The question is what lies behind the hyperbole? What could it even mean to assert that every man suspected his wife of dallying with Moses, of all people? The commentators struggle with this question.[8] I would suggest that one more than plausible reading of this enigmatic passage is that these husbands suspected that Moses' charisma, his force of personality, and

7. Sanhedrin 110a.
8. For a summary of the many explanations, see the *Metivta* edition of the Talmud, ad loc., p. 235.

his deep wisdom inspired wives at their husbands' expense. Charismatic teachers, even unintentionally, may evoke feelings in students, dangerously complicating the relationship between teacher and student, and consequently between student and spouse.[9] The husbands in question took Moses to be a competitor for their wives' respect and admiration, and they suspected Moses – of course falsely – of exploiting that charisma and power to his own ends. Or so the Talmud maintains.

One wonders if a similar dynamic might have been at play in our midrash. The husband was furious not merely because she was late, but because he suspected his wife of harboring too much admiration for the lecturer, whom her husband took to be a competitor for his wife's respect. Indeed, this is a suspicion she perhaps unwittingly confirmed when she reported to him that she had listened to the "voice" of the lecturer, not to the lecture itself. One wonders, too, if his wife used the words she did precisely as he suspected, expressing verbally what she may not have consciously acknowledged, even to herself. On this reading, the husband may not have been too far off the mark, as despicable as his behavior was. As we shall soon see, this is a crucial motif in the aggada, already disclosed in the husband's reaction. What, after all, is the significance of spitting in the face of the teacher? Of all things the husband could have demanded, why this? If he wanted her to embarrass and degrade R. Meir, other means were at his disposal. For example, he could have insisted that she throw a shoe at him, an ancient symbol of disgrace referred to in Psalms.[10] Why then did he demand that she spit in his face?

Not surprisingly, she hesitates to obey his ultimatum, and sits outside the house for three weeks. Interestingly, she does not go to the home of a family member or friend, but remains outside her own home, in a very public exile. Why does she do so? Does she thereby mean to acknowledge that she is at least partially to blame for the failure of her marriage, for which reason she punishes herself through self-exile and public shaming? Notice that the verb the midrash uses is that she "sits"

9. Widely reported clergy sexual abuse would be an example of this phenomenon, except, of course, that in those cases the clergy failed, succumbing to temptation.
10. Psalms 60:8.

outside the house, exactly the same verb she used to describe her "sitting" (*yativa*) at the lecture. Sitting outside the house may be precise penance for sitting at the lecture. One wonders if this was a subtle, even unconscious, *cri de coeur* (cry from the heart). Her marriage was crumbling. Can anyone help her redeem it?

A MARRIAGE REPAIRED?

Indeed, this is exactly what transpires. Her neighbors notice, and respond with a challenge to her: "How long will the two of you remain angry at one another?" They propose that she go to R. Meir and spit in his face, exactly as her husband had demanded, and they very kindly offer to accompany her on this distasteful journey, providing her with emotional support. Notice that the neighbors place the onus for saving the marriage upon her, not him. Is this because they have no access to him? Or is it because in ancient times, and indeed perhaps beyond, wives more than husbands bore the burden of maintaining a healthy marriage?

R. Meir saw them approach and, the midrash reports, looked with the "holy spirit" (*ru'aḥ hakodesh*), and thereby assessed immediately what he must do. He asked the approaching women if any amongst them possessed skill in healing an ailing eye, which, as will be evident, is accomplished by administering saliva. All this is described in a single sentence in the midrash, in which the motif of seeing appears no less than three times. First, R. Meir sees the women approach. Second, R. Meir looks with the holy spirit. Third and finally, he seeks a cure for his ailing eye, the locus of human vision. There can be no doubt that the motif of vision is crucial. Why?

Perhaps because this midrash aims to question the adequacy of R. Meir's own vision, as great as he was. Did he notice that his lecture lasted too long, and did he look at the faces of the audience to properly assess if there was any negative impact to his over-extended lecture? Who was R. Meir looking at? The interests of his audience, or his own personal and perfectly appropriate interest, namely, to expound the Torah he knew so well, great teacher that he was, without full consideration of its consequences for the audience? After all, if R. Meir had focused his "vision" on the other, he might have "observed" that long speeches on

Friday night might be unwelcome by some. And did he see the woman in the audience – the ultimate other amongst a sea of men – rapt with attention, but perhaps making a long-waiting husband very unhappy?

Vision, the midrash suggests, must be directed outward, and not inward. And, one might ask, did R. Meir take even the slightest pleasure in the approving and respectful glances of his audience who absorbed the Torah he loved, and loved to teach? That is perfectly natural, and it is possible that R. Meir did too, even if only with the barest hint of pleasure. Indeed, on this reading, R. Meir's call to cure his eye was not merely a ruse to create peace between husband and wife. Rather, R. Meir, saintly as he was, now understood that his eyes, his vision, really did require a cure, a cure which could emanate only from the person harmed the most by their misdirection. While the average person might not even have perceived any failure at all, R. Meir, by his own lofty standards, did, a manifestation of his moral greatness.

Note that R. Meir is portrayed here as possessing a holy spirit which prophetically informs him of the background behind the visit of this entourage of female supplicants, further confirmation of his greatness. But what is the nature of this holy spirit? Of course, the Talmud may well believe that a man as extraordinary as R. Meir would indeed possess quasi-prophetic status.

Yet a more naturalistic reading is also available. It is altogether likely that R. Meir had noticed a woman in his audience during that fateful Friday night lecture, and when he saw her approaching with her friends, recognized her immediately. This may have triggered in R. Meir a realization that his lecture had gone on too long, and may have brought to the surface an undercurrent of remorse over its consequences. When he saw her, he sensed in a flash what had happened, and took immediate action to address the problem. This is the voice of his conscience, highly developed in a great man like R. Meir, through which God speaks to human beings. On this reading the holy spirit is in all of us, provided we are attuned to the call of our conscience.[11]

11. Of course, this "naturalistic" reading does not fully account for R. Meir's knowledge about the details of the falling out between husband and wife, notably the husband's demand that she spit in the face of the lecturer. Nevertheless, it provides

The neighbors immediately pick up on this cue, and encourage the wife to spit in R. Meir's face. This would cure his ailing eye, and cure her ailing marriage, a marriage ailing precisely because of R. Meir's eye, because of his misdirected vision. Not surprisingly, the wife, "sitting before R. Meir," is too frightened to do so, and asserts that she possesses no skill in curing eyes. Ironically, now she truly does sit before R. Meir, like all the other students did at the lecture, but here she is immobilized by fear. One might say that he has struck the fear of God in her, for R. Meir was the great teacher of God's Torah, His emissary to her. R. Meir nevertheless insists that she spit in his eye a total of seven times, and, he says, "I will be healed."

The wife finally obeys, and spits in R. Meir's eyes seven times. R. Meir then tells her to return to her husband and report that while he had insisted she spit once in R. Meir's face, she went so far as to spit seven times in his face. Surely this would persuade the husband that she is loyal only to him! While the midrash does not say so explicitly, presumably that is exactly what she did.

A new set of characters now appears in the midrash, R. Meir's students, a kind of midrashic Greek chorus. They vehemently object to R. Meir's strategy on the grounds that it debases the Torah. How could the great Torah scholar R. Meir encourage a woman to spit in his face? To spit in R. Meir's face is to spit at the Torah itself.[12] R. Meir's response brings us back to the prologue of the midrash, and constitutes its epilogue. He cites the teaching of R. Yishmael: "Great is peace, for regarding the Great [is]...erased into the water in order to promote peace between a man and his wife!'" Should the honor due to R. Meir be any greater than the honor due to God? If God's name must be erased to bring peace between husband and wife, surely R. Meir could tolerate a little saliva in his eye.

---

a more naturalistic account of how he might have intuited what happened, either with some divine assistance, or by virtue of his knowledge of the men of his era, or by virtue of his intuition that this whole event replicated *sota*, and so would therefore involve water in his face. This may also be an expression of the artifice of the author of the midrash.

12. Kiddushin 32b.

This conclusion illuminates the themes of the midrash. First, consider the difference between R. Meir and his students. They focus on the respect owed the Torah. Of course, that is not wrong in itself, for the Torah and Torah scholars indeed must be respected. But respect is but one value, and not the only one. Sometimes the obligation to respect is trumped by another greater obligation, and that is the obligation to bring peace between a husband and a wife. The students saw the world of obligation in hues of black and white, while R. Meir understood the world of obligation in shades of gray. Sometimes one obligation, as important as it may be, is overridden by other obligations, even if the result appears sacrilegious. And that is because the appearance of sacrilege does not in itself constitute sacrilege. Just the opposite: It would be sacrilegious to insist on one's honor if what is at stake is the relationship between husband and wife. R. Meir thus taught his students a vital lesson about the complexity of moral and religious obligations.[13]

The concluding teaching which cites the ritual of *sota* is crucial. We had asked earlier why the husband chose spitting as a means of debasing the lecturer. The answer is now at hand: Saliva stands in for the waters of the *sota*. Just as God's name is erased with water, so too R. Meir's eye is "erased" with saliva. This is exactly why R. Meir, from his perspective, insisted that the wife spit in his face, despite her natural reluctance to do so. Moreover, this may well have been the intention of the husband in insisting that she spit in the face of the lecturer. This was his way of alluding to the *sota* context of the whole episode, to a wife who listened too intently to the "voice" of the lecturer. He suspected her of disloyalty to him, and he suspected the lecturer of eliciting that disloyalty.

The husband's suspicions were, of course, greatly exaggerated. Yet R. Meir, moral giant that he was, realized that he himself needed some kind of healing, a word he uses himself. Now we have every reason to believe that R. Meir's shortcomings, such as they were, were

13. This is consistent with R. Meir's general valorization of all who make peace between any two people, not only between husband and wife. See Gittin 52a. Note too R. Meir's stress on the value of humility in Mishna *Pirkei Avot* 4:3: "Have humility before everyone." Surely permitting a woman to spit in one's face for the greater good is a remarkable expression of the virtue of humility.

shortcomings only for a man of R. Meir's exceptional stature. He was excessively hard on himself precisely because of his moral stature, precisely because he was capable of the most ruthless self-criticism, virtues of which most of us fall lamentably short. That said, R. Meir did seek healing, and only the woman he harmed could be his healer.

This then constitutes an ironic inversion, for let us recall that the wife approaches R. Meir to heal her marriage, but this healing could come about only if R. Meir himself, who unwittingly harmed her marriage, is himself healed. Only R. Meir could heal their marriage by first expiating his own shortcomings, by confessing to his role, however slight, in the breakdown of the marriage. And only the wife, driven from her home by loyalty to R. Meir's lecture could in turn heal R. Meir, by spitting in his face, thus vividly demonstrating to him his own role in her suffering. Surely that is true beyond the midrash's narrative itself, for in life generally, interpersonal harms can best be healed only by the parties themselves.

We must now consider the duality of R. Meir's role in this midrash. On the one hand, we have argued that within the framework of *sota* he is analogous to the adulterer. Yet on the other hand, R. Meir compares himself to God in the same framework of *sota,* for just as God's name is erased, so too R. Meir's face is erased by the saliva of the wife. What then is R. Meir's role in the midrash? Is he analogous to God, or is he analogous to the adulterer? To complicate this question further, R. Meir takes responsibility for his role in the breakdown of the marriage and seeks healing through the wife who spits in his face. What about God? If the analogy between R. Meir and God is strict, then does God take responsibility too?

Of course, it is possible that the midrash did not mean the analogy to be strict, and that it breaks down on the status of divine responsibility for the failure of human marriages. That is, the midrash may mean to draw the analogy between God and R. Meir in one direction only, from God to R. Meir, and not the reverse. R. Meir is indeed like God in that just like God's name is erased, so too R. Meir must allow his face to be "erased" as well. However, God is not like R. Meir, in that only R. Meir takes responsibility for his shortcomings, but God assumes no responsibility for the failure of the marriage.

Having said that, everything else about this midrash is so precise, so carefully wrought, that I find this approach less likely. The midrash itself uses a very strong term to describe the analogy between God and R. Meir, that they are "equal," which suggests bi-directionality, and this bi-directionality in turn leads to a much richer reading of the midrash, if perhaps not the only one. Such a reading would evoke a profound theological question: What is the role of God in the failure of a marriage? In classical Judaism, God exercises providential governance over the world He created. R. Akiva, the primary teacher of R. Meir, is reported to have taught:

> A person should accustom himself to saying that all that God does, He does for the best. R. Akiva was walking along the road and came to a certain city, he inquired about lodging, and they did not give him any. He said: Everything that God does, He does for the good. He went and slept in a field, and he had with him a rooster, a donkey, and a candle. A gust of wind came and extinguished the candle; a cat came and ate the rooster; and a lion came and ate the donkey. He said: Everything that God does, He does for the best. That night an army came and took the city into captivity. [If the candle had still been lit, if the noisy rooster and donkey had still been alive, they would have given away his location to the invaders (Rashi, ad loc.).] He said to them: Didn't I tell you? Everything that God does, He does for the best.[14]

God is depicted as exercising intimate providential governance over the life of R. Akiva. While there are varying views of divine providence in rabbinic literature, it would be natural for R. Meir to follow his great teacher in this matter.[15] If God indeed exercises such providence, what about His role in human marriages? According to one famous tannaitic tradition, God spends his time arranging them.[16] But if God's providence extends to the arranging of marriages, what then of God's responsibility for failed ones?

---

14. Berakhot 60b–61a.
15. See E. Urbach, *Ḥazal: Pirkei Emunot VeDeot* (Jerusalem, 1975), ch. 11.
16. See, e.g., Genesis Rabba 68:4.

While belief in freedom of choice is a crucial one in rabbinic sources,[17] and human beings make free choices both in whom they marry and how they conduct themselves in marriage, God's role is hardly negligible. How this tension is to be sorted out is well beyond the scope of this volume, but it seems clear that according to many classical sources, including R. Meir's own teacher, God might well bear at least some responsibility for marital failure. One approach to understanding the respective roles of God, husband, and wife might be this: God orchestrates events so that a man meets and falls in love with a woman who will become his wife. Their marriage eventually turns toxic and ends in divorce. While God orchestrated the events leading up to their marriage, nevertheless it was they who made the fateful choices to marry and to conduct themselves during their marriage as they did. There is then more than enough blame for the marriage's failure to go around.

However we are to understand this, if God plays a role in the formation of marriages, then He might well bear some responsibility for their success or failure. Our midrash would understand the erasure of God's name from the Torah as a kind of painful divine expiation of His responsibility for the breakdown of a marriage caught in the throes of the *sota* ritual. This then is the exact analogue to R. Meir. Both confront their respective roles in the breakdown of a marriage. This echoes the portrayal of God in the Torah, where He confronts the limitations of His own handiwork, sees the evil of which humans are capable, and regrets that He created them.[18] Marital failure is but part and parcel of the grander human failure that God so sadly observes.

---

17. Urbach, ibid. Note R. Akiva's own teaching in *Pirkei Avot* 3:19, "Permission is given," usually translated and explained as "freedom of choice is given,"
18. Genesis 6:5–7. Anthropopathic descriptions of God's pain abound in rabbinic literature. For example, in the Introduction (*Petiḥta*) to the Midrash on Lamentations, God is depicted as mourning and crying in a hidden place over the pain He experiences as a consequence of the destruction of the Temple that He Himself decreed. For a recent study of the phenomenon of God crying in rabbinic literature, see Achinoam Jacobs, *"The Description of God Crying in Rabbinic Literature: Literary, Cultural, and Ideological Aspects"* (PhD diss., Hebrew University of Jerusalem, 2016). While not the same, in our context it is worth noting the teaching in Sanhedrin 22a and Gittin 90b, that the sacrificial altar of the Temple cries when a husband divorces his first wife.

Considered from this perspective, God is responsible to some extent not only for the failure of a marriage, but in some measure, for the failure of a suspected adulterer as well. Indeed, this is exactly what He regrets in the book of Genesis, the moral breakdown of the civilization wrought by His creatures. After all, He could have chosen to create human beings less susceptible to temptation, but He did not, and the consequences of that choice for human morality throughout history have been nothing short of disastrous. God's overarching responsibility at some level encompasses a failed marriage, an adulterous man, and a wife who betrays her husband.

Now consider the role of R. Meir once again. We were troubled by his duality: Was R. Meir more like God in the midrash, or more like the adulterer? But on this reading, that duality is a false one, for God Himself is in some sense responsible for marriages, for marital breakdowns, and for adulterers. R. Meir incarnates the complex role of God in the breakdown of a marriage, as he is both divine sage and also analogous to an adulterer. This then is the deepest theological point of the narrative: God, husband, wife, and rabbi all play their own interwoven roles in the failure of this marriage, for which they all bear commensurate responsibility. The wife left her husband Friday night to attend a lecture. R. Meir over-extended the time allotted for his lecture. The husband abused his wife, evicting her from their home. God created them all, with the very human limitations that led to these disparate failures. There are many cooks who spoil the broth of human marriages, including, as it were, God Himself.

But let us also remember that the husband, wife, R. Meir, and God likewise play their interwoven roles in the rehabilitation of the marriage as well. The wife spits in R. Meir's face, exactly as her husband requested. The husband (apparently) admits his wife back into their home. R. Meir, like God, accepts responsibility for his role, and like God in the case of the *sota*, makes it possible for the couple to find healing. God and R. Meir are both humbly "erased" in the cause of marital peace.

Yet the conclusion of this midrash is not as rosy as it might first appear. For consider, again, the husband. He was abusive to his wife, kicks her out of their shared home, and insists that she undertake a ridiculous mission. His wife sits homeless on the doorstep for three weeks, and he never relents. How likely is it, after all, that a man capable of such anger and abuse will transform into a wonderful husband, even after his wife spits in the face of R. Meir? Hardly likely at all. Rather, we must assume that the wife returned to a less than perfect marriage, and to a husband one would not want for one's daughter. We are left to wonder just how repaired this marriage could ever become.

Why is this so? As God Himself observed before the great flood in Genesis, the world in which we live is an imperfect one, and when it comes to deeply troubled marriages, there are no magical potions with which to heal them. God's name is erased in the *sota* ritual to achieve peace, but a suspicious husband who does not trust his wife's fidelity and accuses her of no less a cardinal sin than adultery is likely to never fully trust her again. R. Meir's face received its share of saliva, but the wife he helped save returned to a troubled home.

"Great is peace," teaches the midrash. Why is it so great? In part because once peace dies, its fullest resurrection remains elusive, ever beyond the reach of those who grasp for it.

Chapter 9

Interpreting Fantastical Aggadot: The Giant Who Tried to Slay King David

Sanhedrin 95a

INTRODUCTION

What are we to make of aggadic narratives that tell fantastical tales, which describe events that strike the reader as entirely unlikely and abound with the miraculous? Classical interpreters of aggadot over the centuries have been divided over how best to interpret them. The aggada which is the subject of this chapter will serve as a case study into these different approaches, as it will provide a springboard into considering an alternative approach that I shall propose and elaborate upon here.

The aggada in question, a long and involved one, tells the tale of King David who, during the course of a hunt, pursues a deer into enemy territory, whereupon he is attacked by the giant Ishbibenob (hereinafter, Ishbi), brother of Goliath, whom King David had killed. Ishbi seeks to crush King David under an olive press, but the earth underneath the press miraculously hollows out to save David. In a remarkable turn of events, Avishai, King David's nephew and one of his leading warriors, senses that King David is in trouble, and he sets out to save him. His journey is miraculously shortened, and en route he is attacked by Ishbi's elderly mother who rather helplessly and indeed foolishly, flings a spindle at him, as if a mere spindle could fell a mighty warrior. Ishbi learns of Avishai's approach, plants a sword in the ground upside down, and flings David in the air, expecting him to land impaled on the sword. Avishai arrives just in time, utters God's name, and King David remains suspended in mid-air over the sword, during which he and Avishai converse. Finally, through a puzzling change of heart, King David is freed, and the two of them escape, pursued relentlessly by Ishbi, who is finally killed when informed that his mother has died.

Even this brief summary of the story conveys its fantastical quality, and many of the details not summarized here reinforce this impression. What are we to make of it? What is its significance, and why was it included in the Talmud? What are we the readers to learn from it?

In point of fact, the aggada begins not with a story, but with a message to King David from God. Our giant, Ishbi, was from the city of Nov, in Philistine territory, and for the great Sage Rav, the name of this city recalls another city by the very same name, this one not in the land of the Philistines but in the Land of Israel. Recall that when David had fled from King Saul, who was intent on murdering him, David took refuge in the city of Nov, residence of priests. When King Saul learned that the residents of Nov took David in as a refugee, so incensed was he that in revenge he murdered every resident of the city, man, woman, and child.[1] The question the Talmud takes up is the culpability of David in that slaughter, a slaughter which, the Talmud maintains, led ultimately to the death of King Saul and his three sons. Of course, King Saul bears primary responsibility, for which reason he is punished. But what about David? Should he not have suspected that King Saul would take revenge against the city? How could he have endangered them all, to save his own skin? God accuses King David: "Until when will this sin be concealed in your hand?"

God then presents David with two options: In punishment, he can submit to capture and then death at the hands of the enemy. Or, he

1. I Samuel 21–22.

can save his own life, but only if he agrees to the death of all his descendants. This bitter choice apparently recapitulates the choice David made upon entering Nov. Then too he could either have saved his own life but endangered the residents of the city and all their descendants by taking refuge in the city, or he could have forfeited his own life to the murderous King Saul, but saved the lives of the residents of this city and all their descendants by refusing to enter.[2] In this way, King David is forced to relive that fateful decision he made upon entering Nov. If he chooses to lose his own life and thereby save the lives of his descendants, then he will have de facto repented for that great failure. Not surprisingly, that is exactly what King David decides to do. This background sets the stage for the story that follows.

״וְיִשְׁבִּי בְּנֹב אֲשֶׁר בִּילִידֵי הָרָפָה וּמִשְׁקַל קֵינוֹ שְׁלֹשׁ מֵאוֹת מִשְׁקַל נְחֹשֶׁת וְהוּא חָגוּר חֲדָשָׁה וַיֹּאמֶר לְהַכּוֹת אֶת דָּוִד״ (שְׁמוּאֵל ב כא, טז). מַאי ״וְיִשְׁבִּי בְּנוֹב״? אָמַר רַב יְהוּדָה אָמַר רַב: אִישׁ שֶׁבָּא עַל עִסְקֵי נוֹב. אֲמַר לֵיהּ הַקָּדוֹשׁ בָּרוּךְ הוּא לְדָוִד: ״עַד מָתַי יְהֵיֶה עָוֹן זֶה טָמוּן בְּיָדְךָ? עַל יָדְךָ נֶהֶרְגָה נוֹב עִיר הַכֹּהֲנִים, וְעַל יָדְךָ נִטְרַד דּוֹאֵג הָאֲדוֹמִי, וְעַל יָדְךָ נֶהֶרְגוּ שָׁאוּל וּשְׁלֹשֶׁת בָּנָיו. רְצוֹנְךָ יִכְלוּ זַרְעֲךָ, אוֹ תִּמָּסֵר בְּיַד אוֹיֵב״? אָמַר לְפָנָיו: ״רִבּוֹנוֹ שֶׁל עוֹלָם! מוּטָב אֶמָּסֵר בְּיַד אוֹיֵב, וְלֹא יִכְלֶה זַרְעִי״.

Apropos the massacre of Nov, the Gemara relates: **"And Ishbibenob, who was of the sons of the giant, the weight of whose spear was three hundred shekels of brass; and he was girded with new armor and planned to slay David"** (II Samuel 21:16). The Gemara asks: **What** is the meaning of **Ishbibenob? Rav Yehuda says** that **Rav says:** This is **a man** [*ish*] **who came** to punish David **over matters of Nov. The Holy One, Blessed be He, said to David: Until when will this sin be concealed in your hand** without punishment? **Through your** actions the inhabitants of **Nov, the city of priests, were massacred, and through your** actions, **Doeg the Edomite was banished** from the World to Come, **and through your** actions **Saul and his three sons were killed.** God said to David: Your arrival in Nov

2. See Maharsha, ad loc.

and your misleading Ahimelech the priest generated the chain of events, and therefore you must be punished. You may choose the punishment. **Is it your desire** that **your descendants will cease** to exist **or** that **you will be handed to the enemy?** David **said before Him: Master of the Universe, it is preferable** that **I will be handed to the enemy and my descendants will not cease** to exist.

יוֹמָא חַד נְפַק לְשִׁכּוֹר בַּזַּאי. אֲתָא שָׂטָן וְאִידַּמֵּי לֵיהּ כְּטַבְיָא. פְּתַק בֵּיהּ גִּירָא וְלָא מַטְיֵיהּ. מָשְׁכֵיהּ עַד דְּאַמְטְיֵיהּ לְאֶרֶץ פְּלִשְׁתִּים. כִּדְחַזְיֵיהּ יִשְׁבִּי בְּנוֹב, אֲמַר: הַיְינוּ הַאי דִּקְטַלֵיהּ לְגָלְיָת אָחִי". כַּפְתֵּיהּ, קַמְטֵיהּ, אוֹתְבֵיהּ וְשַׁדְיֵיהּ תּוּתֵי בֵּי בְדַיָּיא. אִתְעֲבֵיד לֵיהּ נִיסָּא, מָכָא לֵיהּ אַרְעָא מִתּוּתֵיהּ. הַיְינוּ דִּכְתִיב (תְּהִלִּים יח, לז): "תַּרְחִיב צַעֲדִי תַחְתָּי וְלֹא מָעֲדוּ קַרְסֻלָּי".

One day David **went to hunt** with **a falcon** [*liskor bazzai*]. **Satan came and appeared to him as a deer. He shot an arrow at** the deer, **and** the arrow **did not reach it.** Satan **led** David to follow the deer **until he reached the land of the Philistines. When Ishbibenob saw** David, **he said: This is that** person **who killed Goliath, my brother. He bound him, doubled him over, and placed him** on the ground, **and** then he **cast him under** the beam **of an olive press** to crush him. **A miracle was performed for him, and the earth opened beneath him** so he was not crushed by the beam. **That is** the meaning of that **which is written: "You have enlarged my steps beneath me, that my feet did not slip"** (Psalms 18:37).

הַהוּא יוֹמָא אַפַּנְיָא דְּמַעֲלֵי שַׁבְּתָא הֲוָה, אֲבִישַׁי בֶּן צְרוּיָה הֲוָה קָא חָיֵיף רֵישֵׁיהּ בְּאַרְבְּעָא גַּרְבֵי דְּמַיָּא. חָזֵינְהוּ כִּתְמֵי דָמָא. אִיכָּא דְּאָמְרִי: אֲתָא יוֹנָה אִיטְרִיף קַמֵּיהּ: אָמַר: "כְּנֶסֶת יִשְׂרָאֵל לְיוֹנָה אִימְתִילָא: שֶׁנֶּאֱמַר: 'כַּנְפֵי יוֹנָה נֶחְפָּה בַכֶּסֶף'. שְׁמַע מִינָּהּ דָּוִד מַלְכָּא דְּיִשְׂרָאֵל בְּצַעֲרָא שָׁרֵי". אֲתָא לְבֵיתֵיהּ וְלָא אַשְׁכְּחֵיהּ. אֲמַר: "תְּנַן: 'אֵין רוֹכְבִין עַל סוּסוֹ וְאֵין יוֹשְׁבִין עַל כִּסְאוֹ וְאֵין מִשְׁתַּמְּשִׁין בְּשַׁרְבִיטוֹ'. בִּשְׁעַת הַסַּכָּנָה מַאי"? אֲתָא שְׁאֵיל בֵּי מִדְרְשָׁא. אֲמַרוּ לֵיהּ: "בִּשְׁעַת הַסַּכָּנָה שַׁפִּיר דָּמִי".רָכְבֵיהּ לְפִרְדֵּיהּ, וְקָם וַאֲזַל, קָפְצָה לֵיהּ אַרְעָא. בַּהֲדֵי דְּקָא מַסְגֵּי חַזְיֵיהּ לְעָרְפָּה אִמֵּיהּ דְּהָוֵות נָוְלָא. כִּי חֲזִיתֵיהּ

פְּסַקְתָּה לְפִילְכָּה שְׁדַתֵּיה עִילָּוֵיה. סְבָרָא לְמִקְטְלֵיה. אֲמָרָה לֵיהּ: "עֲלָם אַיְיתִי לִי פֶּלֶךְ"! פַּתְקֵיה בְּרֵישׁ מוֹחָהּ, וּקְטָלָהּ.

The Gemara relates: **That day at dusk on Shabbat eve, Avishai ben Zeruiah shampooed his hair with four jugs of water** in preparation for Shabbat. **He saw four bloodstains. There are** those **who say: A dove came and fluttered** its wings **before him.** Avishai **said: The congregation of Israel is likened to a dove, as it is stated: "You shall shine as the wings of a dove covered with silver** and her pinions with yellow gold" (Psalms 68:14); **conclude from it** that **David, king of Israel, is in a state of distress. He came to** David's **house and did not find him.** Avishai **said** that **we learned** in a mishna (22a): **One may not ride on** the king's **horse, and one may not sit on his throne, and one may not use his scepter. In a period of danger, what** is the *halakha*? **He came** and **asked** in **the study hall** what the ruling is in that situation. **They said to him: In a period of danger** one may **well** do so. **He mounted** the king's **mule and arose and went** to the land of the Philistines. **The land** miraculously **contracted for him** and he arrived quickly. **As he was progressing he saw Orpah,** Ishbibenob's **mother,** who was **spinning** thread with a spindle. **When she saw him, she removed her spindle and threw it at him, intending to kill** him. After failing to do so, **she said to** Avishai: **Young man, bring me** my **spindle. He threw** the spindle and struck her **at the top of her brain and killed her.**

כַּד חֲזְיֵיהּ יִשְׁבִּי בְּנוֹב, אֲמַר: "הָשְׁתָּא הָווּ בֵּי תְּרֵין, וְקָטְלִין לִי". פַּתְקֵיהּ לְדָוִד לְעֵילָּא, וְדָץ לֵיהּ לְרוּמְחֵיהּ, אֲמַר: "נִיפּוֹל עֲלָהּ וְנִקְטַל". אֲמַר אֲבִישַׁי שֵׁם, אוֹקְמֵיהּ לְדָוִד בֵּין שְׁמַיָּא לְאַרְעָא. וְנֵימָא לֵיהּ אִיהוּ! אֵין חָבוּשׁ מוֹצִיא עַצְמוֹ מִבֵּית הָאֲסוּרִין. אֲמַר לֵיהּ: "מַאי בָּעֵית הָכָא"? אֲמַר לֵיהּ: "הָכִי אֲמַר לִי קוּדְשָׁא בְּרִיךְ הוּא, וְהָכִי אַהְדַּרִי לֵיהּ". אֲמַר לֵיהּ: "אַפֵּיךְ צְלוֹתִיךְ. בַּר בְּרָךְ קִירָא לִיזְבּוֹן וְאַתְּ לָא תִּצְטָעֵר". אֲמַר לֵיהּ: "אִי הָכִי, סַיַּיע בַּהֲדַן". הַיְינוּ דִּכְתִיב (שְׁמוּאֵל ב׳ כא, יז): "וַיַּעֲזָר לוֹ אֲבִישַׁי בֶּן צְרוּיָה". אָמַר רַב יְהוּדָה אָמַר רַב: שֶׁעֲזָרוֹ בִּתְפִלָּה. אֲמַר אֲבִישַׁי שֵׁם וְאַחְתֵּיהּ. הֲוָה קָא רָדֵיף בַּתְרַיְיהוּ. כִּי מְטָא קוּבִּי, אָמְרִי: "קוּם בֵּיהּ". כִּי מְטָא בֵּי תְּרֵי, אָמְרִי: "בִּתְרֵי גּוּרְיָין קַטְלוּהּ לְאַרְיֵא". אָמְרִי לֵיהּ: "זִיל,

אִשְׁתַּכַּח לְעָרְפָּה אִימֵּיךְ בְּקִיבְרָא". כִּי אַדְכַּרוּ לֵיהּ שְׁמָא דְאִימֵּיהּ, כָּחַשׁ חֵילֵיהּ, וְקַטְלֵיהּ. הַיְינוּ דִכְתִיב (שְׁמוּאֵל ב׳ כא, יז): "אָז נִשְׁבְּעוּ אַנְשֵׁי דָוִד לוֹ, לֵאמֹר לֹא תֵצֵא עוֹד אִתָּנוּ לַמִּלְחָמָה וְלֹא תְכַבֶּה אֶת נֵר יִשְׂרָאֵל".

When Ishbibenob saw him, he said: Now they are two, David and Avishai, **and they will kill me. He threw David up** in the air **and stuck his spear** into the ground. **He said: Let** David **fall upon it and die. Avishai recited** a sacred **name** of God and **suspended David between heaven and earth** so that he would not fall. The Gemara asks: **And let** David **himself recite** the name of God and save himself. Why did he need Avishai? The Gemara answers: **A prisoner does not release himself from a prison** but requires someone else to release him. Similarly, one in danger is incapable of rescuing himself. Avishai **said to** David: **What do you seek here** and why did you fall into Ishbibenob's hands? David **said to him: This** is what **the Holy One, Blessed be He, said to me, and this** is what **I responded to Him;** the time to submit to my enemy has arrived. Avishai **said to him: Reverse your prayer** and pray that your descendants will cease to exist rather than that you will be handed to the enemy, in accordance with the adage that people say: **Let your son's son** be a poor peddler and **sell wax, and you will not suffer.** Do not limit your expenses to leave an inheritance for your descendants. David **said to him: If so, help me. That is** the meaning of that **which is written: "And Avishai, son of Zeruiah, came to his aid,** and smote the Philistine and killed him" (II Samuel 21:17). **Rav Yehuda says** that **Rav says:** This means **that he came to his aid in prayer. Avishai recited** another sacred **name** of God **and caused** David to **land** safely after being suspended between heaven and earth, and they fled. Ishbibenob **pursued them,** intending to kill them. **When they reached** the place named **Kuvi they said:** The name of the place is an abbreviation for the phrase meaning: **Stand** and battle **against him** [***kum beih***]. **When they reached** a place called **Bei Terei,** David and Avishai **said: With two** [***bitrei***] **cubs they killed the lion,** meaning they expected to be successful. **They said to** Ishbibenob: **Go find Orpah, your mother, in the grave. When they mentioned**

his mother's name to him and told him she died, **his strength diminished, and they killed him.** The Gemara notes: **It is** after this **that it is written: "Then David's men took an oath to him saying: You shall not go with us to war anymore and you will not douse the lamp of Israel"** (II Samuel 21:17).

ON INTERPRETING FANTASTICAL AGGADOT

Before beginning our examination of this remarkable aggada, we should consider briefly the question of methodology. How have great Jewish commentators in the past interpreted aggadot which tell stories with fantastical elements?[3] One method, the *Literalist*, takes the narratives at face value. God can perform miracles, and the stories told reflect God's miraculous interventions in human, even post-biblical, affairs. What the aggada described literally took place. This approach, especially characteristic of medieval Ashkenaz, is best evidenced by Rashi's commentary to our aggada. Everything described is taken by Rashi at face value, as if it actually transpired. Indeed, this approach represents a long and distinguished hermeneutic tradition in Judaism, although it was one rejected by many rationalists.

A second method is the *Figurative*, according to which texts are interpreted as metaphors or exaggerations. The Figurative method was frequently used during the medieval period, especially by the philosophical rationalists, like Maimonides. For example, the Talmud teaches about the messianic period that "in the future, the Land of Israel will bring forth ready baked rolls and fine woolen garments."[4] Maimonides interprets this to mean that minimal labor will be needed to produce

---

3. For a review, see M. Saperstein, *Decoding the Rabbis* (Cambridge, 1980), 1–20. He does not focus specifically on aggadot of a fantastical nature, but elements of his overview apply. As is well known, and amply discussed by Saperstein, certain distinguished authorities, especially among the *Geonim,* maintained, in the words of R. Shmuel ben Ḥofni Gaon, that "if the words of the Sages contradict reason we are not obligated to accept them" (Saperstein, p. 10). In my discussion below, I focus only on those who did not take this position, who took them to be true, and therefore offered interpretations.
4. Shabbat 30b.

food or clothing in the Messianic Era, during which the "world will follow its natural course."[5] This turn to non-literal readings of such aggadot by Maimonides derives from a scorching methodological critique he delivers against the Literalists in his Introduction to *Perek Ḥelek,* where he writes that some aggadic texts "seem so fantastic and irrational that if one were to repeat them literally, even to the uneducated, let alone to sophisticated scholars, their amazement would prompt them to ask how anyone in the world could believe such things to be true, let alone edifying." Literal readers of such aggadic sources, he writes, "destroy the glory of the Torah and extinguish its light."[6]

A third method, used by medieval rationalists, including Maimonides himself, and kabbalists as well, is the *Allegorical* method, which goes back to Philo of Alexandria. According to this method, abstract concepts, such as good or evil, are represented by concrete images, events, or personae. One of the greatest Allegorists of the Jewish tradition was R. Judah Loew ben Bezalel, the sixteenth-century chief rabbi of Prague popularly known by his acronym, the Maharal. His brilliant and innovative four-volume commentary on aggadot is one of the most comprehensive allegorical interpretations of aggadot in Jewish intellectual history.[7]

The Maharal does not disappoint the reader of our aggada, for he comments on it at great length, and his approach perfectly exemplifies the Allegorical method.[8] He begins by noting: "One can interpret the entire aggada as it sounds, that everything took place in reality, and openly." However, he then asserts, "It is more likely that this is a conceptual matter *(inyan sikhli)*."[9] By that he means that the events described did not take place in reality, but rather are a literary means to reify and convey crucial concepts through concrete narrative form. Specifically, the battle described between King David and Ishbi is the battle between good and evil. Ishbi represented the forces of evil and temptation, the Satan himself, and King David found himself in Philistine territory because

5. Saperstein cites this example, *Decoding the Rabbis,* 15.
6. Ibid.
7. *Ḥiddushei Aggadot* (London, 1960).
8. Ibid., vol. 3, 194–196.
9. Ibid., 194.

he had succumbed to those forces. Satan tempted King David, leading him through the vapidity of desire. The crush of the olive press is the crush of temptation, and King David could ultimately escape Ishbi only when Avishai arrived, whose own goodness supplemented that of King David. Together the two of them could overcome temptation and evil.

While this summary does not do justice to the very rich interpretation the Maharal offers to explain many details of the narrative, it does give the reader a good idea of how the Allegorical method works, and how it can be applied to our text.

The Allegorical method of interpreting fantastical aggadot is indeed a powerful one, and is what I would called Externalist. By that I mean that the allegorist refers to ideas or concepts that are outside the narrative itself. In this case, the main protagonists are King David, Ishbi, and Avishai. They are real people who are being used by the author of the aggada to stand in for abstract concepts such as evil, temptation, and goodness. However, some might argue that those abstractions do not inhere in the real people themselves, with their own life stories and biographies. Put differently, allegory walks the reader away from the characters themselves toward an external domain of abstractions. While this may indeed be a virtue of the method for some readers, as it was for the Maharal and others, some may feel uncomfortable with it. Such abstracting, for these readers, diminishes the humanity of the heroes of the narrative, does not do justice to their unique dilemmas, choices, temptations, personal histories, and relationships, rendering them no more than ciphers for abstract ideas. Later in this chapter, I shall present yet a fourth approach to the interpretation of fantastical aggadot which does address this challenge, but for now let us return to King David and Ishbi.

TROUBLE FINDS KING DAVID

King David goes out to hunt with a falcon, possibly as respite from the stresses of his position.[10] While this in itself is unremarkable, as perhaps

10. See Geoffrey Herman, "One Day David Went Out for a Hunt of the Falconers: Persian Themes in the Babylonian Talmud," in *Shoshannat Yaakov: Jewish and*

King David did hunt, what follows immediately thereafter is remarkable indeed. The Satan appears in the guise of a deer, and King David pursues it with his bow and arrow. However, Satan makes sure the arrows fall short, and King David keeps up his pursuit of the ever-elusive deer. So absorbed is King David in the hunt, that he unwittingly ends up in Philistine territory. Now this is a not a good place for David to be, since he and his people were at war with the Philistines, and David is all alone in enemy territory with no more than a bow and arrow for protection. Remarkably enough, Ishbi the giant happens to be present at exactly the right time and place. He immediately sees David and recognizes him as the man who killed his brother, the even more famous giant Goliath. Ishbi then leaps at the opportunity for revenge.

What method of revenge does he choose? Does he attack David with a weapon? That would be the norm, but in this aggada the norm rarely occurs. Instead, he captures David, binds him up, and then places him underneath an olive press, so as to crush him with its weight. Why would Ishbi choose so unusual a method for avenging his brother's death? And why does the aggada not mention an effort on David's part to resist? After all, he was a skilled warrior, even if his nemesis was a giant, and he did possess a bow and arrow as well. Let us recall that David killed Goliath with a mere slingshot. The aggada almost seems to take it for granted that David succumbed without even putting up a fight. Surely this is surprising.

What happens to David beneath the crushing olive press? The unexpected continues, and the Talmud asserts that a miracle was performed, the soil softens and opens up beneath David and, hidden in the newly formed hole, he survives unscathed. The narrative so far possesses a distinctly far-fetched quality.

Although David is clearly still in danger and the reader is left hanging in anticipation, the scene abruptly shifts from David and Ishbi

---

Iranian Studies in Honor of Yaakov Elman (Leiden, 2012), 111–136, for the Persian background to elements of the literary style of this aggada. Rashi ad loc. notes the Persian origin of the term *sakhar,* translated here as "hunt." See Maharsha ad loc. for another plausible translation of the phrase, which he renders "trap birds and animals in a net."

in the land of the Philistines to Jerusalem, and to a new protagonist, David's nephew, warrior, and advisor Avishai. The aggada now locates the narrative in time and informs the reader that the day these tumultuous events took place is at dusk on Friday, just before Shabbat begins. This in itself is surprising, for why is David going on a hunt so close to Shabbat? Surely that is imprudent. Indeed, later halakha teaches that it is forbidden to depart on a journey close to Shabbat, as the traveler may arrive late.[11] Shouldn't David have been concerned that he might become engrossed in the hunt and return late for Shabbat, which in the end is exactly what transpired?

Be that as it may, the aggada relates that Avishai was washing his hair with four jugs of water in preparation for Shabbat and discovers four bloodstains. An alternative tradition the aggada records is not that Avishai found four bloodstains, but that a dove came and fluttered its wings in front of him. The aggada picks up on this second tradition and depicts Avishai inferring from the fluttering of the wings of the dove that King David is in distress. On what basis? He cites a verse in Psalms which implies that Israel is akin to a dove, and if the dove fluttered its wings – which may imply distress – Israel must be in distress too. But Avishai notices no special distress afflicting the entire people. Therefore, he appears to reason, the distress must be that of their leader, in whose hands their well-being rests.

Clearly this is a bad omen for Avishai, and a meaningful one to him, even if the modern reader might not react in the same way. Avishai therefore sets out on a mission to find and rescue King David. What of the first account the Talmud offers, that Avishai found blood while washing his hair? Presumably, the discovery of blood is so clearly ominous, it requires no talmudic explanation. Yet why would Avishai infer from the blood he finds that David was in danger? Perhaps the bad omen is directed at Avishai himself? To this question the Talmud provides no explanation, and the reader remains puzzled.

The first stop on Avishai's mission is to check David's home, but unfortunately, David is nowhere to be found, so Avishai must seek him out. Since Avishai fears that David is in mortal danger, speed is of the

11. See sources cited in *Mishna Berura* 249:3.

essence, walking by foot will not do, and he wishes to use the king's mule. However, the aggada reports, Avishai encounters a halakhic problem: According to the mishna, citizens are forbidden to use a king's horse, throne, or scepter, all symbols of the king's authority.[12] According to mishnaic law, then, it would be forbidden for Avishai to borrow the king's horse or mule for the chase. The aggada reports that Avishai checked with the halakhic masters in the study hall, was told that under the circumstances, to save David's life, he may do so, and so Avishai borrows David's mule and sets off to find him. A miracle is performed, the land contracts under him, and in no time at all Avishai arrives exactly at the spot that David is held in captivity by Ishbi. Miraculous indeed!

The reader might wonder why Avishai felt the need to inquire of the masters of the study hall to sort out this halakhic problem. Would he not have known that the obligation to save a life trumps the obligation not to use a king's mule, especially since the life to be saved is none other than that of the king himself? Surely the king would have been delighted to offer him permission to save his very own life! Why then was Avishai so troubled by this that he spent precious time to find out, when he could have left immediately to the rescue? This is a problem that bothered several classical commentaries, who proposed various technical solutions.[13] That said, the question is a good one, and the events described may be no more nor less than yet another element of the fantastical quality of the aggada. What then are we to make of this?

ANOTHER APPROACH TO INTERPRETING FANTASTICAL AGGADOT

Before proceeding with the rest of the aggada, now would be a propitious time to introduce a fourth approach to fantastical aggadot, not widely

---

12. While this mishnaic ruling clearly post-dated David, it probably codified an ancient practice. It should be noted that the Talmud somewhat anachronistically often cites, in the context of discussing a biblical passage, teachings which formally post-date the biblical period. This was premised on the conviction that such teachings, the Oral Law, are of ancient origin.
13. See, e.g., Jacob Ettlinger, *Arukh LeNer,* ad loc., and Moshe Feinstein, *Iggrot Moshe, Ḥoshen Mishpat,* vol. 2, Responsum 79:6 (Bnei Brak, 1985).

known or studied, but nevertheless very important indeed. I will suggest that this approach provides a fruitful methodology for interpreting the many bizarre qualities of the aggada we have encountered so far, and will continue to encounter as we progress with our analysis. Moreover, I believe it is fruitful for understanding other fantastical aggadic narratives in rabbinic literature. This approach is to interpret at least some such aggadot as dreams.[14]

This method goes all the way back to Rav Hai Gaon (939–1038), leader of the talmudic academy in Pumpedita, Babylonia. The aggada he interpreted described a dialogue between R. Bibi b. Abaye and the Angel of Death, in which R. Bibi criticized the Angel of Death for bringing death to an undeserving person. Among the interpretations R. Hai Gaon offers is that "it is possible that this episode appeared to R. Bibi in a dream, like many people relate what they saw in their dreams."[15]

Maimonides himself mentions such a possibility in his *Commentary to the Mishna,* noting that he planned to write a future work in which he would explicate puzzling teachings of the Sages, to "explain which are to be taken literally, which are parables, and which occurred in a dream, but were recounted straightforwardly, as if they took place while awake."[16] Maimonides' son Abraham picks up this same theme in an extensive discussion of aggada which offers an important hermeneutic methodology, and in which he archly criticizes the literalists, like his father before him. He likewise teaches that many such fantastical aggadot are really dreams, even though they are recounted as if they actually took place.[17]

The same approach is adopted by the Ritva (R. Yom Tov Asevilli), the Spanish thirteenth–fourteenth-century commentator on the Talmud and student of the Rashba (R. Shlomo ben Aderet). He was troubled by a string of aggadot in Bava Batra 73a describing the extraordinary apparitions of various talmudic Sages while traveling by sea, including

14. See Sokol, *The Snake at the Mouth of the Cave,* chs. 7, 8, for a further discussion of this approach and its application to several aggadic narratives.
15. *Teshuvot HaGeonim,* ed. Abraham Harkavy (Berlin, 1887), 122, no. 245.
16. Y. Shilat, *Introductions to Maimonides' Commentaries to the Mishna* (Jerusalem, 2006), 140 (Heb.). The translation here is mine.
17. "Essay on the *Derashot* of the Rabbis," published in the beginning of the *Ein Yaakov* (Jerusalem, 2008), 29.

frogs the size of a fort, antelopes the size of a mountain, and a bird tall enough to reach the sky. He writes: "When they were at sea they sat alone and thought about the awesome sights they saw, and when they went to sleep they appeared to them like thoughts about wondrous things."[18] Thus the Ritva too takes some fantastical tales as dreams. Numerous other classical sources have taken a similar view.[19]

Why then does the author of the aggada not explicitly announce to the reader that the events recounted took place in a dream? R. Abraham, son of Maimonides, thought that it should be so obvious to the rational reader that it would not even require spelling this out explicitly.[20] Be that explanation as it may, it is also possible that the author of the text might have believed that to announce the events as dreams might undercut their authority for the reader, for which reason he left it open. Note that it was not uncommon in pre-modern times for authors to attribute texts they themselves wrote to earlier historical figures, thereby contributing to the authoritative nature of their own work. Pre-modern and modern writers (and readers) possess different readings of "truth" in texts.

Whatever the answer to this question, the Dream approach is especially important, because it takes the reader not away from the protagonist of the aggada to abstract concepts or ideas, like the Allegorist, but rather back into the protagonist's mind and heart. What does a person dream about? One answer to that question is provided by the Talmud itself: "R. Yonatan said: A person is shown in his dreams only the thoughts of his heart."[21] So on this view, to interpret a dream is to enter into "the thoughts of the heart," the psychology of the protagonist, and so we might call this method the *Psychological*. The Psychological method of interpretation should not be characterized as Externalist, like the Allegorical method, but rather as Internalist. It takes the full measure

18. This is quoted extensively in the *HaKotev* commentary to the *Ein Yaakov*, ad loc.
19. See Z. H. Chayes, *Mevo HaTalmud: The Student's Guide to the Talmud*, trans. Jacob Schachter (London, 1952), ch. 28, for additional sources.
20. Ibid.
21. Berakhot 55b. For a discussion of dreams in talmudic literature, see P. S. Alexander, "Bavli Berakhot 55a–57b," *Journal of Jewish Studies* 46 (1995); and S. Fishbane, *Deviancy in Early Rabbinic Literature* (Leiden, 2007), ch. 11.

of the intricate and complex inner life of the protagonists of surreal aggadot, and thus provides a crucial interpretive key.[22] Moreover, the talmudic rabbis themselves interpret many dreams as full of rich symbols, which they themselves seek to interpret.[23] This in turn gives equally rich license to the interpreter of aggadot that may have been dreams, to seek the symbolic meanings of the fantastical events they record.[24] But how does this work? What is its hermeneutical payoff? Let us now return to our aggada for answers to these questions.

Recall the episode which introduces the narrative proper, a message to King David from God Himself, who holds David responsible for the massacre in Nov. "The Holy One, Blessed be He, said to David: Until when will this sin be concealed in your hand [without punishment]?" God then gives David a tragic choice: "Is it your desire that your descendants will cease to exist, or that you will be handed to the enemy?" David chooses the second option, and the story of his encounter with Ishbi, the enactment of that choice, unfolds.

How does God communicate this message? As we know, prophecy occurs through one of two mediums, a vision or a dream.[25] It is therefore a reasonable reading of our text that its author meant to say that King David received this message from God in a dream. And once we enter the world of dreams, we enter the "thoughts of the heart" of the dreamer, including King David. For dreams, even prophetic ones according to Maimonides, are filtered through the "thoughts of the heart" of the dreamer, through his personal imagination, for which reason, presumably, different

22. For more on the Psychological/Internalist method in another context, see, among other sources, the discussion in S. Harris and G. Platzner, *Classical Mythology* (Mountain View, 1998), 37–43, and sources cited on p. 46.
23. See sources cited in n. 21.
24. Thus, even if some contemporary psychologists would not interpret the details of dreams as rich with symbolic significance, the talmudic rabbis did, and the text we seek to interpret is talmudic, not contemporary. Therefore, in interpreting our text, we must work within the thought-world of its authors and their immediate audience, in which dreams do have symbolic significance, drawing upon the "thoughts of the heart" of the dreamer.
25. See Maimonides, *Guide for the Perplexed,* II:40, and *passim.* In II:45, Maimonides writes that King David possessed *ru'aḥ hakodesh,* the Holy Spirit, a pre-prophetic state.

prophets have very different kinds of dreams.[26] Every person's imagination is shaped by his or her own individual life experiences, and therefore every person's imagination is as unique as his or her own life experiences.

It is possible that the author of our aggada believed that God communicated this message to King David directly, whether or not King David was a prophet, via the medium of a dream (or vision).[27] However, a more naturalistic reading might suggest the following: The author believed that God communicates to all human beings, not only to prophets or visionaries, through the conscience He implanted in them, their *yetzer hatov,* their will to do good. People can be quite conscious of this will, but sometimes they may experience it unconsciously as well. Sometimes feelings of guilt are so painful that people find it difficult to confront those feelings openly. One way of confronting them is in a dream, a dream that derives from the *yetzer hatov* that God implanted in all human beings. Put differently, if King David felt guilty about his role in the massacre at Nov, it would have been God who – indirectly – communicated that feeling to David via his *yetzer hatov.* And David may never have confronted that guilt directly until he first dreamt about it.

This approach draws from psychodynamic psychology. However, it is even more likely that David did indeed confront this guilt directly, and dreamt about it as well, for he may have been haunted by that failure. Indeed, it would have been surprising had King David not dreamt about the massacre at Nov and his role in it. For how could a morally sensitive person like King David not feel pangs of guilt over his complicity in such a tragedy? And would those feelings of guilt not come back to haunt him in his dreams? Consider the guilt David expresses over his relationship with Bathsheba. One of the most moving of all psalms attributed to King David is Psalm 51, in which David expresses the most abject, harrowing guilt over what he painfully describes as his moral failure with Bathsheba. Surely a man of such morally and religiously intense feelings

26. Ibid., II:36 and *passim.* In that chapter, Maimonides writes that even Moses, who did not prophesy through his imaginative faculty, was affected by his mood and did not prophesy when he was depressed. Surely this would apply all the more to all other prophets, who prophesied through their imaginative faculty.

27. See n. 22, above.

would likewise feel guilty about his complicity in the massacre at Nov. Would he not then dream of it? Thus, it seems perfectly natural to suggest that the many classical sources that interpret fantastical aggadot as dreams might do so here, and I shall use the Psychological method to provide a fresh reading of our narrative.

Before returning to the narrative, however, I wish to make two important points. First, the Psychological method as I employ it makes no claims whatsoever about King David himself. How, after all, can a twenty-first-century reader enter into the "thoughts of the heart" of so elevated a figure as King David, one of the greatest men of the biblical period, who lived so long ago, and in such a different world? Psychobiography is a fraught, and perhaps questionable enough enterprise under the best of circumstances, but that is even truer for a man of King David's remarkable stature and place in history.

Rather, what the Psychological method I employ here seeks to do is to interpret the text as we have it, not to interpret King David himself. The author of the aggada wrote the narrative, and the editors of the Talmud included it, because they believed it had an important message to teach the reader, in this case, related to their view about the culpability of King David in a terrible massacre, and his confrontation with that culpability. What then did the author of the aggada mean to teach us in the dream-like sequence of events he narrates? In other words, what does the text mean? These are the questions this method seeks to answer. What King David himself actually thought, felt, or dreamed, we can of course never know. We can only know what the aggada reports, and we can only attempt to interpret that report.

Second, we might ask if the author of the aggada himself believed that David actually dreamt these events. If he did, one wonders how the author could have known this. Or, did the author seek to teach us, the readers, a lesson about moral responsibility and guilt, and self-consciously used the vehicle of a dream-like narration to convey what he believed King David might have experienced?[28] Since we can never

28. Concerning this approach, it is possible that the author drew upon motifs and themes popular in his culture to convey his moral and religious messages, as above in note 10. This may well be true for many other fantastical aggadot as well.

really know what the author of the aggada thought, we must remain agnostic about this question. I shall write as if the text meant that King David actually had a dream as described, but that is mostly for ease of expression, not because I believe it to be truer to the text. For interpretive purposes, it really makes no difference.

Now, to the narrative. According to this reading, King David dreams that he embarks on a hunt before Shabbat and pursues a deer into enemy territory. Why the hunt for a deer? It is surely not without interest that Psalms 42:1, traditionally attributed to David himself, reads: "As a deer longs for flowing streams, so too my soul longs for You, God." David here compares himself to a deer, or more specifically, compares his soul, yearning for God, to a deer longing for water. No doubt the author of the aggada was familiar with this passage, which suggests a deeper meaning to the hunt. For if we follow this metaphor, for David to hunt for a deer is for David to hunt for himself. And is this not what David is doing, in this dream about his own culpability for the Nov massacre? The good David, his *yetzer hatov,* his conscience, pursues the guilty David, like a hunter after his prey, shooting arrow after arrow to punish the David responsible for the massacre at Nov. And David's conscience, his feelings of guilt, are so powerful that they pursue him relentlessly, without respite, until David the target ends up where his conscience tells him he truly belongs, in enemy territory, to be set upon by the vengeful giant, Ishbi. This is what David deserves, or so his guilty conscience tells him.

Moreover, when David enters Philistine territory he is exiled from his homeland. And exile is surely a potent metaphor for the sinner, who is exiled from the good within him, and from God Himself. David leaves the holiness of the Land of Israel behind him, his very own holiness, as a result of his culpability for the deaths in Nov. In this sense, external exile, to Philistine territory, mirrors the internal exile of the sinner.

Why before Shabbat? This is a liminal time, neither sacred nor profane, but a bridge between the two, a perfect metaphor for David himself. For David, too, is suspended between sacred and profane. David knew he possessed the sacred spirituality which would make the Psalms possible, but also knew that he could fail by taking refuge in Nov, as he knew he could fail through his relationship with Bathsheba. Just who then is the real David? Is he the man whose soul yearns for God like a deer for water? Or is he the man who could choose to save himself at the cost of the lives of all the residents of the city of Nov, themselves priests in service of God? To dream of a hunt on Shabbat eve is to dream of a perfect metaphor for David's own self-doubt and torment. Or, so the author of the aggada may be suggesting.

This leads us to Ishbi, the giant tormentor of David. Can there be a better metaphor for the giant guilt a great man like King David might feel than a giant tormentor to punish him for his failures? And how does Ishbi seek to kill David? Not through the usual means of a weapon. Rather, he chooses to crush him, a brilliant metaphor for the crushing weight of guilt that King David feels. Ironically, David is saved from death because the earth miraculously softens and hollows out beneath him. His salvation derives from his falling ever lower into the earth, dirtier than ever, a metaphor for his further descent from the elevated moral station David once occupied into the dust of the earth. To survive his failures, he must feel ever worse about himself, feel that he doesn't even deserve to stand upright upon the land. At this point, he does not put up a fight against Ishbi, as might be expected from a warrior like David, because in the dream he now submits to his guilt, and recognizes its legitimacy.

These metaphors for guilt echo the great penitential Psalm 51, attributed there explicitly to King David himself. Thus, in verse 10 the Psalmist writes that sin crushes the bones. David's sin with Batsheva is described as ever before him (v. 5), as dirt from which he must be cleansed (v. 9). He bemoans the besmirching of the purity of his heart with which he was created by God (v. 12) – the very purity of heart from which in his dream he is now exiled, and which pursues him with his guilt. A "broken spirit and broken and crushed heart" are what God seeks from the penitent (v. 19), exactly the status of David, dirty, broken, and crushed beneath the olive press of his dreams. It is difficult to avoid the feeling that the author of the aggada had this psalm in mind as he wrote the text we have before us. While these may be tropes for the feelings of a penitent soul, their echo from the aggada to Psalms is unavoidable.

Consider too Avishai's experience while washing his hair. This is exactly the metaphor the Psalmist uses, "Wash me, and I shall be whiter than snow" (v. 9). Avishai, David's savior and in some sense surrogate, undergoes the exercise King David himself must undergo; he must wash and cleanse himself to cleanse his uncle King David. And what does Avishai see? The first reading of the Talmud is that he sees bloodstains, the very blood shed in the city of Nov, which comes back to haunt David in his dream. "Deliver me from bloodguilt," the Psalmist writes (v. 16), the very blood Avishai sees in the dream. Of course, in real life Avishai might well have interpreted the appearance of blood as ominous for himself, not his uncle, but in David's own dream, Avishai naturally interprets this as ominous for the dreamer, King David. Similarly, the fluttering wings of the dove vividly express David's deep fright over his culpability for the death of so many priests. If we follow Rashi's interpretation of the text, this reading is even more acute, for Rashi (ad loc.) comments that the dove was "smiting itself," "moaning and in pain," powerful metaphors for David's self-flagellation, his pangs of guilt. Notice that in the text Avishai does not infer from these omens that King David was in danger of losing his life – which was the case – but rather that King David "is in a state of distress," or more literally, "in pain." Exactly!

Why does Avishai seek out the masters in the study hall to permit borrowing King David's steed? Surely he should have known such would be not only permitted, but desired by the king, to save his life. But if David is so consumed by guilt in the dream, might he not feel ambivalent about this effort to save his life? A person responsible for the death of so many innocents might feel, and dream, that he had forfeited his own right to life. Moreover, the eventual granting of permission reflects a diminution in the status of the king, for now a commoner uses his royal steed. And this is exactly what the guilt-ridden king feels he, at the very least, deserves.

AVISHAI SAVES KING DAVID

Through a miraculous intervention, the land contracts under Avishai and he arrives in the land of the Philistines, a turn of events characteristic of dreams generally, in which people move with "miraculous" swiftness from one location to another. Surprisingly, Avishai's first encounter upon arrival is not with Ishbi or King David, but with Ishbi's mother, Horpah. It seems fair to ask why this transpires. That it is not incidental to the narrative becomes even clearer at its end, when David and Avishai succeed in vanquishing Ishbi only after he is informed about his mother's death. Horpah is spinning thread with a spindle, whereupon when seeing Avishai she flings it at him in the vain hope of killing him. She fails, and Avishai returns the favor by using the spindle to kill her. How odd that an elderly woman would think she could kill a mighty warrior with a spindle. Why does she even attempt this, and why is her appearance and eventual death included in the narrative?

Who then is Horpah? At one level, we know from II Samuel that she was not only the mother of Ishbi, but the mother of three other great Philistine warriors, including Goliath.[29] The Talmud elsewhere identifies her with Orpah, the daughter-in-law of Naomi.[30] Numerous talmudic rabbis make this claim, one of them none other than Rav, the original source of at least the first portion of our aggada blaming David for the massacre at Nov.[31] Given the large number of talmudic rabbis who make this identification, and given Rav's role in both sources, it is likely that the author of our narrative too would likewise have believed that Horpah is none other than Orpah.

To further expand the picture, numerous rabbis cited in the Talmud attribute to Orpah/Horpah manifold sexually depraved behaviors.[32] And once again, for the same reasons noted above, it is likely that our source too was familiar with at least some of these attributions. If Horpah is indeed guilty of wild sexual depravity, it may not be all that surprising if she attempted to kill Avishai too, even if the prospects for success were rather dim. Crazed behavior of one sort might well beget crazed behavior of another. Later in this chapter I shall suggest another, stronger link between these two behaviors, and between the identities of Orpah and Horpah, but for now let us return to the narrative.

---

29. II Samuel 21, 15–22.
30. Sota 42b.
31. It is not clear if Rav is author of the narrative with Ishbi that follows, or if this was inserted by the editors of the Talmud. No authorship is cited specifically for this narrative, which follows immediately after Rav's teaching.
32. Ibid., Sota 42b and *Tosafot* s.v. *Me'ah;* Ruth Rabba 2:20.

After killing Horpah, Avishai finally approaches King David. Ishbi catches a glimpse of him from the distance, fears for his own life in a match-up between himself and the two of them, and decides to kill David before Avishai can join him in battle. What does Ishbi do? Instead of killing King David directly with the spear he has handy, he thrusts the spear into the ground upside down, flings David into the air above the inverted spear, to become impaled upon landing to the ground on the sharp point of the sword. Why did Ishbi choose so convoluted a method of killing David? Perhaps because this replicates David's failure with Nov. David did not directly kill the residents of Nov; rather, by taking refuge there he indirectly caused their death, directly brought about not by David but by Saul. Ishbi too does not seek to kill David directly, by piercing him with his sword, but only indirectly, by flinging him into the air, allowing him to fall on the sword. If this is how David failed, this is how David would dream of the death that resulted from his failure.

Avishai arrives just in time, to find King David flung up into the air, ready to fall to his death on the spear. He quickly utters God's sacred name, and David remains suspended in mid-air just above the threatening spear. If this isn't remarkable enough, Avishai and David next proceed to engage in a dialogue, with David suspended in the air. Avishai asks David how he ended up in this predicament, and David responds first by recapitulating the choice God gave him, to submit to his own death or to allow for the death of his descendants. Then he tells Avishai that he chose his own death over the death of his descendants. Avishai tells David to reverse his prayer, that is, to pray for the death of his descendants rather than suffer death himself. He cites a popular adage in support of that recommendation, that it is better for a person's grandson to suffer by becoming a poor peddler who sells wax, instead of the grandfather suffering poverty by providing for his grandchildren. David requests Avishai's help in prayer, Avishai recites another sacred name of God, and David lands safely away from the inverted spear. One wonders what Ishbi was up to during this long dialogue, while David is miraculously suspended in mid-air. What are we to make of this fantastical episode?

To begin with, the image of David hanging suspended in mid-air is not only striking, but fraught as well, for as a dream it might well speak to David's self-doubt. Just who is the real David, the sacred, heavenly author of Psalms, or the very earthbound and flawed man who caused the massacre at Nov, or who failed with Bathsheba? Just as King David could compose the most moving of penitential psalms over his sin with Bathsheba, he would likewise feel much self-doubt following his failure in Nov. This image in space graphically illustrates that self-doubt, much like the timing of his hunting expedition, on Friday, which illustrates that same image in time. For Friday before Shabbat is a liminal time, neither sacred nor profane. So too, David is caught in liminal space, suspended between heaven and earth.

Avishai's use of God's sacred name to save David is telling, for to invoke God's name over David is to evoke God's name within David. Note that a talmudic question interrupts the narrative. Why did David not pronounce God's name and save himself? To this the Talmud answers that a prisoner cannot free himself from prison. The prisoner requires an external agent to liberate him. This is a brilliant metaphor for David himself, who is not impaled on Ishbi's spear, but who is impaled on the spear of his own self-doubt. To switch metaphors, David is the prisoner of his self-doubt, from which he alone could never liberate himself. Only his nephew Avishai could pronounce God's name to David, and thereby convince him of the Godliness that still resides within him, despite his failures. Sometimes people are so mired in doubt or depression that they require the fresh perspective of another person to help them cognitively reframe their experiences. Avishai succeeded in doing this, and thereby liberated David from his suspension between heaven and earth, between his moral failures and his remarkable moral and spiritual achievements. But how exactly did Avishai catalyze David's new self-understanding? How did he reframe David's cognitive experience? Merely by uttering God's name?

In fact, Avishai did more than pronounce God's name. He insisted that David reverse his decision to save himself over his descendants. *Prima facie,* this is deeply puzzling. As I suggested above, the decision to save his descendants over himself recapitulates and reverses the flawed decision he made to save himself while jeopardizing the residents of Nov and their descendants. That reversal was precisely his act of penitence. If so, how could reversing that reversal, and deciding to save himself over his descendants, yield moral and physical salvation? Wouldn't the more noble and self-sacrificial act be to give up his own life on behalf of his many descendants?

The text itself provides no answers. I would suggest that Avishai may have meant to teach his uncle David that David's own life is far more meaningful to the Jewish people, and to the long sweep of Jewish history, than the lives of his descendants. David is more than an individual making his own way in the world. David is king, savior of his brethren from foreign attack, founder of a kingdom which he shaped and led, one which would transform Jewish history long into the future. He is at once a great warrior, leader, and Psalmist too. What would Jewish life and history be without King David? Let us recall that the fluttering wings of the dove, a bird which symbolizes the Jewish people, taught Avishai that King David was in trouble. For if King David is in trouble, then perforce his people are in great trouble too.

Surely a person's descendants matter to him or her a great deal. But should they ever matter as much as the whole of the Jewish people, and the whole of Jewish history? For David to sacrifice himself to save his descendants is to sacrifice the well-being of the whole, not just his own individual life. Conversely, for him to preserve his own life at the cost of the lives of his descendants is to insure the flourishing of the whole. Avishai convinces David that he was not merely a lone singer of Psalms, and that his life must be preserved for the greater good, even at the expense of his own personal descendants, as painful as such a choice might be.

This difficult realization may have been at the heart of the cognitive reframing Avishai sought to achieve for King David. He meant to tell him this: "David, you may have failed in Nov, but your destiny and role in Jewish life far outweigh any failures on your part. God's name is within you, for you are destined to lead and transform the Jewish people and Jewish history. Do not let that failure cloud your understanding of your true identity and just how important you are to Jewish history. God's name rests within you for you have a sacred task, even if that task comes at great personal cost to your own family."

This cognitive reframing liberates David from the self-doubt and guilt that torments him, and therefore ipso facto leads to his salvation from the inverted spear.

Yet their troubles are not over, for Ishbi now pursues the two of them, from pillar to post, from one town to the next. Where was Ishbi during the long dialogue that ensued between David and Avishai? As in a dream, he disappears, only to reappear once again. Now, it is not only David who is in danger, but Avishai too. They are both frightened of the looming and dangerous giant. Guilt, it seems, is not so easily remedied, and now Avishai is implicated as well. His very effort to cleanse David from guilt brings guilt upon himself. Has he too failed to fully acknowledge the catastrophe of Nov? Has he liberated David from guilt prematurely, and in so doing demonstrated that he has not taken full measure of the severity of the sin? If that is the case, then he shares in culpability for the sin itself. Both David and Avishai are now in danger.

They escape from town to town, each of whose names symbolizes to them an encouragement to fight back, but in each town, they are felled by fear, the stuff of dreams. Finally, in a stroke of genius, they inform Ishbi that his mother Horpah has died. This diminishes his strength, and they finally succeed in killing their tormenter. The Talmud notes in a coda to the narrative, and quoting a verse from Samuel, that from this they learned that David as king should never again risk his precious life in war.

We must ask why it is that Ishbi was so weakened upon learning of the death of his mother. Surely a fearsome giant and warrior like Ishbi would hardly wilt in combat at the news. This question in turn leads us back to the identity of Horpah.

Assuming our narrative adopts the widely held position in the Talmud elsewhere, which as I argued above is more than likely, then Horpah is none other than Orpah, sister-in-law to Ruth and second daughter-in-law of Naomi. Both Ruth and Orpah were born gentiles who had married Ruth's two sons while they lived in Moab during the famine in the Land of Israel. Following the death of her husband and sons, impoverished and destitute, Naomi decides to return to the Land of Israel. Both Ruth and Orpah are determined to follow her. Naomi attempts to persuade them to stay in their native country, but both cry bitter tears, and both equally insist on remaining with her. Ruth tries yet again to persuade them to stay, they both cry bitter tears yet again, but in the end, Orpah kisses her mother-in-law and leaves while Ruth remains with Naomi.[33]

Surely a straightforward reading of the biblical text nowhere suggests that Orpah was a terrible person. On the contrary, she remains loyal to Naomi and insists on remaining with her despite Naomi's entreaties, and only in the end is she finally persuaded to remain in Moab. While she may not be an extraordinary heroine like Ruth, she is nevertheless depicted in a positive light. Why then do talmudic and midrashic rabbis insist on attributing the most sexually depraved behaviors to her? While they cite texts in support of their claims, a careful reading makes clear that these texts are no more than suggestive at best. It seems likely, then, that the rabbis took the position they did because they arrived at this conclusion on their own, or they possessed an ancient tradition to that effect. Whatever the origin of their views, however, the question we must ask is what lies behind that tradition. This question is especially acute, since it appears to contradict the simple reading of the biblical text in Ruth.

One possible answer is that a psychological mechanism may have been at work in Orpah's mind. Let us recall the end of the story told in Ruth. Ruth commits herself to the Jewish faith and people, selflessly accompanies Naomi to the Land of Israel and supports her there, demonstrating extraordinary virtue throughout. Eventually, Ruth marries a member of Naomi's family, Boaz, who was a leading member of their community and the tribe of Judah. Ruth and Boaz bear a son together by the name of Oved who, the text reminds us, is the grandfather of none other than King David himself. In short, Ruth is the great-grandmother of King David, founder of the Davidic dynasty which forever shaped and elevated the trajectory of Jewish history. That is quite an impressive achievement for a convert to the Jewish people.

Now let us reflect on how Orpah might have felt in the aftermath of her decision to remain in Moab rather than join Ruth in her enduring loyalty to Naomi and on her journey to the Jewish faith and people. Given her initial insistence that she join Naomi, and the tears she sheds

33. See Ruth, ch. 1.

multiple times preceding her ultimate decision to depart, it seems likely that she might well have felt considerable guilt about that decision. How could she have abandoned her beloved mother-in-law? How could she have abandoned her sister-in-law Ruth? Presumably, they both saw in Naomi, and in their lives with the family, the special qualities of Judaism and the Jewish people to which Ruth explicitly declares fealty. Ruth refused to leave those qualities behind, as did Orpah too, until eventually Orpah relented. Might she not later have felt intense regret about her ultimate decision to abandon the morally and religiously superior life she had seen in Naomi and her family?

Pangs of guilt would then have struck her the moment she turned her back on Naomi and Ruth, and these feelings may only have intensified later. She would likely have learned of the marriage of Ruth to Boaz, a leader of the community, and of the child they had together. Much later, she would have learned that this child became grandfather to no less than the very king of Israel, David. That noble destiny could have been hers, if she had only remained loyal to Naomi. The more time passed, the guiltier she might have felt over her fateful choice to abandon Naomi, Judaism, and the Jewish people, and thereby the destiny that was Ruth's but not hers, due to her fateful choice. Or, at least, this is how the talmudic rabbis could have looked at it.

How does one respond to feelings of acute guilt over a pivotal decision to forever abandon a morally and religiously superior life, or over a decision to forever abandon a great destiny? There are many ways to respond, but one way is to feel intensely angry at oneself for making what in retrospect one comes to see as a corrupt and failed choice. Such intense anger at oneself may eventually lead to self-destructive behavior. The ancient talmudic rabbis were cognizant of this psychological dynamic, for which reason they assumed that Orpah too must have engaged in self-destructive behavior, which they depicted in the most graphic detail. Why? First, given just how elevated a person Orpah apparently had been, they believed that the enormity of her failure could only lead to unmitigated moral disaster. And second, perhaps the rabbis wanted to make abundantly clear to their students and readers the mortal dangers of making the wrong choices. Regret begets guilt, guilt begets anger at self, and anger at self begets self-destructive depravity. Beware of making wrong choices.[34]

This dynamic helps explain Orpah's crazed flinging of the spindle at Avishai, as if a mere spindle could fell a mighty young warrior. Her anger at self erupted into anger at Avishai. But I believe there may well be more to it than that. Consider that in many ways, Ruth was Orpah's alter ego. Ruth was the person that Orpah could have become, but tragically failed. Ruth's loyalty, faith, and success brilliantly illuminate the exact contours of Orpah's failure, for Orpah could have achieved what Ruth did, but failed miserably. Indeed, Orpah herself might have been great-grandmother to the king of Israel, rather than Ruth. For the talmudic rabbis, the Messiah himself will descend from David. From this perspective, Orpah and not Ruth might have become ancestor not only to King David, but to the Messiah as well. Is it any surprise, then, that Orpah bears the most intense animosity toward Ruth and her descendants? They depict her tragic failure more clearly than anyone else. This explains the unbridled hatred toward David and his would-be protector and nephew, Avishai.

Let us recall that it was David who had killed Horpah's son, the giant Goliath, lighting the embers of hatred and the desire for revenge in Horpah ever brighter. The animus between the lines of Orpah and Ruth travel from generation to generation like a Greek tragedy. Goliath, heir to his mother's hatred of the Jews who had precipitated her failures, taunts and torments the Jewish people. Significantly, it is David, scion of Ruth, who rises up in defense and slays him. Once again, it is Ruth and her line who kills the failed Orpah. Next there is Ishbi, Goliath's

34. R. Haim Shmulewitz likewise stresses the initially elevated character of Orpah, but attributes her eventual depravity to the consequences of a breakdown in her sense of self and self-worth, which made her vulnerable to the *yetzer hara,* the evil inclination. See *Siḥot Mussar* (Jerusalem, 1980), Lecture 13, 1971, 41–43. Orpah's depravity may also have been due to her attempt to resolve the cognitive dissonance she would have felt between her aspirations for moral and religious excellence and her failure to live up to those aspirations. One way to resolve that dissonance is by making a radical and all-consuming choice in favor of failure and depravity. I am grateful to Dr. Alan Perry for this observation, and for his discussion of the overall issue with me. One strength of the explanation I offer in the text is that it makes sense of the wild flinging of the spindle in our narrative.

younger brother, who taunts and torments David himself. While Ishbi seeks to avenge his brother's death, his bitter hatred of David is born of deep ancestral hatred, the hatred his mother felt toward Ruth and toward Ruth's line, rendered ever more acute by the success of King David, a success which could have been hers, but for her flawed choice. This hatred she bequeathed to her children, a hatred bred deep within them.

This, finally, explains why Ishbi "loses his strength" and is vanquished by David and Avishai after he learns of his mother's death. The poisonous energy behind his pursuit of David is now gone. His strength derived in part from the overflowing font of his mother's hatred, for hatred imparts strength to the hater. The source of that hatred passed from the world with the death of Orpah. With its passing from the world, the preternatural strength which drove her son to torment King David passed from the world as well, as did the man who bore that hatred from his mother, Ishbi himself. Thus, the rabbinic identification of Horpah with Orpah provides a deep, new meaning to the fantastical narrative which is the subject of this chapter.

Moreover, this identification sheds further light on the striking contrast between Orpah and David. Both Orpah and David confront failure. Yet how does each one cope with that failure? According to our aggada, David thoughtfully confronts that failure, struggles with his own role in the massacre at Nov, and finally comes to terms with his all-too-human limitations, as manifest in that failure. This is healthy, and he moves on with his life. Ishbi is dead. Orpah, on the other hand, never struggles thoughtfully with her failure, never seeks to accept her own limitations as manifest in her decision to abandon Ruth, and emerges depraved and vindictive. The David of our aggada models honest self-appraisal and constructive encounter with past failures. Orpah models the reverse. Is it any wonder that the two become great antagonists through the generations? And is it any wonder that David emerges victorious?

We are left with one final question. The overall theme of the aggada is David's guilt over the massacre at Nov. Does the death of Ishbi reflect in David's mind an expiation of his failure? Does Ishbi's death signify to David in his dream that he can now, finally, feel at peace with himself and his choices? One possible answer to this question is that indeed it does. David's dream ends well for David. He has come to the realization that his well-being is constitutive of the well-being of the Jewish people, and he is willing to sacrifice the life of his descendants for the sake of the whole. Even taking refuge in Nov was the right choice, for it preserved his life and thereby the future well-being of the Jewish people. He no longer needs to be plagued by guilt.

The problem with this answer is that God seems not to be happy with it, for in the dream God explicitly criticizes David for the choice he made. The choice is never justified. David had no right to save his present life, even for a possible better future for the Jewish people, at the expense of the present life of the residents of Nov.

Another possible answer is that the dream conveys no clear message of expiation. Yes, Ishbi is dead, and David's life in the dream is no longer threatened. But that does not entail that David is now liberated fully from his guilt. Perhaps the final message of the narrative is thus an ambiguous one, just as moral life often is, and just as dreams are so often ambiguous too.

Finally, there is a third possible answer to this question. Immediately after the aggada reports that Ishbi was killed, it concludes: "This is what it says,[35] 'Then David's men took an oath to him saying: You should not go with us to war anymore and you will not douse the lamp of Israel'" (II Samuel 21:17). This coda to the narrative is *prima facie* puzzling on two accounts. First, why is this coda here? What does it contribute to the story? Second, and more to the point, it does not follow from the narrative itself. What is the meaning of the introductory phrase "This is what it says"? David did not go out to make war with Ishbi; he had gone on a hunt and only accidentally, and altogether alone and vulnerable, did he appear in the land of the Philistines. Why would David not be permitted to go to war with his whole army, fully armed, just because he almost lost his life to Ishbi?[36]

---

35. This is the literal translation of the text, unlike the more figurative translation in Sefaria.

36. The biblical verse (I Samuel 21:17) itself makes sense in context. Avishai assisted David in vanquishing Ishbi in war, and since David was at risk and succeeded only with the assistance of Avishai, David was made to swear by his assistants that he would never put his life at risk again in war. However, our aggada pointedly does

An answer to these questions, and to the question of David's final moral status, may derive from a conversation King David had with his son and successor Solomon, as reported in I Chronicles 22:8, and with which the author of the aggada would certainly have been familiar. David tells his son that he himself had long wanted to build the Temple, but that he could not do so because "the word of the Lord came to me saying, 'You have shed much blood and fought great battles; you shall not build a House for My name for you have shed much blood on the earth in My sight.'" Only Solomon could build the Temple. Now how did the "word of the Lord" come to him? While the most straightforward reading is that God communicated with him directly, it is also possible that Nathan the Prophet communicated on behalf of God, although there is no record to that effect elsewhere.[37]

If God spoke with him directly, then we have another instance of His doing so, in our own aggada, and the parallels are surely striking.[38] In both cases, God tells David of the limitations of his behavior in regard to the life of other human beings. In our aggada, it is his failure over the massacre at Nov, and in the other prophecy, it is his constant warring. David's wars were justified, and some were even obligatory.[39] Nevertheless, innocents may have been killed during even justified wars, and even soldiers in battle, who must be killed in self-defense, are human beings whose death is regrettable.[40] David is a warrior. Blood is spilled by his hands, and even a warrior who saves his people and leads them to victory may not build God's Temple. Killing, even when justified, is a moral evil. The moral good of such killing may indeed override that evil, as in self-defense, but killing in self-defense is still killing. It is interesting to note that one of the classic commentaries to that passage

not depict David as engaged in a traditional war, but rather as having gone on a hunt alone and fallen accidentally into Ishbi's hands. In that context, the coda makes far less sense.

37. See the commentary of R. David Kimhi (Radak), ad loc.

38. Much the same observations would apply if the prophecy emerged from Nathan, but the point is even more acute if the prophecy is David's alone, for which reason I follow that interpretation in what follows.

39. See comments of Radak, op. cit., *Metzudot David*, Ralbag, and Malbim, ad loc.

40. See Sokol, *Judaism Examined*, ibid., ch. 12, for a fuller discussion of this issue.

in Chronicles explicitly cites the massacre at Nov as an example of the excessive blood spilled by David.[41] The parallel is clearly drawn. Killing directly, or causing the death of others, even if justified, yields enough of a moral stain to preclude the building of the Temple.

David's career as a warrior began with the slaying of Goliath, told in I Samuel 17. His career as a warrior ended with the slaying of Ishbi, told in II Samuel 22, 15–17. Goliath and Ishbi are brothers, sons of Horpah/Orpah. The massacre at Nov took place during David's long years as a warrior, of a moral piece with the many he killed before and after that terrible event. How then expiate his failure at Nov, for which God had originally blamed him? By completely abandoning his life as a warrior in response to God's charges, by divesting himself entirely of responsibility for the shedding of any human blood, directly or indirectly. David's dream ends with the conclusion of his career as a warrior. In so doing, he can expiate the blood on his hands, blood-shedding that began with Goliath, ended with Goliath's brother Ishbi, and the massacre at Nov included in between. The cycle of death is now over, the bloodstain washed away, for David will never shed blood again. David can finally awaken from his dream.

Thus, our analysis of the aggada ends. Is it a true interpretation of the text? Are interpretations of fantastical aggadot using the Psychological method that I have delineated in this chapter true? First, I am not sure what constitutes a true interpretation of any text, a question which has been the subject of interminable scholarly debate and discussion. And even if I knew what a true interpretation of any text might be, I doubt that I would be convinced that this interpretation is true. My argument, however, is that it is a strong interpretation of our aggada and, properly applied to other texts, may likewise be a strong interpretation of them as well.[42] By a "strong" interpretation I mean that it illuminates countless puzzles and nuances in the story and in its careful choice of language; it speaks vividly and authentically to the self-doubt and struggles of any deeply moral sinner; and it draws intertextually upon many other

41. Radak, op. cit.
42. For other examples of the use of this method in aggadic narratives, see Sokol, *The Snake at the Mouth of the Cave.*

biblical and rabbinic texts with which the author of the aggada was likely familiar, thereby enriching the meanings not only of our aggada itself, but also the meaning of those many texts as well.

One final question: If the narrative is indeed told like a dream, did the author of the aggada believe that David actually had this dream? Or did he write the aggada only *as if* David had the dream, in order to convey vividly the moral lessons he wished to teach? I leave that to the reader to ponder.

Chapter 10

R. Yehoshua ben Levi Finds the Messiah

Sanhedrin 98a

INTRODUCTION

Jews throughout the millennia have yearned for the Messiah, and never more so than during periods of great Jewish suffering. The subject of this aggada, the great third-century Sage R. Yehoshua ben Levi, lived in the Land of Israel during a period when the Roman empire began to crumble. Poverty and political insecurity prevailed, and it is hardly surprising, then, that he and others of his generation were so focused on the Messiah.

R. Yehoshua ben Levi was one of the leading scholars of his era, and his views are constantly cited in the Talmud. He was also a man of extraordinary spirituality, frequently visited by none other than Elijah the Prophet[1] and of whom remarkable stories were told, amongst them the aggada which is the subject of this chapter.

---

1. See, e.g., Y. Terumot 8:4, 47b.

The aggada begins with an encounter between R. Yehoshua and Elijah at the cave of R. Shimon bar Yoḥai, whereupon R. Yehoshua hears a voice of the Divine. He asks Elijah what his personal fate will be in the World to Come, and afterward, when the Messiah will arrive. To the latter question, Elijah directs him to ask the Messiah himself, and R. Yehoshua embarks on a journey to find the Messiah. When he finally does find him, the answer he gets from the Messiah is that he will come that very day, which of course he does not.

What are we to make of this strange encounter between R. Yehoshua and Elijah? Where exactly does R. Yehoshua find the Messiah, and what is the Messiah doing when R. Yehoshua finds him? What is the meaning of the Messiah's cryptic response to R. Yehoshua's question? And according to this aggada, when indeed will the Messiah come?

רַבִּי יְהוֹשֻׁעַ בֶּן לֵוִי אַשְׁכַּח לְאֵלִיָּהוּ, דַּהֲוֵי קָיְימִי אַפִּיתְחָא דִמְעָרְתָּא דְּרַבִּי שִׁמְעוֹן בֶּן יוֹחַאי. אֲמַר לֵיהּ: ״אָתֵינָא לְעָלְמָא דְאָתֵי״? אֲמַר לֵיהּ: ״אִם יִרְצֶה אָדוֹן הַזֶּה״. אָמַר רַבִּי יְהוֹשֻׁעַ בֶּן לֵוִי: ״שְׁנַיִם רָאִיתִי וְקוֹל שְׁלֹשָׁה שָׁמַעְתִּי״.

Rabbi Yehoshua ben Levi found Elijah the prophet, **who was standing at the entrance of the** burial **cave of Rabbi Shimon ben Yoḥai.** Rabbi Yehoshua ben Levi **said to him: Will I** be privileged to **come to the World to Come?** Elijah **said to him: If this Master,** the Holy One, Blessed be He, **will wish** it so. **Rabbi Yehoshua ben Levi says: Two I saw,** Elijah and me, **and the voice of three I heard,** as the Divine Presence was also there, and it was in reference to Him that Elijah said: If this Master will wish it so.

אֲמַר לֵיהּ: ״אֵימַת אָתֵי מָשִׁיחַ״? אֲמַר לֵיהּ: ״זִיל שַׁיְילֵיהּ לְדִידֵיהּ״. ״וְהֵיכָא יָתֵיב״? אַפִּיתְחָא דְרוֹמִי. ״וּמַאי סִימָנֵיהּ״? ״יָתֵיב בֵּינֵי עֲנִיִּי סוֹבְלֵי חֳלָאִים, וכוּלָּן שָׁרוּ וַאֲסִירִי בְּחַד זִימְנָא, אִיהוּ שָׁרֵי חַד וְאָסִיר חַד. אֲמַר: דִּילְמָא מִבָּעֵינָא, דְּלָא אִיעַכַּב״.

Rabbi Yehoshua ben Levi **said to** Elijah: **When** will the **Messiah come?** Elijah **said to him: Go ask him.** Rabbi Yehoshua ben Levi asked: **And where is he sitting?** Elijah said to him: **At the entrance of** the city of **Rome.** Rabbi Yehoshua ben Levi asked him: **And what is his** identifying **sign** by means of which I can recognize him? Elijah answered: **He sits among the poor who suffer from illnesses. And all of them untie** their bandages **and tie** them all **at once,** but the Messiah **unties one** bandage **and ties one** at a time. **He says: Perhaps I will be needed** to serve to bring about the redemption. Therefore, I will never tie more than one bandage, so **that I will not be delayed.**

אֲזַל לְגַבֵּיהּ. אֲמַר לֵיהּ: ״שָׁלוֹם עָלֶיךָ רַבִּי וּמוֹרִי״! אֲמַר לֵיהּ: ״שָׁלוֹם עָלֶיךָ בַּר לִיוָאִי״. אֲמַר לֵיהּ: ״לְאֵימַת אָתֵי מָר״? אֲמַר לֵיהּ: ״הַיּוֹם״. אֲתָא לְגַבֵּי אֵלִיָּהוּ. אֲמַר לֵיהּ: ״מַאי אֲמַר לָךְ״? אֲמַר לֵיהּ: ״שָׁלוֹם עָלֶיךָ בַּר לִיוָאִי״. אֲמַר לֵיהּ: ״אַבְטְחָךְ לָךְ וְלַאֲבוּךְ לְעָלְמָא דְּאָתֵי״. אֲמַר לֵיהּ: ״שַׁקּוֹרֵי קָא שַׁקֵּר בִּי, דַּאֲמַר לִי: ׳הַיּוֹם אָתֵינָא׳, וְלָא אֲתָא״! אֲמַר לֵיהּ: ״הָכִי אֲמַר לָךְ (תְּהִלִּים צה, ז): ׳הַיּוֹם אִם בְּקֹלוֹ תִשְׁמָעוּ׳״.

Rabbi Yehoshua ben Levi **went to** the Messiah. **He said to** the Messiah: **Greetings to you, my rabbi and my teacher.** The Messiah **said to him: Greetings to you, bar Leva'i.** Rabbi Yehoshua ben Levi **said to him: When will the Master come?** The Messiah **said to him: Today.** Sometime later, Rabbi Yehoshua ben Levi **came to Elijah.** Elijah **said to him: What did** the Messiah **say to you? He said to** Elijah that the Messiah said: **Greetings** [*shalom*] **to you, bar Leva'i.** Elijah **said to him:** He thereby **guaranteed** that **you and your father** will enter **the World to Come,** as he greeted you with *shalom*. Rabbi Yehoshua ben Levi **said to** Elijah: The Messiah **lied to me, as he said to me: I am coming today, and he did not come.** Elijah **said to him** that **this** is what **he said to you:** He said that he will come **"today, if you will listen to his voice"** (Psalms 95:7).

R. YEHOSHUA MEETS UP WITH ELIJAH THE PROPHET

The overall context of this aggada is a very extensive talmudic discussion of the Messianic Era and the Messiah in the last chapter of Tractate Sanhedrin. In the standard editions of the Talmud, R. Yehoshua here meets Elijah the prophet at the cave of R. Shimon bar Yoḥai, presumably an allusion to where R. Shimon bar Yoḥai was hiding from Roman persecution, or, as the Koren annotated translation above suggests, at

R. Shimon bar Yoḥai's burial cave.[2] R. Yehoshua seizes this opportunity to inquire of Elijah as to whether or not he will gain entrée into the World to Come after he dies.[3] It is surely worth pondering why R. Yehoshua was so concerned. What doubts could a man of such exceptional stature harbor?

Elijah's response is that it depends upon what "this Master" wills, a reference to the *Shekhina*, to the Divine Presence, as Rashi understands it. If the *Shekhina* wills it, Elijah meant to say, then you, R. Yehoshua, will gain entrée into the World to Come. Note that Elijah uses the term "this" in his response, "*this* Master." The use of this term suggests that the Master, the *Shekhina*, is actually present, and indeed R. Yehoshua responds, "Two I saw, and the voice of three I heard."

The two he saw were Elijah and R. Shimon bar Yoḥai, if the latter were still alive. If not, the second person would have been himself.[4] While he could not see the *Shekhina*, R. Yehoshua did say that he heard the voice of yet another party present at the encounter, and that was the *Shekhina*. But what did the *Shekhina* say? The text shares no message with

2. In other editions of the Talmud R. Yehoshua meets R. Shimon and Elijah at the entrance to the Garden of Eden. Yonah Frankel, in "The Image of R. Yehoshua ben Levi in Narratives of the Babylonian Talmud," *Proceedings of the World Congress of Jewish Studies*, 3 (1973): 403–41 (Heb.), identifies five different manuscript versions of this aggada. We will follow the version as it appears in the standard editions of the Talmud. The medieval *Yad Rama* in his commentary to this passage maintains that the encounter took place when R. Shimon bar Yoḥai was hiding in a cave to escape Roman persecution. Frankel, in the article cited just above, suggests that it took place at R. Shimon bar Yoḥai's burial cave, which Koren favors in its annotated translation.

3. That R. Yehoshua ben Levi was centrally concerned with his fate in the World to Come is made amply clear in another remarkable aggada which appears in Ketubot 77b, in which R. Yehoshua leaps into the World to Come with the weapon that the Angel of Death uses to kill people, thereby preventing all human death. There too he meets up with R. Shimon bar Yoḥai, but in the World to Come, and not at the cave. Frankel, op. cit., analyzes that aggada in the context of the aggada which is the subject of this chapter. Here I focus exclusively on the aggada at hand, and find that I am unpersuaded by his otherwise insightful analysis.

4. See too comments of Maharsha, ad loc. Eric Ottenheijm in "Elijah and the Messiah," *Prophecy and Prophets in Stories*, ed. B. Becking and H. Barstad (Leiden, 2015), 204, suggests it might have been the Messiah, but to this reader, at least, that seems rather far-fetched.

the reader. Could the *Shekhina* merely have echoed what Elijah said? Surely it is unlikely that the *Shekhina* would have said "if this master will wish it so," referring to herself. What kind of answer is that? And if that is not what the *Shekhina* said, what then did the *Shekhina* say?

Perhaps what we find here is an instance of "dialogical ellipis," a word or phrase missing from the dialogue. Note that R. Yehoshua says he heard the "voice" of three, but not the "words" of three. He himself may not have heard what the *Shekhina* said, but only that the *Shekhina* said something. Thus, what the author of the aggada may have meant to teach is that the content of the *Shekhina*'s message must remain hidden behind a veil of mystery. Who can truly understand the *Shekhina*'s speech? The very quest to find out from the *Shekhina* herself what was to be one's fate in the World to Come is quixotic, unattainable. Not that there are no answers to this question, for as we shall see at the conclusion of the aggada, there is one. But that answer cannot emanate with any clarity from the inscrutable *Shekhina* herself. R. Yehoshua can ask the *Shekhina* about his fate, but what he will learn is that no answer he can understand will ever come from the *Shekhina* herself, who so transcends R. Yehoshua's personal limitations.

Perhaps, too, Elijah meant to teach R. Yehoshua that if he begins his quest to ascertain the future by asking only about his own fate, then that quest is doomed to failure, for it is too self-centered. R. Yehoshua will never find the answer to that question unless he frames it in a larger, other-centered quest, to ascertain the future of the Jewish people as a whole.[5] R. Yehoshua may take this hint, for his next question is precisely about that: When will the Messiah come? With this question he demonstrates concern not only for himself, but for all fellow Jews.

Before we continue with the narrative, however, we might wonder why, indeed, R. Yehoshua did start with self over others. We know from various sources that R. Yehoshua served as an interlocutor with

5. Frankel, op. cit., takes this to be the key to this aggada, and to the other aggadot about R. Yehoshua that he examines as well. They track R. Yehoshua's development from concern for self to concern also for others. In the body of the chapter, I offer an alternative reading, for reasons that will become apparent.

the Romans on behalf of the Jews in Lod.[6] This in itself suggests concern for the community. As we shall see later in this chapter, R. Yehoshua's own behavior in support of needy others was nothing less than heroic. How then are we to reconcile the seemingly self-centered picture of R. Yehoshua here, with all that we know about him otherwise? Of course, one possible answer might be that R. Yehoshua's deep commitment to the well-being of others was not complete, or that it fully emerged only after the lesson he learned depicted in our aggada. However, for this reader at least, that seems too simplistic. There are so many aggadot which describe the spiritual and moral greatness of R. Yehoshua[7] that it seems unlikely that he was so very self-centered, or that his altruism emerged only after the events described here took place. Rather, it seems more likely that as heroic and other-centered as R. Yehoshua might have been, he still was deeply worried about his own fate, and could not escape that concern for self. Indeed, his concern for his own status in the World to Come is reflected in another aggada as well.[8] Why? After all, he was a man of exemplary religious stature and learning. While we cannot know the answer to this question with any certainty, one clue emerges from a disturbing question that the Talmud reports came before R. Yehoshua, as the leading rabbi in Lod.

One Ulla bar Koshev, probably a criminal, sought refuge in Lod from the hot pursuit of Roman officers. They threatened to destroy the whole city and its inhabitants if they did not turn the fugitive over to the authorities. In order to save the city, R. Yehoshua determined that the halakhically correct decision was to turn him in, and he persuaded the fugitive to submit. While this may seem like a prudent decision, since he thereby saved the lives of all the inhabitants of Lod, it was not without personal repercussions for R. Yehoshua. Elijah chose to suspend his regular visitations with him. Not surprisingly, this deeply troubled R. Yehoshua, and he afflicted himself and fasted, as a result of which

6. E.g., Y. Berakhot 5:1, 37b; Genesis Rabba 78:5.
7. For a full treatment of the biography of R. Yehoshua, see B. Z. Rosenfeld, "R. Yehoshua ben Levi: The Man and His Public Life" (PhD. diss., Bar Ilan University, 1982) (Heb.), cited in Lau, *The Sages*, Vol. IV, 69, and Lau's own discussion, 69–85.
8. Ketubot 77b.

Elijah finally returned. Elijah thereupon said to him, in effect, "Do I reveal myself to a person who hands Jews over to often lawless authorities?" Such a person in rabbinic parlance is a "*moser*," and this behavior is regarded in Jewish law and lore as a despicable act. To accuse R. Yehoshua of such a sin is shocking. R. Yehoshua attempts to justify his behavior, but the accusation itself cuts deeply.[9]

Regardless of how we are to understand this dialogue between Elijah and R. Yehoshua about the rectitude of his choice, one point is amply clear. Elijah ceased his visitations with R. Yehoshua, accused him of despicable behavior, and R. Yehoshua fasted and afflicted himself. While we cannot know when this took place relative to the events described in our aggada, it is surely possible that it took place before our aggada. If it did, then R. Yehoshua might have been so deeply troubled by Elijah's rejection of him, and by the accusations Elijah made, that he would naturally wonder whether or not he could still merit a portion in the World to Come. With this stain on his conscience, R. Yehoshua may well have felt that he must clear his own accounts before he could focus on the Messiah.

It is also worth observing that concern about one's personal fate in the World to Come is not as self-centered as it might first appear. For if one will secure a healthy portion in the World to Come, then that demonstrates that the life he or she leads is a good one in God's eyes, and no corrective course is necessary. On the other hand, if one will fail to secure a place in the World to Come, that would mean that the life he or she is living is seriously flawed, and a corrective course would be necessary. Therefore, to inquire about one's future status in the World to Come is of crucial immediate importance. R. Yehoshua wanted to know whether he must better his ways, repent, make changes to his life, while he still has time to do so. This is a question of major religious import, and not idle, self-centered preoccupation with one's own personal fate.

9. See the commentary *Iyun Yaakov* in *Ein Yaakov* (Jerusalem, 2008), ad loc., for an alternative explanation, based upon Ketubot 77b, according to which R. Yehoshua did not die at the hands of the Angel of Death, which would have served as an atonement for any sins he might have committed, for which reason he was worried about his fate in the World to Come. The explanations I offer above seem more straightforward to this reader.

Finally, yet another way to think about this problem may follow upon reflection about the following question: Just how selfless can a person authentically be? All human beings possess a natural instinct for self-preservation, a natural interest in the well-being of the self. Of course, moral heroes can overcome that instinct, and sacrifice themselves for others. But what is the moral status of someone who doesn't even contend with that instinct, but unthinkingly leaps to perform a heroic act without even fully acknowledging to himself the extent of the cost to him or her? Surely, that is impressive. Yet, one might maintain that for all its impressiveness, it nevertheless lacks a certain degree of authenticity. For one could argue that it is more authentic to fully confront one's own needs, reflect upon them, and then nevertheless choose to sacrifice those needs for others, than it would be to fail even to acknowledge those natural needs. For to fail to acknowledge those needs is to act without full human awareness and moral cognition. Can an act be maximally virtuous if it does not spring from honest, self-aware human reflection? Of course, one could take the contrary position as well, and argue that authenticity and self-awareness do not make any real moral difference at all. Perhaps any selfless act is just that, a virtuous selfless act.

However one relates to this question, and arguments can be made for both sides, it is plausible that R. Yehoshua himself at least initially came out on the side of authenticity. That is, he may have believed that it would be more authentic for him first to ask about his own fate in the World to Come before asking about the Messiah. To do so is to acknowledge the reality of his own natural self-interest, his own personal hope for the future, before looking after the hopes of others. Failing to do so would mean that his interest in the future of the Jewish people would be tainted by a perfectly legitimate, yet unresolved and unconfronted personal need. Once he sorts out his own destiny, then he can faithfully and honestly inquire about the future of the Jewish people.[10]

---

10. In this context, we should recall R. Yoḥanan ben Zakkai's blessing to his students on his deathbed, discussed in chapter 7 of this volume. His blessing was that they fear God as much as they fear human beings. If a person fears God, and feels shame before Him over his failure to obey Him, to the same degree as he or she fears a human being, and feels shame if that person witnesses his or her failure to obey God, then no one would ever sin. Shame before humans is a greater motivator than

R. YEHOSHUA BEN LEVI FINDS THE MESSIAH

In response to R. Yehoshua's query about when the Messiah will come, Elijah tells him to go ask the Messiah himself. The first point to make here is that Elijah does not answer directly either of R. Yehoshua's two questions. He punts. To the first question, he says that R. Yehoshua should ask the master, and to the second question he says that R. Yehoshua should ask the Messiah. The reader surely wonders why Elijah refuses to answer R. Yehoshua directly. But in any case, in order to ask the Messiah when he will come, R. Yehoshua needs to know where he is. Where, then, is the Messiah to be found? That is exactly the question R. Yehoshua next poses to Elijah, who answers that he can be found at the entrance to the city of Rome. This is surely a surprising response. Who would expect the Messiah to be present in this very corrupt world, at the gates of the very civilization that destroyed the Temple, murdered so many Jews, and sent so many others to exile? Would not the ethereal realm of the World to Come be a more suitable location for the Messiah?[11]

In addition, the assertion that the Messiah is residing at the gates of Rome is hardly enough information for R. Yehoshua. No doubt there are many people present at the entrance to Rome. R. Yehoshua wonders how he will recognize him. What are the identifying markers of the Messiah? This is more than a practical question, for by identifying the markers of the Messiah, one can learn much about who he is, and what makes him the Messiah. Is he studying Torah? Is he debating the Romans, or defending the Jews? Many answers suggest themselves, but Elijah's answer is hardly amongst them. Indeed, it is even more surprising than the Messiah's location being found at the entrance to Rome.

---

shame before God. Now note that R. Yoḥanan offered this blessing to his students, who were some of the greatest Jews who ever lived, the likes of R. Yehoshua and R. Eliezer. Yet he still maintained that shame over failure before other human beings is a natural, powerful, and inescapable component of the human experience, which must be confronted and acknowledged. That's just how people are. R. Yehoshua ben Levi may have followed in R. Yoḥanan ben Zakkai's footsteps. To deny the natural instinct for self-preservation, the natural instinct to seek life in the World to Come, is to deny an inescapable element of the human experience. Better to confront it and move on than to make believe it does not exist.

11. Indeed, that is more or less where Rashi locates him, as discussed in note 9, above.

Elijah informs R. Yehoshua that the Messiah sits amongst the poor and sick. They untie and tie their bandages all together, all at the same time. But not the Messiah. He is different from his fellow sufferers, in that he, and only he, unties and ties each wound one by one, not together, and he can therefore be identified as the Messiah. But why does he do this? The Messiah's own explanation, offered directly to no one in particular, but the aggada nevertheless quotes it verbatim, is that he might be called upon at any moment to redeem the Jews. And if he unties all his bandages at once, then it will take him longer to tie them all up, and this could momentarily delay him on his mission to redeem the Jews. He does not want to risk even this momentary delay, so he unties and ties each wound individually.

Notice first that the Messiah is busy with only his own wounds. Nowhere does the text assert that he helped his fellow sufferers with theirs. This is in striking contrast to R. Yehoshua himself. The Talmud[12] notes that many rabbis kept away from those afflicted with a particular serious disease, *ra'atan,* because of fear of contagion. Yet R. Yehoshua ben Levi declared that Torah will protect him, and he attached himself to those afflicted with this disease while studying Torah. The text does not contend that he treated them, or helped them physically with their illness, but clearly he meant to provide them with at least emotional support, for why else would he "attach himself" to them? And why would the Talmud sing his praises for "attaching himself" to them, if he did nothing for them? This, after all, is one of the purposes of the mitzva to visit the ill, which R. Yehoshua courageously fulfilled.[13] On the one hand, R. Yehoshua's vision of the Messiah echoes his own courageous behavior in sitting with the ill. On the other hand, the Messiah is described as engaged in self-care, not care of others. If it were otherwise, why not also write that the Messiah was indeed helping others with their suffering? Surely that too would be at least one of the markers of the Messiah, in addition to his binding his wounds one at a time, as others might be similarly engaged.

Perhaps the key here is that the Messiah is depicted as a suffering servant of God, whose suffering in itself atones for the sins of his

12. Ketubot 77b.

13. See Nedarim 40a.

people. Identifying the Messiah as a sick sufferer has its roots in Isaiah 53:3–5, in describing the servant of God, "He was despised, shunned by men, a man of suffering, familiar with disease.... Yet it was our sickness that he was bearing, our suffering that he endured. We accounted him plagued, smitten, afflicted by God. But he was wounded because of our sins, crushed because of our iniquities. He bore the chastisement that made us whole, and by his bruises we were healed."[14] On this reading, the Messiah is indeed deeply committed to the well-being of his people, and if his fellow sufferers are Jewish (the text is not clear), then he is deeply committed to them. But his commitment manifests itself not in the care he provides, but in the suffering that he undergoes on their behalf. The Messiah is the sacrificial lamb who atones for a sinful people. This comports well with the position R. Yehoshua articulates earlier on the same page in the Talmud, that if the Jews do not merit his arrival by virtue of their model religious behavior, the Messiah will arrive as a poor man riding a donkey. A very unimposing image indeed, as King Shapur is reported there to observe to Samuel, in apparent derision. Indeed, one might argue that this characterization of the Messiah is the perfect mirror image of the suffering Jews he will come to redeem.[15]

This image stands in sharp contrast to the dominant image of the Messiah, as a mighty warrior king who will wage successful war against Israel's oppressors, and re-establish the Davidic monarchy.[16] Moses, the first redeemer, was raised in the palace of Pharaoh, a privileged aristocrat by upbringing. Not so R. Yehoshua's image of the Messiah, a poor, passive sufferer from among the many impoverished sufferers of Israel. Are the two images consistent with one another, or do they represent altogether different models of the Messiah? Is it possible that at the appointed time, the Messiah, like a caterpillar, will slough off his old impoverished, broken self, and emerge as the butterfly of redemption?

14. Frankel makes this obvious connection as well. These verses were long important for Christian interpreters of the Bible, and this theme echoes into our aggada.
15. See also Abraham Berger, "Captive at the Gate of Rome: The Story of a Messianic Motif" PAAJR 44 (1977): 1–17, and *Anaf Yosef* and *Eitz Yosef,* ad loc., commentaries to the *Ein Yaakov,* op. cit.
16. This view is neatly summarized in Maimonides, *Mishneh Torah, Laws of Kings,* ch. 11, based upon various biblical and rabbinic sources.

Let us now turn to the question of location. Why at the gates of Rome? Probably because Rome brought about the almost complete destruction and degradation of the Jewish people, in 70 CE, and continued in R. Yehoshua's time several centuries later to reign sovereign over the Land of Israel. Rome, for the Jews, represents all evil, the nadir of Jewish history, as well as the location where so many Jewish captives were exiled. There, in the very pits of Jewish life, and in the very heart of the great Jewish oppressor, the Messiah awaits his mission. Redemption must begin "from the depths," from Rome itself. The only way to fully defeat evil is to confront its most maximalist incarnation.

Two more crucial observations must be made before we continue with the narrative. First, it is apparent from the aggada that the Messiah himself does not know when he will be called to redeem the Jewish people. Otherwise, why does he keep binding and unbinding his wounds? The Messiah is portrayed as a passive, suffering servant, awaiting a mysterious call from God in some indeterminate future. We might then wish to conclude that Elijah sent R. Yehoshua on a wild goose chase. For Elijah told R. Yehoshua to ask the Messiah when he will come, and even the Messiah himself does not know. Assuming Elijah knows of the Messiah's ignorance on this topic, which seems very likely given Elijah's overall wide-ranging knowledge, why then send R. Yehoshua to ask him? We shall return to this question later in the chapter.

Second, consider how much time the Messiah saves by binding each wound separately, rather than all of them together. It couldn't have been very much at all. Every additional minute the Jews spend suffering was intolerable to him. The Messiah might be a suffering servant, but a sufferer who could bear no unnecessary suffering on the part of the people he will be called to redeem. One of the classic commentaries to the aggada suggests that the Talmud means to teach that the Messiah wanted to publicly demonstrate to his fellow sufferers how certain he was that he would be called to his mission at any moment, a kind of theater of yearning and of trust in God.[17] How better to buttress the waning strength of an afflicted people?

17. Ben Yehoyada, ad loc. The *Anaf Yosef* (ad loc., in *Ein Yaakov*, op. cit.) suggests that there is a specific and precise appointed time for the Messiah's arrival, and with

We can now return to the narrative. R. Yehoshua opens with a formalistic greeting, "Greetings to you, my rabbi and my teacher." He speaks with considerable deference, especially in light of the poverty and suffering the Messiah embodies. R. Yehoshua is not put off or surprised by the Messiah's degraded appearance. Why not? Partly, of course, because Elijah had already warned him, but there might be more to it than that. Another aggada about R. Yehoshua might shed further light on this question. R. Yosef, the son of R. Yehoshua, took very ill, and almost died. When he returned to health, R. Yehoshua asked him what he saw as he approached the World to Come. R. Yosef answered that he saw an inverted world. Those considered important in this world were consigned to a low rank in the World to Come, while those considered unimportant in this world were elevated to a superior rank in the World to Come.[18] Assuming this was a long-held view of his, or that the event described in this passage took place before his encounter with the Messiah, it would come as no surprise to R. Yehoshua if the Messiah were among the impoverished sufferers of the world. That is where the greatest inner purity is to be found, not among the wealthy, healthy, and politically important, distracted as they might be by their worldly good fortune. We find echoes here of the Weltanschauung of R. Ḥanina ben Dosa and R. Shimon ben Ḥalafta, discussed at some length in chapters 5 and 6 of this volume. Indeed, this teaching may shed further light on why R. Yehoshua was so anxious about his status in the World to Come, a question raised earlier in the chapter. As noted, R. Yehoshua was one of the great leaders of the Jewish community in Lod, and represented the community before the nobles in Rome. If his rank in this world was so elevated, then given his theology, might he not have had good reason to worry about his status in the World to Come?

R. Yehoshua treats the Messiah with the utmost deference and respect, appearances notwithstanding. The Messiah responds with equal formality, "Greetings to you, bar Leva'i [the son of Levi]." As we shall see, this response carries with it great significance. Next, R. Yehoshua asks,

---

any slight delay, he might miss the opportunity.

18. Pesaḥim 50a. See also Sota 5b, where R. Yehoshua praises the greatness of those lowly of spirit.

"When will the Master come?" This is the obvious and crucial question, the *raison d'etre* of R. Yehoshua's journey to Rome. As we pointed out above, the Messiah does not know when he will be called to redeem the Jewish people, for which reason he constantly binds and unbinds his wounds one by one. How then can the Messiah answer R. Yehoshua's question truthfully? His answer is "Today." But is that truthful? Did the Messiah come on that day?

Of course, he did not, as the reader knows from Jewish history, and as R. Yehoshua himself angrily asserts when he returns to Elijah. In a flash, R. Yehoshua is next conversing with Elijah. Surely the reader wonders just how Elijah could have traveled so quickly from Rome to Jerusalem, but that is where we find him.

Elijah opens the conversation, and asks R. Yehoshua what the Messiah told him, to which he responds, quite accurately, "Greetings to you, bar Leva'i." From this greeting Elijah infers that R. Yehoshua and his father are both assured a place in the World to Come, an inference he immediately shares with R. Yehoshua. Here the narrative circles back to its beginnings. Recall that R. Yehoshua had first asked Elijah if he would be privileged to occupy a place in the World to Come. Elijah told him to ask the *Shekhina*, but no answer was forthcoming. It is only when R. Yehoshua seeks not his own destiny but the destiny of all the Jews, only when he endeavors to find out when the Messiah will arrive, that he discovers his own personal destiny too. Surprisingly, this no longer seems to concern him, for he does not express joy at those good tidings. Rather, his first reaction is to blurt out to Elijah that the Messiah had lied to him. For the Messiah had told him that he would come on that very day, and that very day has passed. The language he uses is harsh indeed: "The Messiah lied to me." Surely that is a stark and angry indictment of the man who is Messiah of Israel! How are we to explain this puzzling exchange?

Let us begin by first asking about the evidence that R. Yehoshua will indeed find his portion in the World to Come. How did Elijah know? Rashi explains that the Messiah would not have greeted R. Yehoshua so positively, and would not have mentioned his father's name, had the two of them not possessed a portion in the World to Come. Others add that by mentioning only his father's name, the Messiah, who no doubt knew that Levi already had a portion in the World to Come, meant to suggest that R. Yehoshua too, like his father, would have a portion in the World to Come.[19] Whatever the merits of these explanations, R. Yehoshua seems far less interested in his own status, than he is in the "lie" he believes the Messiah told him. Why?

One possibility is that he evolved and grew through these encounters with Elijah, the *Shekhina,* and the Messiah, that he is no longer centrally concerned with self, but is now centrally concerned with all Jews.[20] While R. Yehoshua may indeed have evolved, I have argued above that it is likewise unlikely that he was so completely self-centered at the outset of his experience before he evolved. Indeed, he had good and legitimate reasons, I suggested, to be concerned about his own destiny too. What then transpired over the course of his experiences?

I would suggest that his encounter with the Messiah was transformative. He saw face to face the vivid suffering of the Messiah on behalf of his beloved people. He saw the immediacy of the Messiah's yearning for Jewish salvation, refusing to lose a moment in his great mission to redeem a suffering people. That striking experience sent shock waves through R. Yehoshua. His own personal destiny no longer mattered to him in the shadow of the tragic yearning he saw in the suffering Messiah. How could he even think about himself following that moving encounter? Surely this represents a great change in R. Yehoshua, a transvaluation. What used to matter to him, following this disturbing encounter, mattered no longer. And then, to be lied to by the great Messiah himself? This was outrageous to R. Yehoshua. The embers of messianic yearning were stoked by his encounter with the suffering servant, only to be dashed by the suffering servant's bald lie. Is it surprising that all else faded into the background? All he could do was blurt out to Elijah, no doubt in despair and anger: The Messiah lied! The Messiah said he would come today, but that day has now passed. And the Messiah never came.

Elijah's response is telling, and helps illuminate one of the overall themes of this mysterious aggada: "Today, if you will listen to His voice." The redemption of the Jewish people depends ultimately upon

19. Ben Yehoyada, op. cit. See too Frankel, p. 416, n. 44.
20. This is Frankel's interpretation, op. cit.

the Jewish people themselves. God will activate the Messiah and call him to his mission if and only if the Jews merit the Messiah's arrival by their behavior. The Talmud in this chapter of Sanhedrin cites many differing opinions about when the Messiah will arrive.[21] Is there a specific appointed time when the Messiah will come, irrespective of Jewish behavior? Or, does the Messiah's arrival depend completely upon Jewish repentance? Or does it depend upon some combination of these two factors? Elijah's interpretation of the Messiah's response as recorded in this aggada places it squarely within the tradition of those who maintain that repentance and good deeds are both necessary and sufficient conditions for the arrival of the Messiah.

Yet we might ask why the Messiah himself didn't say so. The Messiah speaks in very terse terms. His answer to R. Yehoshua's question is one word only, "Today." If he meant today, on condition that the Jews repent, why didn't he say so? Surely what he did say was altogether misleading, so much so that R. Yehoshua, gifted man that he was, erupted at Elijah in dismay and anger.

Part of the answer probably turns on the different roles of the Messiah and Elijah in Jewish history. Elijah is the great critic of the Jewish people, perennially reproving them for their disloyalty to God, and their illicit fealty to the Canaanite deity Baal. At the great confrontation on Mount Carmel between himself and the prophets of Baal and Ashera, before all the assembled people of Israel, he approaches the people and famously says, "How long will you keep hopping between two opinions? If the Lord is God, follow Him; and if Baal, follow him!"[22] While Malachi (3:23) prophesizes that Elijah will serve as the harbinger of the Messiah, this is probably related to his crucial historical role in castigating the people for their idolatry, thereby bringing about their repentance, and thus making the arrival of the Messiah possible. It is hardly surprising, then, that the author of the aggada portrays Elijah as teaching that the Messiah will come only if Jews repent.

21. See E. E. Urbach, *The Sages: Chapters in Faith and Belief* (Jerusalem, 1976), 601–623 (Heb.), for an extensive overview and discussion, including comments on the aggada which is the subject of this chapter.

22. I Kings 18:21.

However, the Messiah himself, the great hope of the Jewish people for millennia, is not primarily a person who reproves, but a person who redeems. Why does he unbind and bind his wounds one by one if so little time is really saved? I suggested above that in so doing, he actively nurtures hope among his fellow sufferers that redemption can take place at any moment, that he must be ready to embark upon his great mission without even a minute's delay. For this reason, the Messiah tells R. Yehoshua that he will come today. Today, and not tomorrow. He does not mention repentance because his primary task is to encourage Jews during periods of suffering, to cultivate hope for a better future amidst despair, not to demand repentance.

But what kind of strategy is this? Does it not lead exactly to the anger and frustration that R. Yehoshua experienced? After all, the Messiah did not come yesterday, or the day before yesterday, or the day before that. To further complicate this picture, note that R. Yehoshua himself is cited in the Talmud, just before the aggada which is the subject of this chapter, as teaching that the Messiah will arrive as a poor person riding on donkey if the Jews do not repent, but if they do repent, he will come riding on a cloud in the heavens. This implies that the Messiah will come whether or not the Jews repent, that repentance is not a necessary condition for the arrival of the Messiah. Despite the sins of the Jews, the suffering Messiah waits eagerly, binding his wounds, for the moment he, a poor man riding on his donkey, will be called to redeem the Jews. There is always hope, even if Jews wallow in sin. Likewise, in this passage of the Talmud, R. Yehoshua is also cited as teaching that the Messiah will come in haste if the Jews repent, but if they do not repent, the Messiah will come in the designated time.

That this is the position of R. Yehoshua is reinforced by yet another teaching of his, recorded in some manuscripts on the previous page in the Talmud.[23] There the Talmud cites the great Babylonian teacher Rav as maintaining that the arrival of the Messiah depends upon Jewish repentance. In the standard editions of the Talmud, Shmuel, his Babylonian colleague and frequent disputant, is cited as disagreeing. However, the *Dikdukei Soferim* cites a variant manuscript which reads

23. Sanhedrin 97b.

not Shmuel but R. Yehoshua ben Levi, a reading which appears in a number of medieval sources as well.[24] What does R. Yehoshua (or Shmuel) say? "It is sufficient for the mourner to endure his mourning." This, of course, is cryptic, and Rashi offers two interpretations. According to the first interpretation, the mourner here is God Himself, and R. Yehoshua means to teach that God can endure His mourning, presumably over the destruction of the Temple and the exile of His people, for only so long. At some point, He will intervene to send the Messiah even if the Jews do not repent. According to the second interpretation, it is the Jews who are the mourners, and the pain and suffering the Jews experienced in their mourning and exile itself warrants their redemption, even without their repentance, presumably because their sins are thereby expiated.[25] Even if the Messiah comes like a poor man riding on a donkey because the Jews do not deserve him, he will come nevertheless.

Thus, the author of the aggada portrays Elijah as teaching R. Yehoshua a lesson that R. Yehoshua himself does not quite affirm, at least according to three other sources for his teachings in the Talmud itself (or only two, following the text as it appears in the standard editions of the Talmud, and unlike the text as many medieval commentators had it). What are we to make of this? Possibly that the author of this aggada took the view of Rav (and R. Eliezer, later on the same page of the Talmud), and he wanted to place Elijah and then R. Yehoshua in that camp too, even if according to other traditions (which he may not even have had) R. Yehoshua did not belong there.

Another explanation might emerge from the second interpretation Rashi offers above to explain R. Yehoshua's teaching: The Jewish people endured much torment and exile over the millennia; their mourning never seems to end. The Messiah, the suffering servant, leaves his hiding place at the gates of Rome and, poor and bedraggled, travels by

24. Ad loc., p. 288, and see n. 300, where he cites many medieval sources in which R. Yehoshua ben Levi appears instead of Shmuel.

25. The Maharsha and Rif in their commentaries ad loc. maintain in different ways that even according to R. Yehoshua ben Levi, Jews must repent for the arrival of the Messiah, but the repentance will be brought about by God Himself, forced as it were, since the time for redemption had come. My analysis above is consistent with this reading as well.

humble donkey to join the Jewish people in their collective mourning and pain. They cry and he cries along with them, old bandages covering his wounds. They believe he is the Messiah, because he may so announce himself, but they see their great Messiah suffering too, and they all wail together at the miserable fate of the Jewish people, whose very Messiah suffers along with them. And that experience leads them to rethink their ways and repent. For look what sin has wrought!

Regarding this interpretation, the relationship between repentance and the advent of the Messiah is not that the Jews repent and then the Messiah arrives triumphant. Nor is it that Elijah first comes to bring the Jews to repentance, through his fiery rebuke, following which the Messiah will come, again triumphant. Rather, the public degradation of the Messiah, which mirrors the public degradation of the Jews, itself provokes repentance. God will call the Messiah at the appointed time to provoke, through his own public suffering, the internal transformation of the Jews, which in turn will lead to their redemption.

But what then did the Messiah mean when he told R. Yehoshua that he would come today? For the author of the aggada, Elijah meant that the Jews must actively repent to bring about the Messiah, and if they repent today he will come today, and if they do not repent, he will not come. It is entirely up to the Jews to bring this about, and they may do so today. That is the simplest reading of the text. But what R. Yehoshua himself might have understood Elijah to mean, given what we know about his views, would be something different. He meant to say that if the Jews repent today, the Messiah will come today, but if they fail to repent today, then he will come at God's own appointed time. There is always hope.

Did the Messiah mislead? Why wasn't he clearer? Why didn't he make explicit what Elijah did? Part of the answer, as noted above, is that he is the redeemer, not the reprover; his role is to encourage, not to criticize. But there may be more to it than that. Perhaps the Messiah also meant to teach that he stands ready at any moment to come; every day is the day, should God so decide, to stimulate repentance amongst His sinful people. But, and here is the key point, God and His will are inscrutable. We can never know when God will make that decision. Consider this prophecy of Habakkuk (2:3): "For there is yet a prophecy for a set time. A truthful witness for a time that will come. Even if it tarries, wait for it still; for it will surely come, without delay." R. Natan, reading this prophecy as a reference to the advent of the Messiah, commented: "This verse penetrates and descends to the depths."[26] What did R. Natan mean? Rashi comments: "Just as the depths have no end, so too no human being can gain clarity (*yakhol la'amod*) about the meaning of the end of this verse." All a person can do if the Messiah tarries is await his arrival, Rashi goes on to say, for when the Messiah will come is as inscrutable to human beings as are the depths of the sea.

The Messiah speaks in terse and puzzling riddles because the Messiah himself cannot penetrate to God's will, does not himself know when he will be called. The Messiah says today, because every day could well be the day, and no human being can ever know when that day is. But, as Habakkuk teaches, await the Messiah, for every day could indeed be the day that he arrives. Elijah punts to the Messiah himself R. Yehoshua's question about when the Messiah will come, because Elijah does not know. And it turns out that the Messiah does not know either. Does Elijah know that the Messiah is ignorant? Perhaps. After all, he interprets the Messiah's response, and following his interpretation, either that of the author of the aggada, or how R. Yehoshua might have understood it himself, no one could know when the Messiah will come, even the Messiah himself. For who can know when the Jews will repent, either by virtue of their own internal transformation, or by virtues of the Messiah's, through God's inscrutable intervention? This question requires entrée into the impenetrable depths, to which no human being has access. Why then does Elijah send R. Yehoshua to the Messiah? To teach him exactly this lesson: Even the Messiah does not know.

The reader will recall that when R. Yehoshua asked Elijah about his own destiny in the World to Come, he heard the voice of the *Shekhina*, but did not hear what the *Shekhina* said, for the *Shekhina*, I suggested, was inscrutable. So too is the will of the *Shekhina* with respect to the Messiah. The Messiah might know and be able to communicate directly to R. Yehoshua what his personal destiny will be, but even the Messiah does not know the fullness of the Messiah's own destiny, for God keeps

26. Sanhedrin 97b.

that mystery from the impenetrable depths to Himself. Yet R. Yehoshua indeed seeks it out.

One way to understand this aggada is that it centers around the theme of unrequited quest for unattainable knowledge. R. Yehoshua asks two questions, to the *Shekhina* and the Messiah, respectively, and neither of them provides clear answers to the questions they were asked. Yet nevertheless, Elijah sends R. Yehoshua on a quest to find answers, answers which Elijah might very well know R. Yehoshua will never receive. Why then send him? Perhaps because the quest to seek those answers is itself of great value. To be so concerned about one's destiny in the World to Come would no doubt lead to a life better lived in this world, a life in which R. Yehoshua would never again engage in behavior that could lead to Elijah's abandonment of him, as had occurred in the past. To be so concerned about the Messiah that one seeks him out with the poor sufferers at the gates of Rome can be transformative, as it was for R. Yehoshua. Nothing else mattered to him, even his own destiny, after that shattering encounter with the suffering Messiah.

Elijah was the great mentor and tutor of R. Yehoshua, and in that role he sent him on a quest. The quest would be unrequited, because R. Yehoshua would never receive the answer he sought to the question he asked each of them. Yes, he would get the answer to the first question he asked Elijah, but only incidentally, from his second encounter, with the Messiah, not from Elijah himself or from the *Shekhina*, and also only as interpreted by Elijah, not by himself. On this reading, Elijah meant to teach R. Yehoshua that concrete, immediately understandable answers to his questions are simply not available. Yet the reason one seeks answers to those questions is not to ascertain their answers – which are not forthcoming – but to learn from the very quest to seek them out.

This may be the deepest significance to the cryptic answer "Today." His yearning for the Messiah must be so intense, stoked by his great quest to find him, that he will experience the Messiah's presence on that very day. Note, crucially, that the Messiah is indeed there, on that very day. While he has not yet come to redeem the Jewish people, he exists, is alive, and awaits that moment. R. Yehoshua discovered on his quest that he cannot know when the Messiah will come to redeem the Jews, for the Messiah himself does not know. But he did learn that the Messiah is here, today, forever awaiting the elusive divine call. His intense quest to find the Messiah yielded that great insight.[27]

To ask when the Messiah will come, as R. Yehoshua did, is really ambiguous. Does it mean when he will come to redeem the Jews? Surely that is the usual meaning of the question, and that is no doubt what R. Yehoshua meant. But it can also mean when he will come to live in this world, even if he is not yet called to redeem the Jews. The answer R. Yehoshua received from the Messiah is not the answer to the question that R. Yehoshua intended, but it is nevertheless an answer to a very important question indeed. And one lesson R. Yehoshua learns on this quest is that while he cannot get the answer to the question he intended, he does get an answer to a question his words could have meant, and that is a very important question and answer. The answer to that question is that the Messiah is indeed here today. R. Yehoshua discovers this because he embarked upon the quest that he did. The Messiah is always ready at a moment's notice to redeem the Jews, and he awaits his call on a daily basis, today, because he is here, today. Sometimes the answers one gets fail to answer the question one intended to pose, but are no less important for that failure.

In the end, R. Yehoshua never found out when the Messiah will come to redeem the Jews. In this respect his quest was unrequited. Yet the quest nevertheless revealed profound and important insight. R. Yehoshua returned from his journey a changed man.

27. See too, Ottenheim, pp. 210–211, but his emphasis is that the Messiah is present only for the elite individual like R. Yehoshua, not as in the approach I take here.

The fonts used in this book are from the Arno family

Maggid Books
The best of contemporary Jewish thought from
Koren Publishers Jerusalem Ltd.